EXTREME SCIENCE

SCIENCE

From
Nano

to

Galact

tic

Investigations for Grades 6–12

M. Gail Jones

Amy R. Taylor

Michael R. Falvo

NSTApress
National Science Teachers Association

National Science Teachers Association

Claire Reinburg, Director
Jennifer Horak, Managing Editor
Judy Cusick, Senior Editor
Andrew Cocke, Associate Editor

ART AND DESIGN
Will Thomas Jr., Director
Joseph Butera, Graphic Designer, cover and interior design

PRINTING AND PRODUCTION
Catherine Lorrain, Director
Nguyet Tran, Assistant Production Manager

NATIONAL SCIENCE TEACHERS ASSOCIATION
Francis Q. Eberle, PhD, Executive Director
David Beacom, Publisher

LIBRARY OF CONGRESS CATALOGING-IN-PUBLICATION DATA

Jones, M. Gail, 1955-
  Extreme science: from nano to galactic / by M. Gail Jones, Amy R. Taylor, and Michael R. Falvo.
    p. cm.
  ISBN 978-1-933531-30-4
  1. Science—Methodology—Study and teaching (Middle school) 2. Science—Methodology—Study and teaching
(Secondary) 3. Science—Study and teaching (Middle school)—Activity programs. 4. Science—Study and teaching
(Secondary)—Activity programs. 5. Estimation theory. I. Taylor, Amy R. II. Falvo, Michael R. III. Title.
  LB1585.J66 2009
  507.1'2—dc22

        2009008581

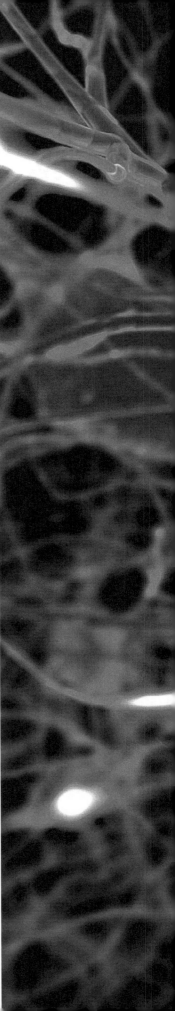

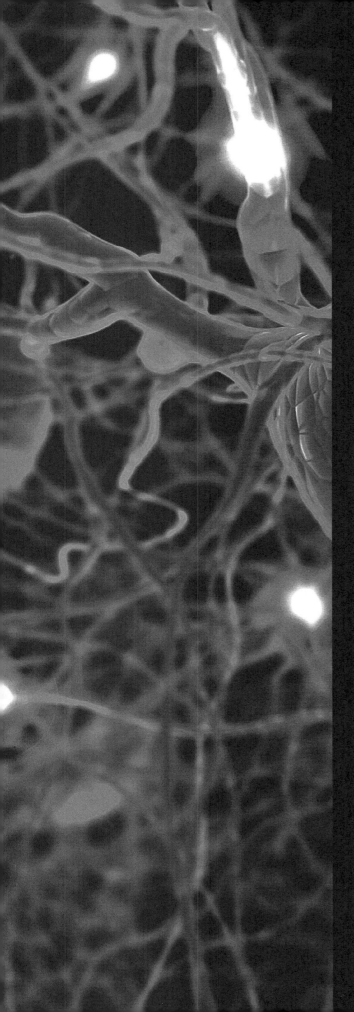

Acknowledgments

This book is the product of the inspiration, encouragement, and work of many people. We offer our thanks to the National Science Foundation for supporting our research in science, science education, and outreach to the community. Its support has enabled us to build classroom investigations that are based on solid research focusing on how people learn and how teachers can teach scale and scaling. We thank Adam Hall for his insightful cartoons, Lamar Mair for scanning electron micrograph images, Dee Dee Whitaker for her contributions related to GIS, and Jennifer Forrester for initial ideas when the book was framed. We want to acknowledge the contributions of Russ Rowlett for co-authoring the Types of Scale investigation. Special appreciation goes to Denise Krebs, Grant Gardner and Laura Robertson for their efforts piloting the investigations and evaluating the exercises for developmental appropriateness. Thanks are extended to the 50 scientists (including Nobel laureates) who allowed us to interview them about how they learned scale and applied it in their scientific work.

Finally, we want to express a most sincere thanks to the many students (from elementary through graduate school) and teachers who have participated in a long series of studies focusing on learning scale and scaling. These individuals have enriched this book in many ways.

This material is based on work supported by the National Science Foundation under Grants Numbers 0411656, 0354578, 0303979, 0507151, and 0634222.

CONTENTS

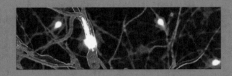

Dedication

This book is dedicated to Carolyn, Herb, Nancy, Tina, Sonia, and Toby, who have supported and inspired us in our work in science and education.

EXTREME SCIENCE

From Nano to Galactic

Whether we are imagining microbes or mammoths, dinosaurs or diatoms, molecules or stars, people of all ages are fascinated with the very large and the very small. Our interest is piqued as we try to imagine the world from a very different perspective—for example, looking up at the world through the eyes of an ant or looking down from the height of a dinosaur. New technologies have enabled scientists to investigate extremes of science previously unknown. Since the development of the telescope nearly 400 years ago we can explore vast worlds beyond our human perception. At the small scale, new advances in microscopy now enable us to manipulate and experiment with individual atoms and molecules. Some of the most striking new developments in science occur at the extreme ranges of scale—the very large (galactic) and the very small (nanoscale). In presenting these new and exciting scientific topics, the teacher faces the additional challenge of introducing the daunting concepts of scale over vast ranges.

Why Scale and Scaling?

An understanding of scale and scaling effects is of central importance to a scientific understanding of the world. Advances in diverse areas such as astrophysics, chemistry, biotechnology, nanoscience, geography, and sociology depend on being able to conceptualize different scales, as well as the effects and laws of nature that apply to each system scale. Most scientific problems cannot be approached without first appreciating the scale of the situation to be investigated. Though scale has always been central in science, an argument can be made that within the currents of scientific thought, it has never been more important than it is right now. A new appreciation of complexity or complex systems has taken hold in all areas of science, from supercon-

xi

ductivity to schooling phenomena in fish, from weather modeling to research on human consciousness (Gallagher and Appenzeller 1999). In 1972, Nobel laureate physicist P. W. Anderson wrote an editorial in *Science* titled "More Is Different" in which he described the concept of "emergent phenomena" (Anderson 1972). As the title suggests, Anderson articulated the idea that completely new rules emerge as the scale of a system changes. In the decades since, this simple yet new idea has influenced all areas of science. This new focus in scientific thinking is driven by advances in scientific technologies such as advanced microscopy and supercomputing, among many others, which have allowed us to access new regimes of scale, to amass huge amounts of data, and to map out systems at a level of detail unimaginable even 20 or 30 years ago. It has also, as Anderson prophetically pointed out in his essay, encouraged an ever-strengthening movement toward cross disciplinarity in science. In this sense, the theme of scaling effects and complex phenomena has acted to bridge disciplines in the world of scientific research in much the same way as the American Association for the Advancement of Science (AAAS) recommends for K–12 science education.

Scaling conceptions are one of four recommended unifying themes in the AAAS Project 2061 Benchmarks for Science Literacy (1993). Understandings of unifying themes such as scaling may serve as a solid framework for students to anchor further learning in a variety of disciplines and allow them to make cross-curricular connections among seemingly disparate topics. Table 1 shows the big ideas about scale that are recommended across the curriculum.

The U.S. science and mathematics curricula have been criticized as lacking coherence (AAAS 1989; National Council of Teachers of Mathematics [NCTM] 2000; National Research Council [NRC] 1996; National Science Teachers Association [NSTA] 1993). The claim that "the present curricula in science and mathematics are overstuffed and undernourished" (AAAS 1989, p. 14) effectively captures a view of the present state of most science curricula in the United States. This lack of coherence is not only a weak point in many science curricula, but also a stumbling block to effective science learning: "The typical U.S. science program discourages real learning not only in its overemphasis on facts, but in its very structure, which inhibits students from making important connections between facts" (NSTA 1993, p. 2).

That lack of coherence may contribute to the underdevelopment of a scientifically literate citizenry able to understand how scientific ways of thinking contribute to our society. An international comparison conducted during the Third International Mathematics and Science Study (TIMSS) reported that the splintering and fractionalization of U.S. science and mathematics curricula are also evident in comparison with those of other countries around the globe (Schmidt, McKnight, and Raizen 1997).

Numerous reform groups have recommended the use of big, overarching, unifying themes to combat the lack of curricular coherence and help students weave a fabric of understanding from the many components of a science and mathematics education (AAAS 1989; NCTM 2000; NRC 1996; NSTA 1993). Rather than representing specific content knowledge within specific disciplines, these themes represent scientifically useful ways of thinking about our world and society. Such unifying themes not only cross traditional disciplinary boundaries, but also develop over the entire course of a K–12 education. Thus these themes need to be well articulated across age groups, as well as across specific disciplinary content, to facilitate the growth of students' knowledge as a rich fabric of understanding rather than isolated bits and pieces of knowledge. For example, an understanding of scale can bridge gaps and provide a framework for concepts in mathematics (e.g., number sense, fractions), geography (e.g., landmass, populations), or Earth science (energy use).

> ## TABLE 1.
> ### Benchmarks for Science Literacy: Concepts of Scale
>
> **What students should know by the end of**
>
> **Grade 2:** Things have very different sizes, weights, ages, and speeds.
>
> **Grade 5:** Things have limits on how big or small they can be.
>
> **Grade 5:** The biggest and smallest values are as revealing as the usual value.
>
> **Grade 8:** Properties depend on volume change out of proportion to properties that depend on area.
>
> **Grade 8:** As the complexity of a system increases, summaries and typical examples are increasingly important.
>
> **Grade 12:** Representing large and small numbers in powers of ten makes it easier to think about and compare things.
>
> **Grade 12:** Large changes in scale change the way that things work.
>
> **Grade 12:** As the parts of a system increase in number, the number of interactions increases much more rapidly.
>
> Summarized from *Benchmarks for Science Literacy* (AAAS 1993, pp. 277–279).

Emerging Nanoscale Developments

A look at just one aspect of scale—nanoscale—shows a need to educate the public about the rapid developments in nanotechnology. The National Science Foundation (NSF), along with 17 other agencies and departments in the National Nanotechnology Initiative, has identified a need to educate students and citizens about advances in the nanoscale sciences. Innovations and changes in nanotechnology are happening very rapidly, and some scientists speculate that nanotechnology will replace genomics as the next scientific revolution. The NSF has committed more than $100 million for nanotechnology research centers, undergraduate education programs, and nanoscale science and edu-

xiii

cation. From the federal level, there is a tremendous demand for students who can fill jobs in nanoscale science and an even greater demand for an educated citizenry that can participate in the decisions that will arise from advances in nanotechnology. Already students can buy clothes in stores that are covered with "nanocare" stain-resistant technology, nanocarbon balls are being sold to keep refrigerators odor free, and nanoscale channels sample glucose levels in small diabetic monitors. Citizens may soon be asked to make decisions about injectable, nanometer-sized blood monitors that will float in the bloodstream, or the potential release of nano-sized pollution scrubbers into the atmosphere, or whether we should use nanotechnology to rearrange atoms in designing molecules. If people don't know how small a nanometer is (10^{-9} meters) and cannot conceptualize the scale of materials of this size, how can they begin to make decisions about the efficacy and ethics of the emerging technologies?

Scaling effects are often complex, and teaching scaling effects is a particular challenge for educators. For example, at the smallest of scales, counterintuitive properties emerge. Along with extensive properties such as mass, volume, and surface area, properties normally thought of as intensive, such as color, conductivity, magnetization, and hardness, change as an object becomes small and approaches the nanometer scale. The color of semiconductor quantum dots can be changed continuously by altering nothing but the size of the particle (Bruchez et al. 1998). If made small enough, a magnetic iron particle will completely lose its magnetism (Majetich and Jin 1999). Individual silicon nanospheres between 40 and 100 nanometers in size exhibit much greater hardness than bulk silicon (Gerberich et al. 2003). At this scale, nature has different rules, some of which are beautiful and unexpected.

At the nanoscale, properties of objects are dramatically different from those at the macroscale. These properties include ***bumpiness:*** Things tend to be *bumpy* rather than *smooth*. "Bumpiness" not only refers to geometrical bumpiness but also includes bumpiness in the magnetic, electronic, optical, and mechanical properties. ***Stickiness*** takes over at the nanoscale, and everything sticks together; gravity is irrelevant. At this scale relevant forces include the van der Waals forces, hydrogen bonding, and hydrophobic bonding. For very tiny objects at the nanoscale, ***shakiness*** dominates; everything shivers and shakes, and nothing stands still.

Size and Scale

The influence of scaling effects on size acts as a limiting factor for many flora and fauna (Stevens 1976; Brown and West 2000). The recent discovery of the dime-sized world's smallest lizard highlights an example of scaling effects determining a physiological lower size limit for such an animal. As the biologist who discovered it remarked, "If we don't provide a moist environment when we collect them, they rapidly shrivel right up and die by evaporation from the proportionally large area of their surface" (NSF 2002, p. 14). At an intersection of biology, chemistry, and physics, gecko setae—the millions of tiny hairs that branch off the toes of a gecko—provide enough adhesive force for geckos to climb virtually anything using van der Waals forces. These forces become significant only at very small scales, and that is why the small size of the setae is vital for the gecko's climbing ability. Scientists have nanofabricated artificial setal tips from different materials and observed the strong adhesive properties that are due to their size and shape, potentially leading to the manufacture of the first dry adhesive microstructures (Autumn et al. 2002). As Thompson writes about scaling effects in his classic work *On Magnitude*, "The predominant factors are no longer those of our [human] scale; we have come to the edge of a world of which we have no experience, and where all our preconceptions must be recast" (Thompson 1917/1961, p.48).

Limits to Size

Humans have long been curious about creatures of minuscule or gargantuan extremes of size, as is evident in the themes of many movies and books. Could a person shrink to the size of an ant and survive? Could a butterfly grow to the size of an airplane? Why or why not? Answers to these questions and many others that students ponder can be illuminated through investigating limits to size. Limits to the size of physical structures, especially that of living organisms, are influenced by factors such as surface tension, gravity, allometry (differing growth rates), diffusion, support structures (i.e., bones), and surface area-to-volume ratios. These limits to size can be applied at the cellular level or to the whole organism. The same factors that limit the size of a cell also limit the size of the organism. Body temperature regulation, metabolism, uptake of nutrients, disposal of waste products, cell growth, enzymatic activity, and bone structure/length are all scale dependent.

An animal's mass and the stress on its bones must also be considered. Structural support for our bodies (bones) cannot be scaled up to the size of a skyscraper and still function properly. For example, imagine holding down one end of a meterstick on the edge of a table. The stick will remain almost straight, bending only very slightly by its own weight, even if cantilevered out most of its length. If we simply scale a meter stick up 200 times, so that it is 200 m long and perhaps 1.0 m thick, this scaled-up version will break under its own weight if most of its length is cantilevered and unsupported. Simply put, the larger the mechanical supports, the more they distort under their own weight, even if scaled proportionally. So an organism's bones, if scaled to large enough size, would simply break under their own weight. Even though larger land animals have thicker leg and arm bones in proportion to their body size,

XV

there is a certain body size above which bones become too weak to support the body.

Limits to size and surface area-to-volume ratios obviously play a role in processes occurring in living things. These relationships play a role in physical and chemical reactions that occur as well. The dominant forces and types of bonding may shift as one's investigations move from the macroscale to the nanoscale. Rates of chemical reactions also change depending on surface area-to-volume relationships.

The Habit of Quantitative Thinking: Scale and Understanding Our World

Dealing comfortably with large and small numbers and appreciating the absolute and relative scales of those numbers are essential skills not only in the sciences but in any endeavor where quantitative evaluation is important. A goal of this book is to help students develop those skills through quantitative exploration of groups of numbers that are particularly interesting (the fastest animals, the tallest buildings) and particularly important (the populations of the largest cities, the population of the entire earth, the age of the Earth). Exploring these concepts not only provides an interesting context in which to practice quantitative manipulations and comparisons, but also provides content knowledge for students in subjects of scientific, social, political, and economic importance. In the context of populations, developing a quantitative conceptualization of the absolute scale of national and world populations will undoubtedly come in handy as the students start wrestling with social and political issues including globalization, economics, and environmentalism. Developing an understanding of absolute time scales and benchmarks (from human and historical time scales to geological and evolutionary time scales) will inform and greatly enhance students' understanding of subjects as varied as history, geology, and evolution.

It is also crucial for students to gain an understanding of the appropriate degree of precision for discussing quantitative information and to recognize the power and utility of estimation. For example, there are between 6 billion and 7 billion people currently living on Earth. Knowing that there are 6.62 billion is of little additional utility in most contexts and can in fact imply greater precision than is appropriate (by they time you read this it might be 6.63 billion). Exercises providing students practice in the art of rough estimation, or "order of magnitude" estimates of quantities in question, will help them gain comfort with the habit of quantitative thinking while simultaneously familiarizing them with the size of important numbers that describe their world. The numbers that describe our world cover a mind-boggling spectrum of magni-

NATIONAL SCIENCE TEACHERS ASSOCIATION

tudes; identifying the correct scale is the essential first step. A student with the skill to make an educated guess at the magnitude or scale of a problem can reach into her toolbox and pick the proper ruler.

Overview of Investigations

This book is organized into a developmental framework that includes the following sections: an introduction to types of scale, measurement, powers of ten, estimation and models of scale, surface area-to-volume relationships, limits to size, and behaviors at different scales. These sections are designed to help students develop skills in measuring and applying scale, an appreciation for the value of different scales in scientific work, and an understanding of the powerful role that scale has in limiting natural systems, as well as to lay a foundation for students to investigate more complex issues in scaling, such as how phenomena and materials behave differently at different scales.

The instruction is designed so that it can be used flexibly at the middle and high school levels. Each investigation is designed around a modified learning cycle (engage, explore, explain, extend, and evaluate) that begins with background information for the teacher and lists of specific objectives and process skills. The "Engage" section presents a question, challenge, or phenomenon for students to consider. It is followed by the "Explore" section, in which students actively investigate an area of scale. Students then attempt to make sense of their investigation, in collaboration with their peers and the teacher, in the "Explain" section. The "Extend" part of the lesson guides students into thinking of new or different applications or uses for scale. Finally the students are presented with a series of questions that evaluate their understandings of the investigation. The lessons are designed to build scale concepts across the different science domains (see Table 2, p. xxiii).

Introduction to Scale

The book begins with an investigation, *What Is Scale?* in which the range of extreme scales is explored by a fact-or-fiction activity. In the activity *Types of Scale*, students examine the array of different scales that exist for measuring time, mass, volume, and length, as well as less-well-known scales that are used for rating and measuring things such as clouds, wind, earthquakes, or the hardness of rocks.

Measurement

Measurement skills are taught in various investigations. However, in the activity *Oops! I Did It Again: Errors in Measurement*, students measure using different metric and English units, explore the history of measurement, and examine errors in measurement by looking at repeated measurements and random errors.

xvii

Powers of Ten

Students' examination of the powers of ten begins with the card-sorting activity, *Sort It Out*, in which the students think about objects from the very large to the very small and sort them according to size. This investigation challenges them to think about both horizontal and vertical scale. For example, they must decide which is larger—the height of the Empire State Building or the diameter of the Earth. The next challenge is to compare relative and absolute sizes of things in the investigation *It's Not All Relative: Relative Versus Absolute*. This task involves students in placing objects on a string number line, first with relative size and then by adding the appropriate power of ten to each object. Students have to think about the meaning of 10^0 and how to order a series of objects that range in size from 10^{-5} meters to 10^5 meters. *Scaling the Solar System* involves students in scaling the solar system down to the size of a large field and determining the relative size and location of each planet. In the activity *Time Flies*, students explore the geological time scale in the context of major events from the biological, physical, and Earth sciences, as well as from their own personal lives. What are the largest cities on Earth? How do the sizes of other cities compare with the size of your hometown? By pursuing these questions in depth in the activity *Billions of Us*, students also gain knowledge of the absolute scale of important numbers that will help them better interpret their world.

Estimation and Modeling

Skills in estimation and modeling are extended in a series of investigations. Through the lesson *Scale It!* students learn how to create models at different scales, as well as map the school environment at different scales. *Mega Virus* takes students from the nano world (10^{-9} meters) to the macroworld (10^0 meters) as they build a giant icosahedral virus model.

Your World or Mine? Different Perspectives involves students in examining objects and environments from different perspectives. Students draw the environment looking down from a bird's nest high in a tree and looking up at a potted plant from the perspective of an ant. They draw the phases of the Moon as viewed from Earth. Large scale is examined in the investigations using GIS (Geographic Information Systems). In the lesson *Eye in the Sky* students use satellite data to look at the environment. With a zooming tool they are able to map the increasing detail that is revealed about their environment such as tree canopies, Africanized honeybees, and topography. In *Drops to the Ocean* students investigate river basins and map scale using GIS as a tool. They work first with paper maps, establishing relationships between terrain and water flow. Next they investigate how map scale determines the level of detail shown on paper and interactive GIS maps. Magnification is explored in *Zoom Zoom: Magnification* with hand lenses, video cameras, and microscopes, as students examine and draw different objects at varying magnifications.

Surface Area-to-Volume Relationships

Limits to the size of organisms and their structures go hand and hand with surface area-to-volume ratios. Because this relationship affects so many aspects not only of living organisms but also of physical and chemical processes, students investigate various scenarios in which surface area-to-volume relationships are evident. By completing the activity *That's Hot!*, students begin to understand that surface area size affects the rates of evaporation, heat loss, diffusion, and water loss. In the investigation *SWEET! Exploring Surface Area of Sugar Molecules* the phenomenon of gravity is examined in relation to surface area-to-volume ratios of various structures.

Limits to Size

Students learn how scale limits a number of processes and phenomena in the natural world through investigating the pore size of eggs or the exoskeletons of insects and other structures found in living organisms. Processes that occur in living things are only efficient under certain conditions. For example in the activity *Captivating Cubes* students model the efficiency of diffusion into and out of a cell, as determined by the cell's surface area-to-volume ratio. This principle is explored by students in activities such as *Eggsactly* (investigating diffusion of gases to the chick embryo in eggs of various sizes) and *Attack of the Giant Bug?* (investigating how the size of an insect is limited by processes of respiration, as well as the weight of the exoskeleton).

Behaviors and Scale

One of the more challenging ideas that students need to become acquainted with is that materials may behave differently at different scales. For example, gravity and magnetism, although present, may play minor roles on the behavior of materials at the nanoscale, where electrostatics or friction has significant influence on materials. Students explore the movement of materials such as Styrofoam of various sizes in *Flying Foam: The Scale of Forces*. The influence of static on balls of different sizes is investigated in *Stick With It*, which models the changes in behavior that take place at very small scales.

Students investigate self-similarity of geometrical features at different scales for fractal objects in *Fractals: Self-Similar at Different Scales*. This investigation involves students in examining fern fronds, tree symmetry, and river patterns, as well as creating fractals from basic patterns. This lesson sets the groundwork for more complex systems levels of scaling that are often used in science. Light is just one type of electromagnetic radiation and belongs to what scientists call the *visible* portion of the electromagnetic (EM) spectrum. In the activity *Screening My Calls: Scale and the Electromagnetic Spectrum* students explore the properties that vary dramatically as the scale of the wavelength changes. Using the electro-

xix

magnetic spectrum as an example, students consider how different scales give rise to very different phenomena. *Stringy Chemistry and States of Matter* explores the important concept that molecules come in many different sizes. The size of molecules is one of the most important of the parameters that determine the properties of a substance. Scaling is applied in *Our Amazing Senses*, in which students examine the magnitude of difference in our perceptions of soft and loud sounds. They explore how few particles our senses of smell and sight can detect. The investigation *Beetlemice Multitudes!!! Power Law and Exponential Scaling* uses an imaginary population to explore exponential growth. Students determine the population growth over time and the amount of space that would be needed to contain it. Students are then challenged to apply power law to figure out whether a set of cubes and spheres are hollow or solid.

A Sense of Scale

One of the goals of science education is to help students develop a meaningful *sense of scale*. Students should be able to measure, estimate, and apply scale in different contexts. To have a meaningful sense of scale means that students are able to predict and monitor their investigations to know when their quantitative measurements are significantly in error.

One way we gain an intellectual understanding of our world is through numbers. Quantitative scales are where the world and numbers meet; they serve as the standards for measuring that world. A scale is ultimately a magnitude (a pure number) and a unit (a chunk of the world) tied together in a useful way. To measure, or quantitatively understand, something requires the ability to identify the appropriate unit (what kind of thing is it? what ruler should I use to measure it?) and the appropriate magnitude (how big is it?). Professionals ranging from physicists, to earth scientists, to social scientists, to politicians who use numbers as a part of their daily work gain skill in identifying these appropriate units and magnitudes. Comfort with the ability to estimate and evaluate quantitatively is crucial in a wide range of intellectual efforts, and it comes down to identifying the appropriate scale: What unit? What magnitude?

Research on learning is beginning to document the skills and concepts that students need to master as they develop a sense of scale (see Figure 1). Learning scale begins with learning about quantities and numbers. For young children this translates into learning about sizes and amounts. From early in school, measurement skills are critical if students are to be able to understand size and scale. Learning what measurement tool to use and how to use tools accurately continues throughout schooling. Our research has found that scientists report childhood experiences building and making models as very important in their development of a sense of scale. Scientists also report that frequent

xx

FIGURE 1.
Skills and Concepts to Develop a Sense of Scale.

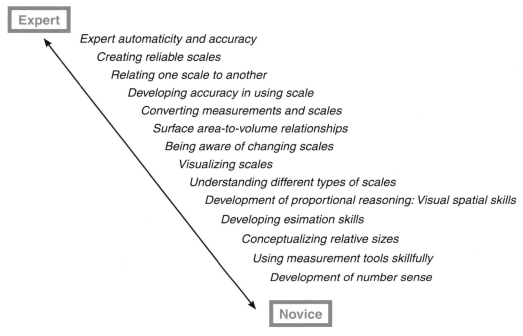

Expert

Expert automaticity and accuracy
Creating reliable scales
Relating one scale to another
Developing accuracy in using scale
Converting measurements and scales
Surface area-to-volume relationships
Being aware of changing scales
Visualizing scales
Understanding different types of scales
Development of proportional reasoning: Visual spatial skills
Developing esimation skills
Conceptualizing relative sizes
Using measurement tools skillfully
Development of number sense

Novice

opportunities to explore the outdoor world through hiking, biking, and traveling in cars and planes helped them understand scale and how perspectives of size change with distance (like watching a ship come across the horizon). In middle school, students' increased proportional reasoning and visual spatial skills enable them to conceptualize more complicated aspects of scale, such as surface area-to-volume relationships. This includes being able to visualize mentally and to manipulate scales and changes in scales. At the more expert levels of scale use, scientists learn to invent reliable scales (not unlike operationally defining variables in experiments) as well as to use measurements with rapid automaticity. Experts in science report that they use "body benchmarks" as conceptual rulers to make estimations quickly, measuring with their fingers or arms or pacing off distances. Other critical strategies included developing conceptual anchors (such as the size of a carbon nanotube or the size of a cell) that helped scientists navigate from the human-sized world to smaller worlds at the micro- or nanoscale. These skills of inventing scales, developing benchmarks, learning to estimate, and applying body rulers can be taught throughout schooling and can help students learn and apply scale in different science contexts.

The investigations in this book are designed to help students develop a comprehensive and flexible sense of scale through experiences with the quan-

xxi

titative units and tools of science. The investigations build on our research, which has documented how people learn scale. The goal of the book is for all students to develop a meaningful *sense of scale*. Understanding scale is where a quantitative understanding of the world begins.

References

American Association for the Advancement of Science (AAAS). 1989. *Science for all Americans.* Washington, DC: AAAS.

American Association for the Advancement of Science (AAAS). 1993. *Benchmarks for science literacy.* New York: Oxford University Press.

Anderson, P. W. 1972. More is different. *Science* 177: 393–396.

Autumn, K., M. Sitti, Y. A. Liang, A. M. Peattie, W. R. Hansen, S. Sponberg, T. W. Kenny, R. Fearing, J. N. Israelachvili, and R. J. Full. 2002. Evidence for van der Waals adhesion in gecko setae. *Proceedings of the National Academy of Sciences of the United States of America* 99 (19): 12252–12256.

Brown, J. H., and G. B. West, eds. 2000. *Scaling in biology.* New York: Oxford University Press.

Bruchez, M., M. Moronee, P. Gin, S. Weiss, and A. Alivisatos. 1998. Semiconductor nanocrystals as florescent biological labels. *Science* 281 (5385): 2013–2016.

Gallagher, R., and T. Appenzeller, eds. 1999. Special Issue on Complex Systems. *Science* 284: 79–109.

Gerberich, W. W., W. M. Mook, C. R. Perrey, C. B. Carter, M. I. Baskes, R. Mukherjee, A. Gidwani, J. Heberlein, P. H. McMurry, and S. L. Girshick. 2003. Superhard silicon nanospheres. *Journal of the Mechanics and Physics of Solids* 51 (6): 979–992.

Majetich, S., and Y. Jin. 1999. Magnetization directions of individual nanoparticles. *Science* 284: 470–473.

National Council of Teachers of Mathematics (NCTM). 2000. *Principles and standards for school mathematics.* Reston, VA: NCTM.

National Research Council (NRC). 1996. *National science education standards.* Washington, DC: National Academy Press.

National Science Foundation (NSF). 2002. A little lizard. *The Science Teacher* 69 (2): 14.

National Science Teachers Association (NSTA). 1993. *Scope, sequence and coordination of secondary school science. Vol. 1. The content core: A guide for curriculum designers (revised).* Washington, DC: NSTA Press.

Schmidt, W. H., C. C. McKnight, and S. A. Raizen. 1997. *A splintered vision: An investigation of U.S. science and mathematics education.* Boston: Kluwer Academic Publishers.

Stevens, P. S. 1976. *Patterns in nature.* New York: Penguin Books.

Thompson, D.'A. W. 1917/1961. *On growth and form.* London: Cambridge University Press.

TABLE 2.
Investigations and Science Domains

Investigations	Biology	Physics	Chemistry	Mathematics	Earth Science
Introduction to Scale					
What Is Scale?	•	•	•	•	•
Types of Scale	•	•	•	•	•
Measurement					
Oops, I Did It Again: Errors in Measurement	•	•	•	•	•
Powers of Ten					
Sort It Out				•	
It's Not All Relative: Relative Versus Absolute					
Scaling the Solar System				•	•
Time Flies When You're Learning About Scale!	•				•
Billions of Us: Scale & Population				•	•
Estimation & Models					
Scale it!				•	
Mega Virus	•			•	
Your World or Mine? Different Perspectives				•	
Eye in the Sky: An Introduction to GIS & Scale					•
Drops to the Ocean: A GIS Study of River Basins					•
Zoom Zoom: Magnification	•	•		•	•
Surface Area-to-Volume Relationships					
That's Hot! The Effect of Size on Rate of Heat Loss	•	•	•		•
SWEET! Exploring Surface Area of Sugar Molecules		•	•	•	
Limits to Size					
Captivating Cubes: Investigating Surface Area-to-Volume Ratio	•	•		•	
Eggsactly	•			•	
Attack of the Giant Bug?	•			•	
Behaviors & Scale					
Flying Foam: The Scale of Forces		•		•	
Stick With It		•		•	
Fractals: Self-Similar at Different Scales	•	•		•	
Screening My Calls: Scale & the Electromagnetic Spectrum		•		•	
Stringy Chemistry & States of Matter		•	•	•	
Our Amazing Senses	•	•	•	•	
Beetlemice Multitudes!!! Power Law & Exponential Scaling	•	•		•	

INTRODUCTION TO SCALE

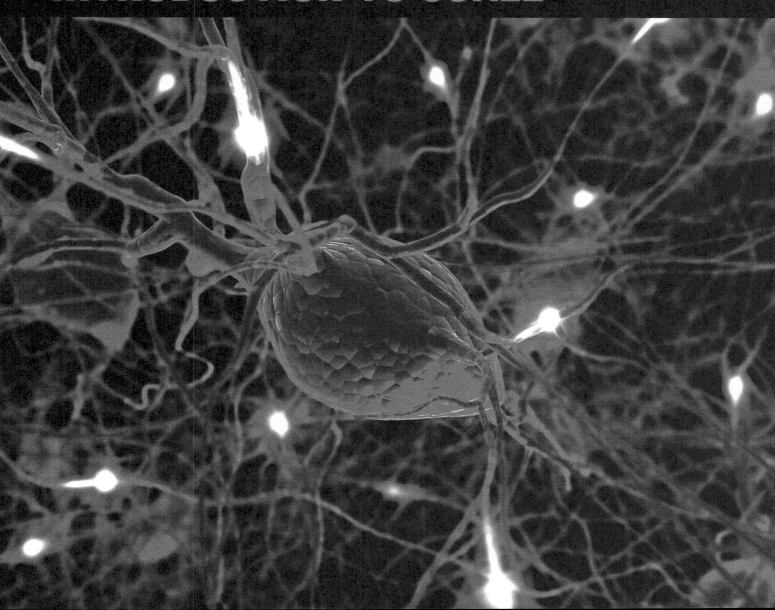

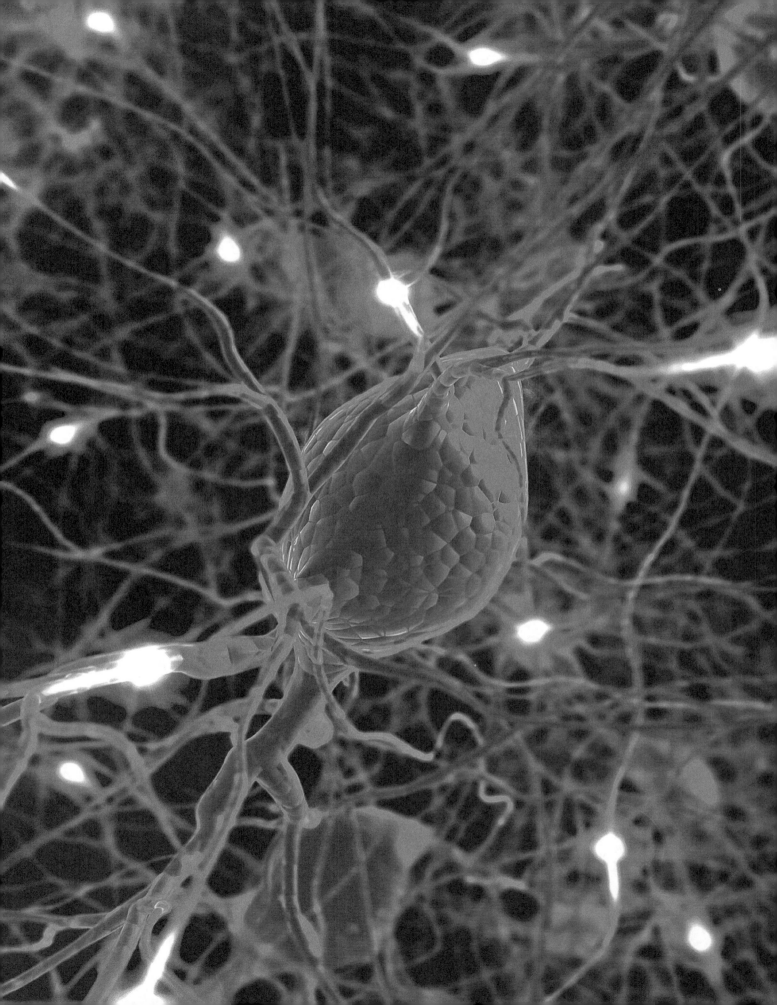

Chapter 1
What Is Scale?

Overview

Scale is one of the big ideas that cross the science domains. Whether one is talking about the weight of a blue whale, the size of a galaxy or a molecule, or the age of a mountain range, scale is an essential tool in understanding the universe in a scientific way. But what exactly is scale, and why is it important? In this investigation students explore size and scale by examining the wide range of scales that are investigated in science.

Objectives

- To develop an understanding of the range of sizes and scales that exists.
- To understand the extremes of size for different living and nonliving things.

Process Skills

- Observing
- Predicting
- Analyzing data

Activity Duration

30 minutes total

Background

The American Association for the Advancement of Science has identified scale as one of the four major unifying themes of science in *Benchmarks for Science Literacy* (AAAS 1993). Understanding scaling is essential for learning life, physical, and Earth/space sciences. Not only are these ideas useful within the various science disciplines, but they also cut across the curriculum in such subjects as mathematics, history, or English literature. An understanding of scale can help students make cross-curricular connections in the different science domains.

This investigation is designed to interest students in thinking about scale and scaling by examining the amazing range of sizes and distances that scientists study today. After completing this introduction to scale, students should complete the investigation *Types of Scale* to survey the different types of scales and then invent their own unique scales.

Materials

Each student will need:
- Fact or Fiction Extreme Size Card tied with string
- Student Data Sheets

Engage

Ask students, *What was the largest animal ever to live on Earth? Was it the dinosaur, the whale, or perhaps the mammoth?* As they brainstorm, record their predictions and ideas about the sizes of very large animals on the board. You may want to discuss how to define *largest*. Would this be length, volume, or mass?

Ask the students, *How tall was the largest tree ever to live?* Encourage them to give their best estimation if they are uncertain.

3

Explain that in this investigation they will explore the wide range of sizes and distances that scientists investigate in doing research.

Also explain that one of the crucial skills in science is making estimates of scale. Sometimes these estimates are quite rough. Scientists sometimes call this an "order of magnitude estimate," which roughly translates as an estimate of which power of ten a number belongs to.

Explore
Part I

Begin the activity by passing out Student Data Sheet for Part I: Estimating Size. Ask each student to predict the truth of each statement by indicating whether it is fact or fiction. Answers should be recorded on the Student Data Sheet.

Part II

Give each student a Fact or Fiction Extreme Size Card. Instruct them to walk around the room and ask at least five other people to give their best estimate of whether the statement on the card is fact or is fiction and to discuss their responses. Each student should record the responses on Part II of the Student Data Sheet.

After students have had a chance to circulate and discuss the answers, have them return to their seats. Ask them to share their best guess as to whether the statement on their card is fact or fiction. Following the student responses, the correct answer can be shared and filled in on the Student Data Sheet.

Part III

Before engaging the students in the multiple-choice order of magnitude exercise of Part III, introduce the idea and motivation for such estimates. Sometimes we just want to know roughly how large a number is. Gaining this skill is very important to a student's development of a scientific sense. If absolute precision is emphasized too much, students will have the sense that they know nothing unless they know the exact number (the distance to the moon, or the weight of a blue whale). Knowing how to estimate roughly, based on prior knowledge, is usually more important than knowing a precise number. As we will explore in the *Errors in Measurement* investigation, often a precise number is not really known or cannot be known. You could provide an illustration to help the students understand this concept by asking the question, *How many people live on Earth today?* Explain that no one knows the answer to this to the nearest person or even to the nearest hundred. In fact, actual population is changing second to second (with deaths and births). However, we do know that there are between 6 billion and 7 billion people on Earth (in the "ones of

4

billions"). Knowing that there are a few billion people on Earth, rather than a few trillion or a few million, is what is important in this exercise.

The challenge problems require the students to do a rough calculation. This again is a crucial skill in science. Emphasize that to answer the challenge questions correctly, one does not need to measure the size of a piece of paper or the floor of the classroom precisely but does need to make a reasonably good guess. One should be able to do these challenge problems using pencil and paper but with no actual measurements.

Explain

It is important to tell students that the goal of this investigation is to develop a broad sense of number and scale and not to memorize exact numbers. For example, it is worth knowing approximately how many millions or billions of people there are on Earth but not critical to know the number to the exact person. Scientists often use what is known as an "order of magnitude estimate." This is a very rough assessment of the magnitude of a quantity. For example, a question might be posed this way: *Do you think the tallest tree in the world is several feet tall, several tens of feet tall, several hundreds of feet tall, or several thousands of feet tall?* Though imprecise, these types of estimates help scientists gauge the scale of a parameter that helps refine questions and proceed deeper into a problem. It's also a very powerful exercise for helping students learn to think critically and creatively, rather than simply memorize magnitudes.

People have a natural fascination with extremes of size, and many of the examples given in this investigation can be found on the internet with accompanying photos and video clips. You may want to show students a photo of the giant dog that weighs 282 pounds or the rabbit with 31-inch ears (website references provided on the answer sheet). It is also worth pointing out that although these are the extremes of size today, there is always the potential for a new, record-breaking size to appear in the future.

5

Fact or Fiction?
Answer Sheet

1. **The blue whale is the largest of all the living animals.**

   Answer: Fact

   Explanation: The largest blue whale recorded was 108 feet in length. A very heavy whale was recorded as weighing 190 tons.

   Source: *http://nationalzoo.si.edu/Animals/AnimalRecords*

2. **The smallest dog known is 6 inches from nose to tail.**

   Answer: Fact

   Explanation: The smallest dog recorded was a Chihuahua named Brandy that was 6 inches from the nose to the tip of the tail.

   Source: *www.guinnessworldrecords.com/records/natural_world/animal_extremes/smallest_dog_living_(length).aspx*

3. **The longest ears ever measured on a rabbit were 31 inches long.**

   Answer: Fact

   Explanation: An English Lop rabbit named Geronimo had giant ears that were more than 31 inches in length.

   Source: *www.guinnessworldrecords.com/records/natural_world/animal_extremes/longest_ears_on_a_rabbit.aspx*

4. **The tallest tree ever to live was a giant sequoia at 275 feet.**

   Answer: False

   Explanation: The largest single tree in height is a redwood, known as the Mendocino Tree, that measures 367 feet and 6 inches. This tree is thought to be more than 1,000 years old. The most massive tree was the giant sequoia tree known as General Sherman, which was 275 feet tall with a girth of 102 feet and 8 inches.

   Source: *http://www.zilkha.com/superlativetrees.html*

5. **The tallest living woman is 8 feet 2 inches tall.**

   Answer: Fiction

   Explanation: The tallest living woman was Sandy Allen, who was 7 feet 7 inches in height at her death on August 13, 2008. She had a pituitary gland disorder that contributed to her unusual growth.

   Source: *www.guinnessworldrecords.com/records/human_body/extreme_bodies/tallest_man_-_living.aspx*

6

6. **The tallest living man is 8 feet 5 inches tall.**

   Answer: Fact

   Explanation: The tallest living man is Leonid Stadnyk, who is 8 feet 5 inches tall.

   Source: *www.guinnessworldrecords.com/records/human_body/extreme_bodies/ tallest_man_-_living.aspx*

7. **The smallest bird is the hummingbird at 2 inches long.**

   Answer: Fact

   Explanation: The smallest bird is the bee hummingbird of Cuba, which is about 2 inches long and weighs less than a dime.

   Source: *http://en.wikipedia.org/wiki/Bee_Hummingbird*

8. **The largest known invertebrate is the coconut crab at 2.5 feet.**

   Answer: Fiction

   Explanation: The largest invertebrate is the giant squid, which can be up to 43 feet long. The coconut crab is the largest land invertebrate and can reach up to 2.5 feet.

   Source: *http://nationalzoo.si.edu/Animals/AnimalRecords*

9. **The smallest frog is 2 millimeters in length.**

   Answer: Fiction

   Explanation: The smallest frog in the Northern Hemisphere is the tiny black frog with orange stripes *Eleutherodactylus Iberia,* which is only about 1 centimeter long (10 millimeters). The tiny frog was discovered in 1996 living under leaf litter in Cuba.

   Source: *www.nsf.gov/news/news_summ.jsp?cntn_id=101828*

10. **The shortest adult cat is 6.1 inches tall.**

    Answer: Fact

    Explanation: Mr. Peebles, the cat, lives in Illinois and holds the world record as the smallest cat.

    Source: *www.cat-world.com.au/CatRecords.htm*

7

Fact or Fiction?
Answer Sheet

11. The smallest horse is 2 feet tall.

Answer: Fiction

Explanation: The world's smallest dwarf miniature horse, named Thumbelina, is 17.5 inches tall.

Source: *www.reuters.com/news/video/videoStory?videoId=55080*

12. The world's tallest building is the Empire State Building at 1,250 feet.

Answer: Fiction

Explanation: The tallest building (as of 2008) is the Taipei 101 Tower that stands 1,670 feet tall. The Burj Dubai Tower is under construction in Dubai and is expected to be the tallest building when completed.

Source: *http://architecture.about.com/library/bltall.htm*

13. The tallest mountain is Mt. Everest, which is 29,035 feet tall.

Answer: Fact

Explanation: Mt. Everest is the tallest mountain above sea level. Mauna Kea, in Hawaii, is the tallest from base to peak, but much of it lies beneath the ocean. Mauna Kea is a total of 33,480 feet tall.

Source: *http://geography.about.com/library/faq/blqzmanuakea.htm*

14. The world's largest spider is the tarantula at 1 foot long.

Answer: Fact

Explanation: The goliath bird-eating tarantula is the largest spider. This spider can grow up to a foot long.

Source: *http://news.nationalgeographic.com/news/2006/10/061027-tarantula-video.html*

15. The Madagascar hissing cockroach is the largest roach in the world.

Answer: Fiction

Explanation: The Madagascar hissing cockroach is large, but the largest is the giant burrowing cockroach, which can reach up to 80 millimeters (3.15 inches).

Source: *www.abc.net.au/creaturefeatures/facts/cockroach.htm*

8

16. **The deepest part of the ocean is 1 mile deep.**

Answer: Fiction

Explanation: The deepest part of the ocean is the Mariana Trench in the Pacific Ocean, which is about 6.8 miles deep (36,090 feet).

Source: *http://en.wikipedia.org/wiki/List_of_deepest_ocean_trenches*

17. The largest single cell is the ostrich egg.

Answer: Fact

Explanation: The unfertilized ostrich egg is a single cell and is the largest single cell known.

Source: *http://wiki.answers.com/Q/What_is_the_largest_single_cell*

18. The longest snake ever found was 60 feet long.

Answer: Fiction

Explanation: The longest snake ever found was the green anaconda that was measured and found to be 11.5 meters (37.7 feet).

Source: *www.thewildclassroom.com/biodiversity/snakes/main/giantsnakes.html*

19. The longest bridge in the world is the bridge from Miami to Key West, Florida.

Answer: Fiction

Explanation: The longest bridge is the new bridge that China has opened that spans Hangzhou Bay and is 36 kilometers long (22.37 miles).

Source: *http://entertainment.timesonline.co.uk/tol/arts_and_entertainment/visual_arts/architecture_and_design/article3858256.ece*

20. The distance from the center of the Earth to the Moon is about 230,000 miles.

Answer: Fact

Explanation: The Moon is about 230,000 miles from the center of the Earth, but because the Moon moves around the Earth in an ellipse, the distance will be a bit smaller or greater depending on where the Moon is in its orbit around the Earth.

Source: *www.universetoday.com/2008/04/21/what-is-the-distance-to-the-moon*

9

21. There are about 3 million people on Earth.

Answer: Fiction

Explanation: It is estimated that there are about 6.5 billion people on Earth.

Source: *www.ined.fr/en/everything_about_population/faq/theme_1/*

22. The biggest dinosaur was *Tyrannosaurus rex*.

Answer: Fiction

Explanation: The largest dinosaur was *Brachiosaurus*, which was 75.4 feet long. *T. Rex* was about 40 feet long.

Source: *http://pubs.usgs.gov/gip/dinosaurs/sizes.html*

23. The longest domestic cat is 5 feet from nose to tail.

Answer: Fiction

Explanation: The longest cat in 2006 was a Maine Coon cat named Verismo that was 48 inches long and weighed 35 pounds.

Source: *www.verismocat.com/htmscripts/leo-guinness.htm*

24. An atom is about 100 picometers (0.0000000001 meters) in size.

Answer: Fact

Explanation: The atom is about 0.1 nanometers or 100 picometers in size.

Source: *http://wiki.answers.com/Q/What_is_the_size_of_the_atom*

25. The fastest mammal on land is the cheetah, which can run 70 miles per hour.

Answer: Fact

Explanation: Cheetahs are very fast and can run up to 70 miles per hour.

Source: *http://nationalzoo.si.edu/Animals/AnimalRecords*

10

Part III. The Skill of Estimating

1. How tall is the tallest building in the world?
    a. Tens of meters tall (10 m–99 m)
    b. Hundreds of meters tall (100 m–999 m)
    c. Thousands of meters tall (1,000 m–9,999 m)
    d. Tens of thousands of meters tall (10,000 m–99,999 m)

2. How fast can the fastest car in the world go?
    a. Tens of miles per hour
    b. Hundreds of miles per hour
    c. Thousands of miles per hour
    d. Tens of thousands of miles per hour

3. How fast can the fastest land animal (cheetah) go?
    a. Tens of miles per hour
    b. Hundreds of miles per hour
    c. Thousands of miles per hour
    d. Tens of thousands of miles per hour

4. How fast can the fastest bird go?
    a. Tens of miles per hour
    b. Hundreds of miles per hour
    c. Thousands of miles per hour
    d. Tens of thousands of miles per hour

5. What is the population of the whole Earth?
    a. Hundreds of thousands
    a. Millions
    b. Billions
    c. Hundreds of billions

6. What is the population of the United States?
    a. Thousands
    b. Hundreds of thousands
    c. Hundreds of millions
    d. Billions

11

7. What is the population of your city or town?
   a. Hundreds
   b. Thousands
   c. Tens of thousands
   d. Hundreds of thousands
   e. Millions

8. How far is it from New York City to Los Angeles (across the country)?
   a. Hundreds of kilometers
   b. Thousands of kilometers
   c. Tens of thousands of kilometers
   d. Hundreds of thousands of kilometers

9. How far would you travel if you went once around the Earth at the equator?
   a. Hundreds of kilometers
   b. Thousands of kilometers
   c. Tens of thousands of kilometers
   d. Hundreds of thousands of kilometers

10. How long ago was the United States founded?
   a. A few years ago
   b. Tens of years ago
   c. Hundreds of years ago
   d. Thousands of years ago

11. How long ago were the Egyptian pyramids built?
   a. Tens of years ago
   b. Hundreds of years ago
   c. Thousands of years ago
   d. Tens of thousands of years ago

12. How long ago did life emerge on Earth?
   a. Thousands of years ago
   b. Hundreds of thousands of years ago
   c. Millions of years ago
   d. Billions of years ago

12

13. How old is the universe?
   a. Hundreds of thousands of years old
   b. Millions of years old
   c. Billions of years old
   d. Tens of billions of years old

14. **CHALLENGE:**
   What is the volume of your classroom in cubic meters?

   Your classroom is likely to be about 10 m × 10 m (100 m² floor area) and ~3 m from floor to ceiling. The volume of your classroom is then: Volume = 10 m × 10 m × 3 m = 300 m³.

   Answer: c. Hundreds of cubic meters

   Note that this answer would be arrived at even with very different (but reasonable) guesses for room size. For example a floor area of 15 m × 15 m and a room height of 4 m (a very large classroom) yields:

   Volume = 15 m × 15 m × 4 m = 900 m³. Still in the hundreds of cubic meters.

15. **CHALLENGE:**
   What is the area of this piece of paper in square centimeters?

   The typical piece of notebook paper is roughly 20 cm × 30 cm.
   This yields 600 cm².

   Answer: a. Hundreds of square centimeters

16. **CHALLENGE:**
   What is the area of the floor of your classroom in square centimeters?

   Again, your classroom is likely to be roughly 10 m × 10 m. This is 1,000 cm by 1,000 cm. This yields an area of 1,000 cm × 1,000 cm, or 1 million cm². Depending on how large a room you are in and what numbers you used to estimate, your answer could be just below this or just above this, so either c or d would work.

   Answer: c. Hundreds of thousands of cm² or d. Millions of cm².

13

Extend

Challenge your students to find other examples of living and nonliving things that are at the extremes of size. Encourage them to find video clips or photos of new examples.

Many of the living organisms that are extremely large or small have genetic mutations, and there are often health complications that accompany these changes. Have students research acromegaly or gigantism. This condition results from a chronic exposure to growth hormone and can result in a person's growing to unusual heights.

Evaluate

1. Which environment is associated with the largest animals, the ocean or the land? Why do you think this is so?
2. Why are most living things found in a relatively narrow range of sizes?
3. How have miniature animals such as dogs evolved? Why is this?
4. How many people are on Earth? Is it thousands, millions, or billions? How many people live in the United States? China? India?

Resources

For more information on the sizes of things:

http://nationalzoo.si.edu/Animals/AnimalRecords/

www.guinnessworldrecords.com/records/natural_world/animal_extremes

www.zilkha.com/superlativetrees.html

www.cat-world.com.au/CatRecords.htm

http://architecture.about.com/library/bltall.htm

Source: *http://pubs.usgs.gov/gip/dinosaurs/sizes.html*

14

Name _____

Part I: Estimating Size

Directions

Complete the chart below, indicating in column 2 your best estimate of whether the statement is a fact or is fiction.

Exteme Size Statement	I think... *Fact or Fiction*	Answer
1. The blue whale is the largest of all the living animals.		
2. The smallest dog known is 6 inches from nose to tail.		
3. The longest ears ever measured on a rabbit were 31 inches long.		
4. The tallest tree ever to live was a giant sequoia at 275 feet.		
5. The tallest living woman is 8 feet 2 inches tall.		
6. The tallest living man is 8 feet 5 inches tall.		
7. The smallest bird is the hummingbird at 2 inches long.		
8. The largest known invertebrate is the coconut crab at 2.5 feet.		
9. The smallest frog is 2 millimeters in length.		
10. The shortest adult cat is 6.1 inches tall.		
11. The smallest horse is 2 feet tall.		
12. The world's tallest building is the Empire State Building at 1,250 feet.		
13. The tallest mountain is Mt. Everest, which is 29,035 feet tall.		
14. The world's largest spider is the tarantula at 1 foot long.		
15. The Madagascar hissing cockroach is the largest roach in the world.		
16. The deepest part of the ocean is 1 mile deep.		
17. The largest single cell is the ostrich egg.		
18. The longest snake ever found was 60 feet long.		
19. The longest bridge in the world is the bridge from Miami to Key West, Florida.		
20. The distance from the center of the Earth to the Moon is about 230,000 miles.		
21. There are about 3 million people on Earth.		
22. The biggest dinosaur was *Tyrannosaurus rex*.		
23. The longest domestic cat is 5 feet from nose to tail.		
24. An atom is about 100 picometers in size.		
25. The fastest mammal on land is the cheetah, which can run 70 miles per hour.		

15

Part II: Class Estimates of Size

Directions

Record your statement in the space below. Walk around the room and ask at least five different people to give you their best estimate about whether the statement is fact or fiction and why.

My Extreme Size Card

_____

Estimated Responses

1. _____

2. _____

3. _____

4. _____

5. _____

Questions for Discussion

1. Which Extreme Size Card answer surprised you the most?

2. Why do you think marine animals may be larger than land animals?

3. Are there limits to how tall we can build a building?

4. Why do people who are unusually large often have health problems?

16

Part III: The Skill of Estimating

Scientists often make rough guesses at the size of things or categorize the size or magnitude of a number based on its "order of magnitude" or "power of ten."

1. How tall is the tallest building in the world?

      a. Tens of meters tall (10 m–99 m)

      b. Hundreds of meters tall (100 m–999 m)

      c. Thousands of meters tall (1,000 m–9,999 m)

      d. Tens of thousands of meters tall (10,000 m–99,999 m)

2. How fast can the fastest car in the world go?

      a. Tens of miles per hour

      b. Hundreds of miles per hour

      c. Thousands of miles per hour

      d. Tens of thousands of miles per hour

3. How fast can the fastest land animal (cheetah) go?

      a. Tens of miles per hour

      b. Hundreds of miles per hour

      c. Thousands of miles per hour

      d. Tens of thousands of miles per hour

4. How fast can the fastest bird go?

      a. Tens of miles per hour

      b. Hundreds of miles per hour

      c. Thousands of miles per hour

      d. Tens of thousands of miles per hour

5. What is the population of the whole Earth?

      a. Hundreds of thousands

      b. Millions

      c. Billions

      d. Hundreds of billions

17

6. What is the population of the United States?

a. Thousands

b. Hundreds of thousands

c. Hundreds of millions

d. Billions

7. What is the population of your city or town?

a. Hundreds

b. Thousands

c. Tens of thousands

d. Hundreds of thousands

e. Millions

8. How far is it from New York City to Los Angeles (across the country)?

a. Hundreds of kilometers

b. Thousands of kilometers

c. Tens of thousands of kilometers

d. Hundreds of thousands of kilometers

9. How far would you travel if you went once around the Earth at the equator?

a. Hundreds of kilometers

b. Thousands of kilometers

c. Tens of thousands of kilometers

d. Hundreds of thousands of kilometers

10. How long ago was the United States founded?

a. A few years ago

b. Tens of years ago

c. Hundreds of years ago

d. Thousands of years ago

11. How long ago were the Egyptian pyramids built?

a. Tens of years ago

b. Hundreds of years ago

c. Thousands of years ago

d. Tens of thousands of years ago

18

12. How long ago did life emerge on Earth?
- a. Thousands of years ago
- b. Hundreds of thousands of years ago
- c. Millions of years ago
- d. Billions of years ago

13. How old is the universe?
- a. Hundreds of thousands of years old
- b. Millions of years old
- c. Billions of years old
- d. Tens of billions of years old

14. **CHALLENGE:**
What is the volume of your classroom in cubic meters?
- a. A few cubic meters
- b. Tens of cubic meters
- c. Hundreds of cubic meters
- d. Thousands of cubic meters.

15. **CHALLENGE:**
What is the area of this piece of paper in square centimeters?
- a. Hundreds of square centimeters
- b. Thousands of square centimeters
- c. Hundreds of thousands of square centimeters
- d. Millions of square centimeters

19

16. **CHALLENGE:**
What is the area of the floor of your classroom in square centimeters?
- a. Hundreds of square centimeters
- b. Thousands of square centimeters
- c. Hundreds of thousands of square centimeters
- d. Millions of square centimeters

Chapter 2
Types of Scale

Overview

Across the different sciences one of the common challenges that researchers encounter is defining and measuring different variables. An essential part of that process is creating and using scales. In this investigation students learn about a range of different scales that are used in everyday life. In addition, they create a unique scale to measure a new and novel variable.

Objectives

- To be able to describe nominal, ordinal, and interval scales.
- To be able to create a valid and reliable scale.

Process Skills

- Observing
- Predicting
- Analyzing data

Activity Duration

40 minutes total

Background

Researchers frequently face the need to accurately measure variables they encounter when studying phenomena. Measuring changes during experiments is dependent on having valid and reliable measurement tools and scales.

One of the first challenges in designing an experiment is to operationally define variables. In some cases this has already been done and is a standard part of scientific practice. An example is the measurement of temperature. In other cases the variables are less well known or have not been defined. Determining how to measure variables of interest is often interwoven with the process of defining the variable. We know how to measure temperature because the variable has been defined, the range of possible values has been determined, and tools have been developed with which we can measure temperature in consistent ways. But other variables of interest may be less well defined. For example, as we have developed new techniques for exploring the nano-sized world, we have discovered that things are very bumpy, shaky, and sticky. But what does it mean to say that something is bumpy, shaky, or sticky? How can we measure these variables so that we can figure out just how bumpy, shaky, or sticky things are at this very tiny scale?

Materials

Each student will need:
- Scale Card tied with string (one per student)

Engage

Ask students, *Have you have ever heard of a unit of measurement called a "smoot"?* The smoot is a unit of linear measurement that has become famous at the Massachusetts Insti-

21

tute of Technology (MIT). In 1958 a group of students was given the task of measuring the length of the bridge that connects MIT to Boston. The students decided to use the height of one of the students as the unit of measurement. This student, Oliver Smoot, was picked because he was the shortest student (5 feet 7 inches, or 5.58 feet). The students called his length a "smoot" because it sounded like other units, such as a watt or a meter. The group laid Oliver down over and over again across the bridge and figured out that the bridge was 364.4 smoots and one ear in length. Since then the smoot has become a famous unit of measurement.

Members of the MIT running club train for the Boston Marathon in smoot units and not miles. How many smoots would equal the length of the traditional marathon? (A marathon is 42.195 kilometers, which equals 138,435 feet. Dividing 138,435 feet by 5.58, the feet in a smoot, gives an answer of 24,809 smoots.)

Continue with your students: *Suppose we invent a new unit for this class. What would you want to call it? A Chris, a Madison, or a Mike? How many Mike's would we measure for the length of this room?*

One of the challenges that scientists have is creating scales that can be used to measure properties of things. In this lesson you will learn about a variety of different scales.

Explore

Different Types of Scale

Hang a scale card on the back of each student (see the template for cards on page 29). Instruct students not to look at their own cards until they have walked around and asked five other students to read their cards and make their best guesses as to what the scale measures. The students should record the different responses. After at least five answers have been given, the students should return to their seats, look at their scale card, and see if they can figure out what the scale measures. As a class, review the different cards and explain how the scales are used.

Explain

See the explanations for the different types of scales on the scale cards in the Types of Scale Answer Sheet (p. 24). Challenge students to determine whether the scale measures nominal, ordinal, interval, or ratio variables.

- *Nominal scales* are names or labels that describe a category. This type of scale does not have an order. An example of nominal data is gender or color.
- *Ordinal scales* have directionality or order. However, there is no consistent

distance between one measurement and the next. Ordering a group of people by height would be an example of an ordinal measurement.

- *Interval scales* have consistent distances between one measurement and the next but no zero point. An example of an interval scale is Fahrenheit temperature.
- *Ratio scales* have intervals between measurements and have a zero starting point. Age is an example of a ratio scale.

23

Types of Scale

1. **Apgar**

   Explanation: The Apgar scale is used to assess the health of newborn babies immediately upon birth. The scale ranges from 0 to 2 on five criteria (appearance, pulse, grimace, activity, respiration). Low scores quickly let physicians and nurses know that the baby needs attention.

   Apgar Scores

   0 Blue all over, no heart rate, no responsiveness to stimulation, no muscle tone, breathing absent

   1 Body pink but extremities blue, heart rate less than 100, feeble cry, some muscle tone, weak breathing

   2 Body and extremities pink, heart rate greater than 100, reacts when stimulated, actively moves, and strong breathing

   Source: *http://en.wikipedia.org/wiki/Apgar_score*

2. **Beaufort**

   Explanation: Measures the velocity of the wind. Describes how the wind would appear at sea and on land.

   Source: *www.unc.edu/~rowlett/units/scales/beaufort.html*

3. **Danjon**

   Explanation: A scale of lunar eclipse brightness from very dark (Moon almost invisible) to very bright copper-red.

   L = 0 Very dark eclipse.
     Moon almost invisible, especially at mid-totality.

   L = 1 Dark eclipse; gray or brownish in coloration.
     Details distinguishable only with difficulty.

   L = 2 Deep red or rust-colored eclipse.
     Very dark central shadow, while outer edge of umbra is relatively bright.

   L = 3 Brick-red eclipse.
     Umbral shadow usually has a bright or yellow rim.

   L = 4 Very bright copper-red or orange eclipse.
     Umbral shadow has a bluish, very bright rim.

   Source: *http://eclipse.gsfc.nasa.gov/OH/Danjon.html*

4. **Fujita Scale**

   Explanation: This scale measures the intensity of a tornado in terms of wind gusts.

   * F0 (Gale)
   * F1 (Weak)

* F2 (Strong)
* F3 (Severe)
* F4 (Devastating)
* F5 (Incredible)

Source: *www.spc.noaa.gov/efscale*

5. Mercalli Scale

Explanation: Measures the severity of an earthquake on a scale from 1 (not felt except by a few) to 12 (total destruction).

Source: U.S. Geological Survey pamphlet *The Severity of an Earthquake* (1986).

6. Saffir-Simpson Hurricane Intensity Scale

Explanation: The Saffir-Simpson Hurricane Scale measures a hurricane's intensity on a 1–5 rating. The scale is used to estimate the possible property damage and flooding that may occur as a hurricane comes ashore. Variables that go into the score are wind speed, slope of the continental shelf, and shape of the coastline.

Category 1 Hurricane:
Winds 74–95 mph (64–82 kt or 119–153 km/hr.)
Storm surge generally 4–5 ft. above normal

Category 2 Hurricane:
Winds 96–110 mph (83–95 kt or 154–177 km/hr.)
Storm surge generally 6–8 ft. above normal

Category 3 Hurricane:
Winds 111–130 mph (96–113 kt or 178–209 km/hr.)
Storm surge generally 9–12 ft. above normal

Category 4 Hurricane:
Winds 131–155 mph (114–135 kt or 210–249 km/hr.)
Storm surge generally 13–18 ft. above normal

Category 5 Hurricane:
Winds greater than 155 mph (135 kt or 249 km/hr.)
Storm surge generally greater than 18 ft. above normal

Source: *www.nhc.noaa.gov/aboutsshs.shtml*

7. Torino Scale

Explanation: Assesses asteroid and comet impact hazards from 0 (no hazard) to 10 (collision is certain).

Source: *http://neo.jpl.nasa.gov/torino_scale.html*

25

8. **Kelvin**

   Explanation: The Kelvin temperature scale (K) uses a zero point equal to −273.16°C. This zero point is known as "absolute zero" and is the lowest possible temperature. It is also known as the "absolute temperature scale." At the freezing point of water, the Kelvin scale reads 273 K. At the boiling point of water, the Kelvin scale reads 373 K.

   Source: *www.windows.ucar.edu/earth/Atmosphere/temperature/kelvin.html*

9. **Rankine**

   Explanation: The Rankine is a temperature scale that begins with absolute zero. The Rankine scale has degrees that equal 1 degree Fahrenheit. Zero Rankine is equal to −459.67°F.

   Source: *http://en.wikipedia.org/wiki/Rankine_scale*

10. **Richter Scale**

    Explanation: The Richter scale is a measure of the amount of seismic energy released by an earthquake. It is based on the displacement of a Wood-Anderson torsion seismometer.

    Source: *http://en.wikipedia.org/wiki/Richter_magnitude_scale*

11. **UV Index Scale**

    Explanation: A rating of the amount of ultraviolet radiation that is expected to reach the surface of the Earth at solar noon (when the sun is directly overhead). The amount of radiation depends on the amount of ozone in the stratosphere, the elevation of the Sun, and the amount of cloud cover. The scale ranges from 0 (night) to 16 (in the tropics at high elevations).

    Source: *www.cpc.ncep.noaa.gov/products/stratosphere/uv_index/uv_what.shtml*

12. **TNM Staging Scale**

    Explanation: The TNM Staging Scale is the scale that is used to describe stages of cancer. TNM stands for Tumor, Node, Metastasis. This scale describes the size of a tumor, whether or not there are affected lymph nodes, and whether or not the cancer has spread. The rating is important because it helps the physician know how to treat the cancer.
    Stage 1 = Cancer is relatively small and contained within the organ.
    Stage 2 = Cancer is localized, but the tumor is larger than in stage 1. There may be cancer in nearby lymph nodes.
    Stage 3 = Cancer is larger and cancer cells are found in the lymph nodes.
    Stage 4 = Cancer has spread to another organ.

26

Source: *www.cancerhelp.org.uk/help/default.asp?page=3779*

13. BMI Scale

Explanation: The BMI (body mass index) measures the amount of body fat based on a person's height and weight. The categories are

Underweight = < 18.5
Normal weight = 18.5–24.9
Overweight = 25–29.9
Obesity = BMI of 30 or greater

Source: *www.nhlbisupport.com/bmi*

14. pH Scale

Explanation: This scale measures the degree to which something is an acid or a base. This is determined by the activity of dissolved hydrogen ions (H+). The scale is the negative log of the hydrogen ion concentration. Water is considered to be the neutral point and has a pH of 7.0. Acids are solutions with a pH of less than 7.0, and bases are solutions with a pH of greater than 7.0.

Source: *http://en.wikipedia.org/wiki/PH*

15. Decibel Scale

Explanation: The decibel is often used to measure sound but is also used in electronics. The decibel is a logarithmic measurement of the magnitude of a quantity (such as intensity) relative to a specified reference level. The decibel is a ratio of two quantities.

The decibel is often used to measure sound. In humans the Decibel Sound Pressure Level (dBSPL) is used to measure hearing. One KHz is the weakest sound level a person with normal hearing can hear, and normal speech is typically 60 dBSPL.

Source: *www.phys.unsw.edu.au/jw/dB.html*

27

Extend

Create a Scale

For a recent science fair a student conducted a study to determine which lipstick stayed on the longest. The project appeared to be well done, but the student never described how she defined and measured "stayed on the longest," and as a result the project did not win a prize at the fair.

Design a strategy that can be reliably and validly used to measure this variable. What are the challenges and issues? Would different people have behaviors (such as biting their lips) that would give different results? What if one person had chapped lips—would that change the results? How can you decide how much lipstick stayed on the lips and how much came off the lips?

In another case, students at Lewis and Clark College conducted a test to see which potato chip students liked the most *(www.lclark.edu/~nilsen/kern. html)*. They took three types of chips (regular, low fat, and no fat) to the dining hall and asked the students to taste them and rate them on a scale from 1 to 7 (a 1 is yuck, and 7 is yum). Ask your students, *What do you think of this scale? Do you think a 3 is the same from one student to the next? What could you do to increase the accuracy of the rating scale?*

Challenge your students to design other measurement units for novel questions. They might explore how to measure which potato chip tastes the saltiest or how sweet different varieties of apples are. How do you quantify sweetness or saltiness?

Evaluate

Check for student understanding:

1. Why do scientists need numbers to measure variables?
2. What is the value of using ordinal or interval scales?
3. Why do scales need to be reliable (used by more than one person in the same way)?
4. What is an example of a nominal scale?
5. What would be the drawbacks of using a unit such as a smoot to measure the lengths of different large and small things?

Resources

For more information:
Measurement
www.unc.edu/~rowlett/units
Smoot Units
http://web.mit.edu/newsoffice/2003/smoots-0312.html
http://web.mit.edu/spotlight/smoot-salute

Scale Cards

1. Apgar	2. Beaufort
3. Danjon	4. Fujita Scale

Student Data Sheet

Types of Scale

5. Mercalli Scale	6. Saffir-Simpson Hurricane Intensity Scale
7. Torino Scale	8. Kelvin
9. Rankine	10. Richter Scale

11. UV Index Scale	12. TNM Staging Scale
13. BMI Scale	14. pH Scale
15. Decibel Scale	

e^FUN!
THE WATERSLIDE WITH THE EXPONENTIAL DROPOFF!
2.72 SECONDS OF FREEFALL!
MAYBE THIS ISN'T SUCH A GOOD IDEA...

MEASUREMENT

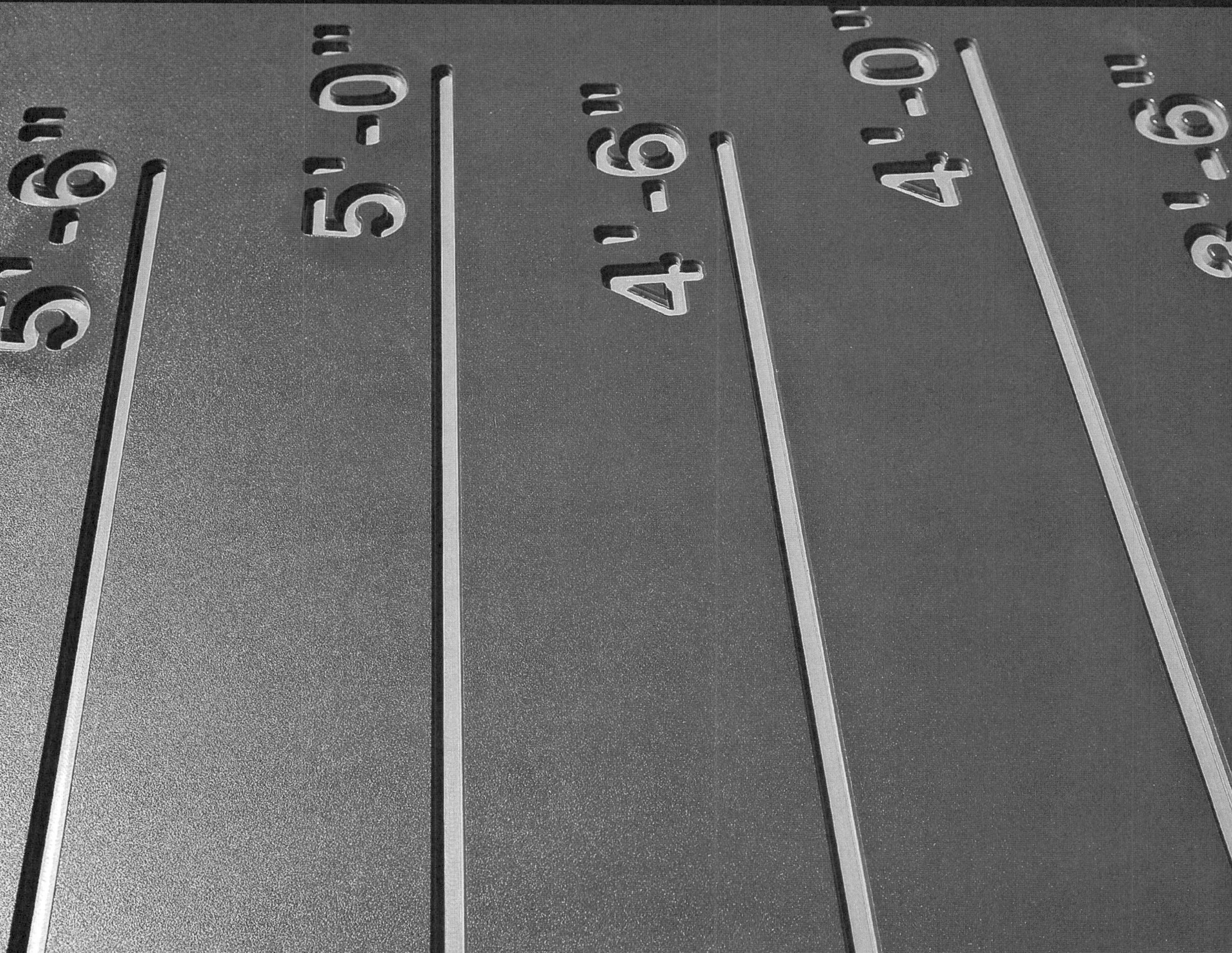

5'-6"

5'-0"

4'-6"

4'-0"

3'-6"

Chapter 3
Oops, I Did It Again: Errors in Measurement

Overview

Understanding the precision and accuracy of measurements is a crucial skill that scientists must develop to do their work. All measurements involve some degree of error. Knowing how to assess and work with error is an essential part of making sense of scientific observations. What is accuracy? What is precision? How do we make our measurements more accurate or precise? Why would two measurements of the same object yield different values? How can error in measurement be reduced? Students investigate these questions through a series of measurement tasks involving heights, mass, and different scales of measurement.

Objectives

- To develop skills in measuring.
- To become familiar with properties of materials that can be measured.
- To develop an understanding of accuracy, precision, and measurement error.
- To develop an understanding of how measurement error changes with the instrument used to make measurements.

Process Skills

- Observing
- Measuring
- Communicating

Activity Duration

60 minutes

Background

If you ask 30 people to measure the width of a room, it is likely that there will be many different answers. Variation in measurement is always present and is a part of doing science. Why does this variation in measurement occur? How much measurement variation is tolerable? These questions are considered as students make measurements and compare their measurements with those of other students.

It is important for students to recognize how errors in measurement occur and to be able to describe how to minimize both random and systematic errors. Ultimately there will always be some error or level of uncertainty. Students must also learn that this is a fundamental part of science. Nothing is known with quantitative exactness. A level of uncertainty in measurement is usually referred to as the "error." A sophisticated understanding of the occurrence of random errors develops after students have many opportunities to make repeated measurements and see the patterns of data that emerge. Encouraging students to check their own measurements, as well as to compare them with those made by others, is a fundamental part of this developmental process.

35

Materials

Each group will need:
- 1 thermometer (inexpensive alcohol thermometers work best)
- Metric measuring tape
- Scale for measuring mass

Class materials needed:
- Shoe box
- Egg (hard-boiled)
- Metric ruler
- 2 meter sticks
- Centimeter ruler
- Yarn
- Meter tape

Engage

Pass out one thermometer to every two students. For this activity, very inexpensive thermometers work best. Ask the students to record the temperature of the room. Then record the temperatures from the different groups on the board in a table. Look across the data and ask the students to explain why there is variation in the temperature measurements. Make note of the different reasons that they provide. Possible explanations include readings to the nearest half-degree versus the nearest whole degree, thermometers that have various calibrations, inaccurate thermometers, variations in temperature throughout the room, thermometers being under a vent or in the sunlight, and readings of thermometers from different angles.

Explore how the different thermometers give different readings by laying the thermometers side by side on a table and having the students view them as a group. Ask, *Why do different thermometers show different temperatures?*

Explain that in this lesson they will investigate the different sources of errors in measurement and the different types of errors that occur. In the case of the thermometers, the differences are due in part to their manufacturing, which results in variable readings. However, other human sources of error are inherent in the act of measurement.

Explore

Divide the class into groups of two students each. Explain that the focus is to make accurate measurements for the following: (a) a student's height in meters; (b) a shoe box length measured in centimeters; (c) a shoe box length measured in millimeters; (d) a shoe box length measured in meters; and (e) the mass of an egg in grams. Each measurement should be recorded on the Student Data Sheet.

36

A. *How Tall Am I?* Select a student volunteer who is willing to have his or her height measured. The first measurement task is to measure the student's height in centimeters. Provide Group 1 with a meter stick, Group 2 with meter tape, Group 3 with a ruler marked in inches and centimeters, Group 4 with yarn and a meter stick taped down to a table, and Group 5 with a small centimeter ruler (approximately 25 cm). Remind them to convert units to centimeters if they use a different unit for their initial measurement.

After the students make measurements, have the groups report their measurements to the class. Record the different measurements on the board on a chart (see Figure 1). Note the variation in students' measurements. Discuss possible sources of error. Students should note that some of the differences in the answers are the result of different measurement tools. Ask, *Which tool is the most accurate? Why?* Discuss the ways that students made the measurements and how they could be more consistent in their measurement strategy.

Extend the discussion by taking the mean of the different values and asking the students if the mean is more likely to be accurate than an individual measurement.

B, C, and D. *Shoe Box Measurements.* Each group should measure the same shoe box length (long side) in centimeters, millimeters, and meters, using either a ruler or metric tape. Record the measurements on the Student Data Sheet. Ask, *Which unit gave the most consistent measurements across the different groups—the centimeter, millimeter, or meter units? Which unit of measurement gave the most precise measurement? Why would the smaller unit of measurement be more precise?*

E. *Egg Mass.* Each group should measure the egg in grams using a scale. Note: Use hard-boiled eggs to avoid possible breakage and mess. Why did different groups get different measurements? What are the possible sources of errors that students could make when measuring with a scale? How could they increase both the precision and the accuracy of the measurement?

FIGURE 1.

Measurement Tool	Height in Centimeters
Group 1- meter stick	
Group 2- meter tape	
Group 3- metric ruler	
Group 4- yarn/meter stick	
Group 5- centimeter ruler	

Explain

Accuracy in Measurement. Most of the time we want our measurements to be as "true" or accurate as possible. When we make a measurement we want to know that the value we determine is close to the real value. If our bathroom scale at home consistently measures our weight as higher than we know it to be, the measurement is inaccurate. Students may have noticed that when they are weighed in the doctor's office the weight there is heavier or lighter than the value they get on their bathroom scales. This inconsistency exemplifies differences in accuracy due to the measurement tool.

Figure 2.
Archery Analogy
The relationship between precision and accuracy in target shooting.

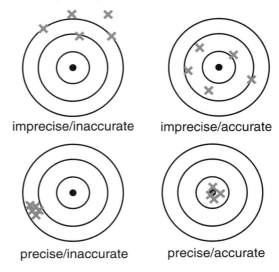

imprecise/inaccurate

imprecise/accurate

precise/inaccurate

precise/accurate

Calibration. How do we know if our measurements are accurate? With any instrument we use for measurement, whether it is a ruler, a weight scale, or a thermometer, we need a method of *calibration.* Calibration is a process in which a known standard is measured with the instrument in question. If the instrument doesn't agree with the standard, we adjust the instrument, or calibrate it, so that it does agree as closely as possible. For example, for a thermometer we know that at standard pressure, water freezes at 0° C and boils at 100° C. If the thermometer is designed to withstand these temperatures, we dunk it in a glass of ice water and in boiling water to determine if it reads accurately (ice water and boiling water, for thermodynamic reasons, maintain a constant temperature very near the freezing and boiling temperatures respectively). A second option is to calibrate our thermometer against a thermometer that we are reasonably sure is calibrated (if such an instrument is available). For a scale or balance, we need weights of known mass (e.g., 100 g, or 5 lbs.) for calibration. For length measurements, there are fewer options for standards. One option is simply to check our ruler or meter stick against other rulers and meter sticks. Have students check the rulers and see if they are all in reasonable agreement. Can they detect any variation in the rulers or meter sticks? You may be surprised to find real variations. How large are they?

Precision in Measurement. Precision is a term that refers to the degree of fineness or coarseness of a measurement. If we use a meter stick that just has centimeter tick marks, then our measurement will have less precision than if we use a meter stick with millimeter marks. Precision is independent of accuracy. We can have cases of high precision and low accuracy and vice versa. The figure on page 38 illustrates this point with a target-shooting analogy. Precision in this case is how close together the shots are (independent of whether they are on target). In the case of measurement, high precision means that the measurement technique is very fine grained. It provides more significant digits than a lower-precision measurement.

In some cases, high precision is not necessarily desired or meaningful. If I want to know how much I weigh, it may be enough to say I weigh 125 lbs. I may not care to know that I weigh 125.255 lbs. In fact, these extra digits imply a precision that may be misleading. Our instrument may provide weight readings to the nearest thousandth of a pound, but it is unlikely that this precision is meaningful (especially in the case of a bathroom scale). However, if I wanted to know how much gold there was in my gold nugget, I would want very high precision. First I would select an instrument that can accurately weigh objects with high precision (not a bathroom scale, but a high-precision balance). If I simply measured my nugget to the nearest ounce, I might find it weighed 1 oz. However if I used a tool that accurately measured to the nearest thousandth of an ounce, I would find that my nugget weighed 1.458 oz. At the time of writing, gold is selling for \$871.16 per ounce. If I used my low-precision measurement of 1 oz, instead of my high-precision measurement of 1.458 oz, I would loose \$398.99 of value. Precision is often noted by the last digit of the measurement value. In the case of my weight measurement, the level of precision is the nearest pound, whereas the level of precision for my gold nugget weight measurement is the nearest thousandth of an ounce.

Types of Error. Virtually all measurements have some degree of error. There are a number of sources of error, some that are random and some that are systematic. *Random error* results from fluctuations that occur in making measurements; it is related to the inability of the person making the measurements to do it in exactly the same way each time. By definition, random errors are neither biased high nor low; you are as likely to make a measurement that is too high as you are to make one that is low. A measurement is considered to have *high precision* if it has low random error.

Systematic error happens when the same error is made over and over again in the process of measuring. An example of systematic error would be using a ruler by measuring from the end of the ruler, rather than from the first tick mark, or zero on the ruler. By using the ruler improperly the person measuring would make the same mistake consistently, over and over again with different measurements. As this example indicates, a systematic error tends to bias a set of measurements either high or low. Reducing systematic error can produce measurements that are more accurate.

Measurements are likely to involve a degree of both kinds of error. Again using the ruler analogy, if a student was making a set of measurements using the end of the ruler rather than the zero mark, there would be a variation around an average in that set of measurements that would be called the *random error.* There would also be an offset (due to the extra length between the end of the ruler and the zero tick mark being erroneously added) to the whole set of measurements that is called the systematic error.

Extend

Extend these ideas by exploring how measurements have evolved over time. Earlier measurement standards used the span of a person's hand or the length of the foot. How might these types of measurements decrease the accuracy of the measurement? Today many commercial scales are inspected to ensure that they weigh purchased items consistently and accurately. Have students research how scales were altered in past times to allow merchants to overcharge for products being sold.

Hubble Space Telescope. There have been a number of very public and highly significant errors in measurement that students can research. The $1.5 billion Hubble Space Telescope was sent into space with a significant flaw in the telescope's main mirror. This flaw resulted from a 1.3 mm spacing error in the assembly of an instrument used to guide the grinding of the mirror. As a result of this error, the mirror was deformed and the telescope did not produce precise images.

For more information on the Hubble Telescope:
- *www.newscientist.com/article/mg12717301.000-the-testing-error-that-led-to-hubble-mirror-fiasco-.html*

Mars Climate Orbiter. Another significant error in measurement caused the crash of NASA's Mars Climate Orbiter in 1999. The spacecraft entered a much lower orbit around Mars than intended, was captured by the Martian atmosphere, and likely crashed. An independent investigation found that NASA engineers did not convert English measurements of the rocket thrusts to metric measurements in Newtons. The difference in the two values was enough to cause the spacecraft rocket to misfire, allowing the craft to be destroyed by entering the atmosphere of Mars instead of going into orbit.

For more information on the Mars Climate Orbiter:
- *www.cnn.com/TECH/space/9911/10/orbiter.02*
- *http://mars.jpl.nasa.gov/msp98/orbiter*

40

What would happen? After discussing famous errors in measurement that have been reported to the public, ask students to think about different technologies in our world and imagine what would happen if an error in measurement had occurred in the design or manufacture of the product. Ask the students to write a story about the source of error and the possible impact that the error could have on the people who use the technology.

Evaluate

Check for student understanding:

1. What is error of measurement?

2. How can measurements be made more accurate?

3. How can measurements be made more precise?

4. What are potential sources of error when using a metric stick?

5. Does precision increase as the unit of measurement gets larger or smaller? Explain.

41

Name _____

Measure Up!

In this investigation you will make a series of measurements of different objects. Record your measurements below.

Procedure

A. *How Tall Am I?*

      Measure the height of the student volunteer in centimeters. Make sure that everyone in the group agrees with the measurement before recording the height.

      Student height: _____ cm

What are possible sources of error that could influence the measurement?

B. *Shoe Box Length—Centimeters*

      Measure the long side of the shoe box. How many centimeters long is the box?
      Shoe box length: _____ cm

C. *Shoe Box Length—Millimeters*

      Measure the long side of the shoe box. How many millimeters long is the box?
      Shoe box length: _____ mm

D. *Shoe Box Length—Meters*

      Measure the long side of the shoe box. How many meters long is the box?
      Shoe box length: _____ m

E. *Egg Mass*

      Measure the mass of the egg in grams.
      Egg mass: _____ grams

Compare your measurements with those of other students.
Did you agree or disagree?

42

Questions

1. When you measured the shoe box, which unit do you think gave you the most precise measurement?

2. When you measured the shoe box, what were possible sources of error in your measurement?

3. Another teacher had five of her classes measure the mass of the egg. Each class reported a different mass. What could explain these different measurements?

43

POWERS OF TEN

Chapter 4
Sort It Out

Overview

Is a virus bigger than a bacterium? Is the distance from the Earth to the Moon greater than the diameter of the Earth? In this investigation students explore the relative sizes of things through a card-sorting activity. The goal is to raise students' awareness of metric distance scales and to promote the development of a series of conceptual anchors that they can use to estimate the sizes of objects.

Objectives

- To develop a sense of scale and the sizes of things.
- To use existing knowledge to make inferences about the sizes of different objects.

Process Skills

- Inferring
- Analyzing data

Activity Duration

30 minutes

Background

Developing a sophisticated understanding of the sizes of things involves many skills. They include knowing the names of the measurement units and what they mean, knowing how to compare sizes and convert from one measurement unit to another, and having a framework of size references to use when encountering a new size or distance. Research on how students learn scale (Jones et al. 2008) suggests that students learn relative sizes before they learn absolute sizes. This skill is tied both to the development of both number sense and proportional reasoning.

In this investigation students apply their knowledge of the relative sizes of known objects to infer the relative sizes of less-well-known objects and distances.

Materials

Each pair of students will need:
- Set of Student Investigation Object Cards
- Set of Metric Unit Cards
- Relative-Size Data Table
- Unlined index cards (1 per student)
- Colored pencils or markers

ENGAGE

Ask the students to predict which is larger: A cell or an atom? A fruit fly or a mite? The height of the Washington Monument or the height of the Empire State Building? After giving them a chance to share their responses, explain that the goal of this investigation is to consider the relative sizes and distances of different things.

47

Encourage the students to memorize the sizes and distances of a few objects and locations that they can use as mental anchors to apply throughout life. Examples of some common references for small objects are proteins (nanometers), viruses (10s of nanometers), cells (micrometers), fleas (millimeter), and a child (meter).

EXPLORE
Part I: Relative Size

Assign students to work in pairs for this activity. Explain that the goal for Part I is to order the set of Object Cards by size, from smallest to largest. Invite them not only to consider whether the object on the card is bigger or smaller than another, but also to think about how much larger (proportionally) one object size is than another. Pass out the cards and encourage the students to discuss the sizes as they reach consensus on their sorting rationale.

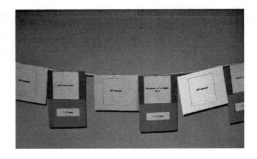

After they complete the sorting task, have the students explain their sorting rationale for a subset of cards (cell, molecule, and diameter).

EXPLAIN

After students complete their card sort, review the correct ordering of the cards. Encourage the students to share the reasoning they used to place one object as larger or smaller than another object.

Part I. Answer Sheet: Relative Size Data Table

Smallest	Object or Distance (Relative Order)	Actual Size (Average)
1	Diameter of a proton	10^{-15} m
2	Size of a hydrogen atom	50×10^{-12} m
3	Size of a typical small molecule	$2^{-10} \times 10^{-10}$ m
4	Range of virus sizes	2×10^{-8} -2×10^{-7} m
5	Diameter of a strand of DNA	2×10^{-9} m
6	Diameter of a typical cell	2×10^{-5} m
7	Diameter of a human hair	7.5×10^{-5} m
8	Thickness of a penny	0.0015 m
9	Width of an adult's hand	0.22 m
10	Height of a typical human	1.71 m
11	Length of longest snake	11.5 m
12	Length of a school bus	10 m
13	Width of a football field	47.97 m
14	Height of Empire State Building	381 m
15	Distance you could walk in 10 minutes	1,000 m
16	Distance from the Earth to the International Space Station	400,000 m
17	Distance from New York to London	5,590,000 m
18	Diameter of the Earth	12,800,000 m
19	Distance from the Earth to the Moon (center to center)	385,000,000 m*
20	Distance from the Earth to the Sun	150,000,000,000 m
Largest		

* This is mean value. The distance from Earth to the Moon varies ~10% over the course of the year (357,000 km to 407,000 km). *http://nssdc.gsfc.nasa.gov/planetary/factsheet/moonfact.html*

Part II: Metric Measurements

Part of learning about metric measurements is learning the metric prefixes. This part of the investigation repeats the card-sort activity, but now students sort the metric units with different prefixes from smallest to largest. After the students have had a chance to predict the placement of the metric cards, review the different prefixes. Then have students reexamine their sorting order, making changes where needed.

Part II. Answer Sheet: Prefixes and Metric Measurements

Prefix	Description	Decimal	Scientific	Unit in Meters
femto	quadrillionth	0.000000000000001	10^{-15}	femtometer
pico	trillionth	0.000000000001	10^{-12}	picometer
nano	billionth	0.000000001	10^{-9}	nanometer
micro	millionth	0.000001	10^{-6}	micrometer
milli	thousandth	0.001	10^{-3}	millimeter
kilo	thousand	1,000	10^{3}	kilometer
mega	million	1,000,000	10^{6}	megameter
giga	billion	1,000,000,000	10^{9}	gigameter
tera	trillion	1,000,000,000,000	10^{12}	terameter
peta	quadrillion	1,000,000,000,000,000	10^{15}	petameter

EXTEND

Prefix Creatures

Invite the student teams to create an imaginary creature based on an assigned prefix. The creature's name and some characteristic of the creature should be based on the prefix. Provide each team with a large index card. The front of the card should be used to make a drawing of the unknown creature, and the back should be used for a description of it. After the cards are complete, have student teams exchange cards and, as a class, order the cards from smallest to largest. For further extensions of this activity have the students write creative stories about the habitats of their creatures as well as the creatures' adaptations to the environment.

Evaluate the ordering of the imaginary creatures based on the correct ordering of the

Example of a Prefix Creature:
Duck-Billed Gigabeast

name prefixes. Display examples of creative and imaginative creatures on the board.

Further Exploration

Community Speakers

To explore this lesson further, invite people who use measurement frequently in their jobs to visit the class and discuss techniques used for measuring in their fields. For example, surveyors have to measure land for new roads or neighborhoods, cartographers measure land to create maps, and foresters measure large tracts of land to estimate the amount of wood that can be harvested from a forest. Speakers from the community help stress the relevance of the topic as well as help students think abut future careers.

Web Investigations

For a visual comparison of different scales (large and small) explore the website A Sense of Scale: *http://www.falstad.com/scale*

EVALUATE

To test their knowledge of prefixes and metric units have students fill in the missing cells on the chart.

Prefix	Description	Decimal	Unit in Meters
1._____	quadrillionth	0.000000000000001	femtometer
tera	trillion	2. _____	terameter
mega	3. _____	1,000,000	megameter
milli	thousandth	0.001	4. _____
giga	5. _____	1,000,000,000	gigameter
pico	6. _____	0.000000000001	picometer
7. _____	thousand	1,000	8. _____
nano	9. _____	0.000000001	nanometer
peta	10. _____	1,000,000,000,000,000	petameter
11._____	millionth	0.000001	micrometer

Note: This investigation is adapted in part from Tretter, T., and M. G. Jones. 2003. A sense of scale. *The Science Teacher* (Jan.) 2003: 22–25.

51

References

Jones, M. G., T. Tretter, A. Taylor, and T. Oppewal. Forthcoming. Experienced and novice teachers' concepts of spatial scale. *International Journal of Science Education*.

Jones, M. G., A. Taylor, and B. Broadwell. Forthcoming. Estimating linear size and scale: Body rulers. *International Journal of Science Education*.

Jones, M. G., A. Taylor, J. Minogue, B. Broadwell, E. Wiebe, and G. Carter. 2007. Understanding scale: Powers of ten. *Journal of Science Education and Technology Education* 16 (2): 191–202.

52

Student Investigation Object Cards

Directions: Distribute one object card to each pair of students.

Part I **Directions:** Place these cards in order of relative size from smallest to largest.	
Diameter of a cell	Diameter of a proton

53

Height of a typical human	Diameter of a strand of DNA
Diameter of the Earth	Size of a typical molecule
Size of a hydrogen atom	Width of a football field

54

Height of Empire State Building	Length of the longest snake
Distance you could walk in 10 minutes	Size of a typical virus
Width of an adult's hand	Distance from New York to London

55

Thickness of a penny	Distance from the Earth to the International Space Station
Diameter of a human hair	Length of a school bus
Distance from the Earth to the Moon	Distance from the Earth to the Sun

56

Student Data Sheet
Sort It Out

Name _____

1. Record your card sort into the data table below.

Relative-Size Data Table

Smallest	Object or Distance
1	
2	
3	
4	
5	
6	
7	
8	
9	
10	
11	
12	
13	
14	
15	
16	
17	
18	
19	
20	
Largest	

Metric Unit Cards

Directions: Sort the metric unit cards from smallest to largest.

femtometer	kilometer
nanometer	micrometer
millimeter	petameter

58

gigameter	terameter
picometer	

Chapter 5
It's Not All Relative: Relative Versus Absolute

Overview

Learning about the sizes of things and scale engages students in thinking about conceptual benchmarks for sizes. In this investigation students learn to order objects on a relative scale, as well as to accurately label actual or absolute sizes. In addition, students apply their knowledge of the powers of ten as they sequence objects and distances by size.

Objectives

- To use knowledge of the sizes of things to rank-order objects according to size.
- To explore the meaning of powers of ten.

Process Skills

- Comparing and contrasting
- Measuring
- Modeling

Activity Duration

30 minutes

Background

This investigation involves students in placing objects on a string number-line according to relative size as well as the corresponding power of ten. Students think about the meaning of notations such as 10^1 and 10^0 and where these powers of ten lie when they have to order a series of objects ranging from 10^{-5} meters to 10^5 meters.

The goal of this investigation is to help students develop conceptual benchmarks or anchors for the sizes of things. Once we move beyond the human scale, it becomes increasingly difficult to conceptualize very large and very small scales. The challenge is further complicated when we ask students to apply a metric scale to things that they may be more familiar with in English units. If they develop a sense of scale with a few distinctive, representative objects for set sizes, students can use those anchors to reason about the sizes of other, less well known objects.

Materials

The class will need:
- A 4 m clothesline
- Clothespins or paper clips (for attaching cards)

Each student or group will need:
- Large index cards with representative objects (Part A, Student Object Cards)
- Powers of Ten Cards (Part B) with sizes in meters
- Index cards with absolute sizes for objects and distances (Part C, Metric Size Labels)

61

ENGAGE

Explain that the purpose of this investigation is to explore the sizes of things. Begin by asking, *Does anyone know how big a red blood cell is?* If students are not sure, ask them if a red blood cell is bigger or smaller than a flea. Is it bigger or smaller than a virus? What is its size relative to an atom?

Prepare for the activity by hanging a clothesline across the room and labeling each end with cards indicating "smallest" and "largest."

EXPLORE

Part A. Relative Size

Explain that each team of three to four students will be given a card with the name of an object or a distance on it (such as the size of a flea) and that the task is to place the objects on the clothesline in order by size. Each team of students will have a different object. They should consider the size of their object and compare it with the size of other teams' objects. You may want to complete the *Sort It Out* activity (Chapter 4) first to lay the conceptual foundation for this activity. Pass out the Part A, Student Object Cards and ask the students to clip their cards to the clothesline in a location according to the object's size relative to the other objects.

Once the students have had a chance to place their cards on the line, invite the class to review the relative ordering and see if there are any cards that need to be moved. Allow the students to openly discuss and explain the sorting rationale. Once the class is in agreement, check the relative ordering of the cards and move those that are in the incorrect location or sequence (see Table 1).

TABLE 1.
Representative Object Sizes

Object Card	Size	Power of Ten	Size in Meters
Proton	1 fm (femtometer)	10^{-15}	1×10^{-15} meters
Size of an atom	.1 nm (nanometer)	10^{-10}	1×10^{-10} meters
Water molecule	0.1 nm	10^{-10}	1×10^{-10} meters
Cold virus	80 nm	10^{-8}	8×10^{-8} meters
Bacterium	5 μm (micron)	10^{-6}	5×10^{-6} meters
Red blood cell	10 μm	10^{-5}	1×10^{-5} meters
Grain of sand	1 mm	10^{-3}	1×10^{-3}
Thickness of a human hair	.1 mm	10^{-4}	1×10^{-4} meters
Thickness of a penny	1.55 mm	10^{-3}	1.55×10^{-3} meters
Diameter of a quarter	25 mm	10^{-3}	2.5×10^{-3} meters
Adult human	1.5 m	10^{0}	1.5 meters
Length of a typical car	4.5 m	10^{0}	4.5 meters
Height of a male giraffe	5.5 m	10^{0}	5.5 meters
Length of Tyrannosaurus rex	13 m	10^{1}	13 meters
Length of a blue whale	25 m	10^{1}	25 meters
Length of a football field (including end zones)	110 m	10^{2}	110 meters
Distance around an athletic track	400 m	10^{2}	400 meters
Distance from Los Angeles to New York	3,960 km	10^{6}	3.96×10^{6} meters
Distance from Earth to the Moon	384,400 km	10^{8}	3.844×10^{8} meters
Distance from Earth to the Sun	$1,496 \times 1011$m	10^{14}	$1,496 \times 10^{11}$ meters

EXPLAIN

Part B. Powers of Ten

Next explain that each group will receive a card with a power of ten printed on it. Explain that they are to order the cards from smallest to largest on the same clothesline they used in Part A. Explain that they will add the Powers of Ten Cards to the correct place on the line relative to the objects already on the line. Explain that these powers of ten refer to the scale in meters.

Note: If the students have previously been instructed about the powers of ten, do not review the notation but instead allow them to review their knowledge by ordering the cards. Allow them to think through with their team what 10^0 means.

Review the proper ordering of the Powers of Ten Cards and help the students make corrections in the sequencing of the cards. Before moving to Part C, in which they use metric labels with the powers of ten, review the powers of ten and the prefixes that correspond to the different measurements.

Explain how to read scientific notation. For example, 10^4 reads, "ten to the fourth" and is written out as 1 followed by four zeros or 10,000. Remind the students that 10^0 meters represents 1 meter and that 10^1 is another way of writing 10 meters (see Tables 2 and 3). Review the terminology for metric measurements to help the students develop an understanding of what "a kilo" means or how large a nanometer is.

TABLE 2.
Powers of Ten: 1 Meter to 100,000 Meters

10^0	1	1 meter (m)
10^1	10	10 meters
10^2	100	100 meters
10^3	1,000	1 kilometer (km)
10^4	10,000	10 kilometers
10^5	100,000	100 kilometers

TABLE 3.
Powers of Ten: 1 Meter to 0.00001 Meters

10^0	1	1 meter (m)
10^{-1}	0.1	100 millimeters (mm)
10^{-2}	0.01	10 mm or 1 cm
10^{-3}	0.001	1 millimeter (mm)
10^{-4}	0.0001	100 micrometers
10^{-5}	0.00001	10 micrometers

Next pass out the Metric Size Labels and encourage the students to talk to other teams to decide which object or distance matches the metric measurement. By combining knowledge and reasoning rationales, students can often infer the correct placement of the measurement label. If needed, you may want to give them a few representative placements to get them started (e.g., bacteria are typically micrometer in size). Check their placements of the metric measurements labels against Table 1. Hand out copies of Table 4, Powers of Ten, and discuss the usefulness of scientific notation in representing very large and very small numbers.

(Continued from p. 65)

Power of Ten	Number	Unit in Meters	Representatives of Sizes
10^{-1}	0.1	100 millimeters	Hand
10^{-2}	0.01	10 millimeters	Tip of finger
10^{-3}	0.001	1 millimeter (mm)	White line thumb nail
10^{-4}	0.0001	100 micrometers	Hair thickness
10^{-5}	0.00001	10 micrometers	Cell
10^{-6}	0.000001	1 micrometer (µm)	Organelle
10^{-7}	0.0000001	100 nanometers	Virus
10^{-8}	0.00000001	10 nanometers	Large protein
10^{-9}	0.000000001	1 nanometer (nm)	Medium size molecule; DNA width
10^{-10}	0.0000000001	100 picometers (1 angstrom)	Atom
10^{-11}	0.00000000001	10 picometers	
10^{-12}	0.000000000001	1 picometer (pm)	
10^{-13}	0.0000000000001	100 femtometers	
10^{-14}	0.00000000000001	10 femtometers	Nucleus of a large atom
10^{-15}	0.000000000000001	1 femtometer (fm)	Diameter of a proton

EXTEND

Explore the Powers of Ten With Science Fiction

Challenge your students to figure out how many powers of ten the disproportionately sized creatures in popular movies are. By inferring the creature's
size, it is possible to calculate the number of times larger or smaller it is than
the "real world." For example, in the movie *Godzilla*, the creature's size can be
calculated by comparing it to the size of the buildings and cars in the movie.
This activity can be extended further to determine whether or not it is possible
for the character to exist. In the case of *Godzilla*, the creature's legs are too
slender to sustain its mass. Students enjoy applying their knowledge to movie
characters in movies such as *Antz, A Bug's Life, Mothra, Honey, I Shrunk the Kids,*
or *Gulliver's Travels.*

66

TABLE 4.
Powers of Ten

Power of Ten	Number	Unit in Meters	Representatives of Sizes
10^{24}	1,000,000,000,000,000,000,000,000	1 yottameter (Ym)	100 million light years
10^{23}	100,000,000,000,000,000,000,000	100 zettameters	10 million light years; distance to Ursa Major
10^{22}	10,000,000,000,000,000,000,000	10 zettameters	Distance to Andromeda Galaxy
10^{21}	1,000,000,000,000,000,000,000	1 zettameter (Zm)	Size of the Milky Way Galaxy
10^{20}	100,000,000,000,000,000,000	100 exameters	10,000 light years
10^{19}	10,000,000,000,000,000,000	10 exameters	1,000 light years
10^{18}	1,000,000,000,000,000,000	1 exameter (Em)	100 light years
10^{17}	100,000,000,000,000,000	100 petameters	10 light years
10^{16}	10,000,000,000,000,000	10 petameters	Distance light travels in a year
10^{15}	1,000,000,000,000,000	1 petameter (Pm)	
10^{14}	100,000,000,000,000	100 terameters	
10^{13}	10,000,000,000,000	10 terameters	Width of the solar system
10^{12}	1,000,000,000,000	1 terameter (Tm)	
10^{11}	100,000,000,000	100 gigameters	Distance from Earth to Sun
10^{10}	10,000,000,000	10 gigameters	
10^{9}	1,000,000,000	1 gigameter (Gm)	Distance from Earth to Moon
10^{8}	100,000,000	100 megameters	
10^{7}	10,000,000	10 megameters	Diameter of Earth
10^{6}	1,000,000	1 megameter (Mm)	Size of Lake Michigan
10^{5}	100,000	100 kilometers	Estimated number of hairs on your head
10^{4}	10,000	10 kilometers	6.2 miles
10^{3}	1,000	1 kilometer (km)	Six blocks
10^{2}	100	100 meters	Building
10^{1}	10	10 meters	Truck
10^{0}	1	1 meter (m)	Size of small child

(Continued on p. 66)

65

Interactive Websites

There are a number of interesting websites that allow students to explore the powers of ten visually.

1. Zoom in and out on different powers of ten on a ruler:
   http://microcosm.web.cern.ch/microcosm/P10/english/welcome.html

2. Zoom in from the Milky Way toward the Earth in successive orders of magnitude and then move into a leaf down to subatomic levels:
   http://micro.magnet.fsu.edu/primer/java/scienceopticsu/powersof10

3. Zoom into the universe in 40 jumps. This website uses graphics to move through the universe to the edge of infinity in one direction and to the nucleus of the atom in the other:
   www.vendian.org/mncharity/cosmicview

4. This original website includes images from the video *Powers of Ten* as well as a game for students to play in which they put pictures in order from the farthest away to the closest:
   www.powersof10.com

It's Not All Relative
Answer Sheet

EVALUATE
Check for student understanding with the following quiz:

Understanding the Sizes of Things
Directions: Circle the response that best represents your answer.

1. **The number 24,327 can also be correctly written as which of the following:**
   A. 24.327×10^4
   B. 2.4327×10^4
   C. 243.27×10^3
   D. 2432.7×10^5

2. ***Kilometer* means which of the following:**
   A. 1 million meters
   B. 1,000,000 meters
   C. 100 meters
   D. 1,000 meters

3. **The number 1 can be represented accurately as which of the following:**
   A. 1×10^0
   B. 1×10^1
   C. 1×10^{-1}
   D. 1×10^{-2}

4. **The number 0.00044 can be represented accurately as which of the following:**
   A. 0.44×10^{-4}
   B. 4.4×10^3
   C. 4.4×10^4
   D. 4.4×10^{-4}

5. **The number 1,000,000 can be represented accurately as which of the following:**
   A. 10×10^7
   B. 10×10^6
   C. 1×10^7
   D. 1×10^6

68

6. *Millimeter* would represent which of the following:
   A. 1 million meters
   B. 1×10^3 meters
   C. 0.001 meter
   D. 1,000 meters

7. The number 0.0001 can be represented accurately as which of the following:
   A. 1×10^{-4}
   B. 10×10^4
   C. 1×10^{-3}
   D. 1×10^3

8. The number 10 can be represented accurately as which of the following:
   A. 1×10^{-1}
   B. 10×10^1
   C. 1×10^0
   D. 1×10^1

9. The number 0.01 can be represented accurately as which of the following:
   A. 1×10^{-3}
   B. 10×10^2
   C. 1×10^{-2}
   D. 1×10

69

Part A. Student Object Cards

Water molecule	Adult human
Nucleus of a hydrogen atom	Grain of sand
Red blood cell	Cold virus

70

Student Data Sheet

It's Not All Relative

Length of a typical car	Length of a football field
Thickness of a penny	Distance from Earth to the Moon
Thickness of a human hair	Distance from Los Angeles to New York

Size of an atom	Distance from Earth to the Sun
Diameter of a quarter	Bacterium
Distance around an athletic track	Height of a male giraffe

72

Length of a blue whale	Length of *Tyrannosaurus rex*

Part B. Powers of Ten Cards

10^0 meters	10^1 meters
10^2 meters	10^3 meters

73

10^4 meters

10^5 meters

10^6 meters

10^7 meters

10^8 meters

10^9 meters

10^{10} meters	10^{11} meters
10^{12} meters	10^{13} meters
10^{14} meters	10^{-1} meters

75

10^{-2} meters	10^{-3} meters
10^{-4} meters	10^{-5} meters
10^{-6} meters	10^{-7} meters

10^{-8} meters	10^{-9} meters
10^{-10} meters	

Student Data Sheet

It's Not All Relative

Part C. Metric Size Labels

1×10^{-10} meters	2.5×10^{-3} meters
1×10^{-10} meters	109.7 meters
1×10^{-5} meters	3.844×10^{8} meters
1.5 meters	3.961×10^{6} meters
1×10^{-3} meters	$1,496 \times 10^{11}$ meters
8×10^{-8} meters	5×10^{-6} meters
4.5 meters	400 meters
1.55×10^{-3} meters	25 meters
1×10^{-4} meters	5.5 meters
1×10^{-10} meters	13 meters

78

Chapter 6
Scaling the Solar System

Overview
How big is the solar system? Are there eight planets or nine? How big are the other planets compared to the Earth? How far are the planets from each other? In this activity students explore the answers to these questions as they create a large-scale model of the solar system outside of the classroom.

Background
For thousands of years people have looked up at the night sky and pondered the size and structure of the heavens. Even today, with all we know about the structure of the solar system, the galaxy, and beyond, it is hard to get an accurate mental picture. Making physical models helps! Making models is an effective way for researchers to study very large or very small phenomena. The importance of modeling is significant when we try to conceptualize things we cannot see, whether at the nanoscale or the astronomical scale. Many misconceptions may arise as students try to imagine how our solar system is arranged. Unfortunately some models are inaccurate in their representation of the placement or sizes of the planets. Some pictures and models portray the planets as equally spaced and in a straight line. Although that technique is effective for visualizing all the planets at once, it is important to convey to students that the solar system is more complex than that in its structure. Planets are not spaced at regular intervals, their orbits are elliptical and on slightly different elliptical planes, and their distance from the Sun varies throughout their orbit.

Besides the planets, this activity includes the asteroid belt and dwarf planets (as Pluto is currently considered). Students should be aware of the other objects in our solar system besides the major planets, as well as the relative sizes of those celestial bodies. The Earth is of intermediate size; some objects are much larger (e.g., Jupiter), and some are much smaller (e.g., Pluto and the dwarf planets). What is a planet? According to the International Astronomical Union, "A planet is an object that must have the following three traits: orbits the sun, be massive enough that its own gravity pulls it into a nearly round shape, and be dominant enough to clear away objects in its neighborhood" (NASA 2006, p. 6). Pluto has only two of those traits (it orbits the Sun and is massive enough that its own gravity pulls it into a nearly round shape), and therefore it is considered a dwarf planet.

Objectives
- To make a large-scale model of the solar system.
- To compare and contrast the distances of the planets in the solar system.
- To create measurement conversions for astronomical units.

Process Skills
- Modeling
- Measurement conversions
- Comparing and contrasting

Activity Duration
90 minutes

Students can create models to explore the relative distance from the Sun to both the inner planets (Mercury, Venus, Earth, and Mars) and outer planets (Jupiter, Saturn, Uranus, Neptune, and Pluto) and explore how those distances compare to the planet diameters. Even though scientists have chosen a unit of measure representing the distance from Earth to the Sun (called an *astronomical unit* or AU), students should also be able to create scales to represent the diameters of the planets and the distances between the planets using meters and miles. This activity helps them to explore the concept of large distances and to practice the skill of scaling large sizes to something more conceivable.

Materials

- 12 large pieces of unlined paper (or large index cards)
- Metric rulers
- Meter stick
- Calculators
- Large retractable measuring tape
- Colored pencils or markers
- Duct tape
- 9 stakes or stands for posters (see note)
- Encyclopedias
- Internet access

Note: Instead of making posters of the scaled planet sizes, you may choose to have your students make three-dimensional scaled models of planets using everyday items (such as sports balls, seeds, marbles, or clay). A variety of items may be used to hold planet posters in place, such as stakes, dowel rods, meter sticks, or large ring stands.

Engage

Divide the class into 10 groups and give each student an information collection sheet (Student Data Sheet 1). Assign each group a different celestial body; they will research and answer specific questions about the object (see list below). Using textbooks, reference books, and the internet, students should complete the information chart on Student Data Sheet 1. After collecting information and answering questions, the students will make a color drawing of the celestial body. Have student groups share, compare, and contrast their information (e.g., diameters, distances). Discuss the answers to the questions and encourage

80

the students to think about the astronomical distances in our solar system and how one could begin to represent this information in a model. Can you really fathom the distance an airliner would travel in 20 years at 600 miles per hour? Can the light we see from stars today have been created over 100 years ago?

Celestial Body Research
- Sun
- Mercury
- Venus
- Earth
- Mars
- Asteroid Belt
- Jupiter
- Saturn
- Uranus
- Neptune
- Pluto
- Eris

Explore

Ask the students to describe solar system models they have seen in books or in physical model form. Have them begin to explain how they think one goes about planning and building such a model. What factors should someone making a model take into account (e.g., sizes of planets, distances of planets from the Sun and each other, the location of the planets in the solar system)? What issues arise when one tries to make the solar system model accurate? How does one create a scaled model from the astronomical distances and sizes found in the solar system?

Now explain to the students that they are going to take the information they collected in their groups about the celestial bodies and create a scale model of the solar system *outside*! A typical football field is about 92 meters long. The solar system that the students will make outside will be scaled down to the size of a football field. (Any large, open area may be used if a football field is not available, and various scaling factors may be calculated. See other options in the list of references at the end of this activity.)

Each group will be responsible for making a planet sign with an accurately scaled picture (or a 3-D model) of the celestial body that was assigned to them in the previous section. All students are also responsible for calculating the scaled sizes and distances for all of the celestial bodies. See the celestial body size and distance information in Tables 1 and 2 on pages 82 and 83, scaled using 92 meters of space outside. Note that in our example we have two sepa-

81

rate scaling factors. The first scaling factor determines the size of each model planet based on a model Sun diameter of 500 mm. The second scaling factor determines the distance of each planet from the Sun based on a 92 m (football field length) distance from the Sun to Pluto. So in this model scheme, the planets and Sun are exaggerated in size (by a factor of ~23) to make them large enough to model practically.

(More advanced students should try to calculate the scaling factor for distance on their own based on a 92 m Sun-Pluto orbit distance and a 500 mm Sun diameter. An example may need to be provided for other students.)

TABLE 1.

Celestial Body	Actual Diameter (km)	Scaled Diameter (mm)
Sun	1,390,000	500.0
Mercury	4,890	1.8
Venus	12,100	4.3
Earth	12,800	4.6
Mars	6,800	2.4
Ceres	950	0.3
Jupiter	143,000	51.3
Saturn	121,000	43.3
Uranus	51,100	18.4
Neptune	49,500	17.8
Pluto	2,300	0.8
Eris	2,500	0.9

To calculate the scaled diameter of the Sun (500 mm) for the football field–sized model, divide 500 mm by the actual diameter of the Sun (1,392,000 km), and the answer is your scaling factor. Multiply the scaling factor by the actual diameter of the celestial body and record. See example:

500 mm / 1,392,000 km = **0.000359 mm/km**, or
(3.59×10^{-4} mm/km, or 1: 3.59×10^{10})

To calculate the scaled diameter of Mercury:

4, 878 km $\times$ **0.000359 mm/km = 1.75 mm**

TABLE 2.

Celestial Body	Actual Distance From Sun (km)	Scaled Distance (m)	Actual Distance in Astronomical Units (AU)
Sun	0	0.00	0.00
Mercury	58,000,000	.72	0.4
Venus	108, 000, 000	1.69	0.7
Earth	150, 000,000	2.35	1.0
Mars	228,000,000	3.57	1.5
Ceres	420,000,000	6.59	2.8
Jupiter	778,000,000	12.21	5.2
Saturn	1,430,500,000	21.21	9.5
Uranus	2,870,000,000	45.04	19.0
Neptune	4,500,000,000	70.48	30.0
Pluto	5,900,000,000	92.02	39.0
Eris	14,000,000,000	219.52	96.7

Sources:
http://solarsystem.nasa.gov/planets/charchart.cfm
http://solarsystem.nasa.gov/planets/profile.cfm?Object=Pluto
http://rst.gsfc.nasa.gov/Sect19/Sect19_21.html

To calculate the scaled distance for a football field of 92 meters, divide 92 m by the distance from the Sun to Pluto (this is your scaling factor). Multiply the scaling factor by the actual distances from the Sun to each planet and record. See example:

92 meters / 5,869,000,000 km = **.0000000157 m/km** or
(1.57×10^{-8} m/km, or 1: 1.57×10^{11})

To calculate the distance from the Sun to Mercury:

46,000,000 km $\times$ **.0000000157 m/km** = **.72 m**

After each group has calculated the accurate scaled size and distance for all the celestial bodies and recorded them on Student Data Sheet 2, have volunteers record the answers on a "community" data table (on a chalkboard or overhead transparency) for the class to check for accuracy.

Now the groups should make either a poster with a scaled drawing representing their celestial bodies or, if time and materials permit, a scaled 3-D model using everyday items such as balls, marbles, or seeds.

83

Once the posters (or models) are completed and all groups have the scaled sizes and distances recorded on the information tables on their Student Data Sheets, it's time to head outside!

*Remind students to remember safety procedures for activities outside and to bring materials such as calculators and measuring tapes.

Find the edge of the open area where you will recreate the solar system, and have the Sun group place their scaled poster or model there. From this point, using the scaled distances and a tape measure, each group should place their poster or model the appropriate distance from the Sun. (See student examples in Figures 1 and 2.)

Once the placements have been made, have the students gather around a central location for discussion. They will immediately see that the first few planets are fairly "close" to the Sun, whereas the others are spaced farther out, and none is spaced at equal distances. How does the outside model compare with how the students answered question 7 on Student Sheet 1 earlier? The students should then complete Part II of Student Sheet 2.

FIGURE 1.
Inner planets.

FIGURE 2.
View from outer planet.

Explain

The importance of modeling is significant when we try to conceptualize things we cannot see, whether they are microscopic or astronomical in size. Many misconceptions may arise as students try to imagine how our solar system is arranged. Unfortunately, some models are inaccurate in their representations of the placement of the planets or of the sizes of the planets. As this exercise illustrates, it is difficult to use a *single* scaling factor to represent effectively both the distances between the celestial bodies and their sizes. For example, if the same scale used for creating a football field–sized solar system was used to represent the diameters of the planets, the planets would be too small for us even to distinguish among their sizes (Jupiter would be ~2mm and Mercury 0.07 mm, the width of a human hair!). As students complete the various sections in this activity, try to make them aware of the issue of using one scaling factor.

At this extreme scale, there are units of measure that may or may not be familiar to the students, such as light years, parsecs, and astronomical units. An astronomical unit (AU) is a unit to measure distances in space. One AU equals 150,000,000 km or 93,000,000 miles and represents the average distance between the Sun and the Earth. The distances of the planets from the Sun in astronomical units appear in Table 2 on page 83. Part II on Student Sheet 2 is designed to get students to think about other units of measurement and how scientists sometimes simplify quantities. It is easier to say that the Earth is one AU away from the Sun than to remember 150,000,000 km. Students will create their own units of measurement while outside to measure the distances from the Sun to the planets (paces may be the most common unit).

There are many variations of activities for students to model the solar system. See the references below for more information.

To help you consider how to make a large-scale model outside with the space you have available, there are websites to help you calculate the scaling factor, such as:
- *http://thinkzone.wlonk.com/Space/SolarSystemModel.htm*
- *www.exploratorium.edu/ronh/solar_system*

Other activities for building a large-scale solar system can be found at:
- *www.nasa.gov/audience/foreducators/9-12/features/F_Solar_System_Scale.html*
- *http://epswww.unm.edu/iom/epo/scale/outdoorscale.pdf*
- *www.morehead.unc.edu/Shows/SSA/model_solar_system.htm*
- *http://mars.jpl.nasa.gov/education/modules/webpages/activity2.htm*
- *www.worsleyschool.net/science/files/scale/model.html*
- *www.freewebs.com/vagabondastronomer/solsys1.htm*

For more traditional methods of modeling the solar system go to:
- *http://stereo.gsfc.nasa.gov/classroom/scales.shtml*
- *www.fi.edu/fellows/fellow9/dec98/art2.htm*
- *www.nasaexplores.com/show_k4_teacher_st.php?id=021220104924*
- *http://mars.jpl.nasa.gov/classroom/pdfs/solarsystembeaddistance.pdf*
- *http://serch.cofc.edu/special/matmods/ssbead.pdf*
- *www.exploratorium.edu/ronh/solar_system/*
- *www.astrosociety.org/education/family/materials/toiletpaper.pdf*

85

For more information about whether or not Pluto is a planet:

- *www.nineplanets.org*
- *http://news.nationalgeographic.com/news/2006/08/060824-pluto-planet.html*
- *www.universetoday.com/2008/04/10/why-pluto-is-no-longer-a-planet*

Reference

NASA. 2006. Honey, I shrunk the solar system. Mission News. Available online at *www.nasa.gov/vision/universe/solarsystem/planetsf-20060824.html.*

Extend

Part A

Have the students choose and calculate the scale of the solar system with their school, home, or some other favorite place representing the Sun. Depending on what scale they choose, Mercury could be located just down the street or in another state! Have the students create a data table to record this new information. They will have to use the internet and maps to determine distances.

Another exercise can be performed that illustrates the magnitude of the diameter of the planets relative to the vast distances of these planets from the Sun. You can simply repeat the outdoor solar system modeling activity but place only the three inner planets (Mercury, Venus, and Earth) across a football field. In this case, Earth would be placed at 92 m (or 100 m). (Scaling: 6.13×10^{-7} m/km. Remember to convert m to mm when doing planet diameters.)

TABLE 3.

Planet	Diameter (km)	Scaled Diameter (mm)	Orbit Distance (km)	Scaled Orbit Distance (m)
Sun	1,390,000	85.2	-	-
Mercury	4,890	3.0	58,000,000	35.6
Venus	12,100	7.4	108,000,000	66.2
Earth	12,800	8.0	150,000,000	92.0

Part B

Ask students to compare and contrast the definitions for mass, weight, and gravity. Have the students first predict what their own weights or those of some other object (e.g., dog, car) would be on each planet, and then have them calculate the actual figures. Gravity on Earth is considered to be 1, for comparisons with other planets. You can have the students calculate in pounds and kilograms by multiplying actual weight by the factor of gravity.

TABLE 4.

Planet	Factor of Gravity	How Much Do You Think the Bbject Would Weigh?	Actual Weight on Other Planets (lbs)	Actual Weight on Other Planets (kg)
Sun	27.00			
Mercury	.38			
Venus	.90			
Earth	1.00			
Mars	.39			
Jupiter	2.60			
Saturn	.95			
Uranus	.91			
Neptune	1.14			
Pluto	.03			

Evaluate

Check for student understanding:

1. If the Sun were the size of a soccer ball (25 cm), what would be the comparative sizes of the planets?

2. What is an AU?

3. Is it farther from Mars to Venus, or from Saturn to Neptune?

4. Calculate the scaled distance from Jupiter to Mars if one AU equals 20 km.

5. List the inner planets. List the outer planets.

6. What does it mean to create a scaled model?

7. Write a paragraph comparing and contrasting the distances and spacing of the planets in our solar system.

87

Student Data Sheet
Scaling the Solar System

Using the materials provided, complete the Student Data Sheet below about the celestial body assigned to your group. You may use the internet, reference books, or textbook.

Location in Solar System	Diameter	Distance From the Sun (in km and AU)
Characteristics	Natural Satellites	Three Unique Facts

88

Answer the following questions:

1. **What is a celestial body? Give examples.**

2. **Distinguish between a dwarf planet and a planet.**

3. **What is meant by "inner planets" and "outer planets"?**

4. **What is an astronomical unit (AU)?**

5. **How long do you think it would take to travel from your celestial body to the Sun? If your group is researching the Sun, how long do you think it would take to travel from the Sun to Mars?**

6. **The distance from the Earth to the Sun is 150,000,000 km. Could a person walk this distance in a lifetime?**

7. **Describe in your own words how you think the planets are spaced in relation to each other in the solar system. Are they the same distances from the Sun?**

89

8. Describe the orbit of your celestial body around the Sun.

9. To which planet have space exploration rovers been sent most recently?

10. What problems are presented when scientists attempt to study the outer planets?

11. To which planet have scientists most recently sent space exploration missions? How does that planet compare to Earth?

12. Draw a color sketch of your celestial body below:

90

Modeling the Solar System OUTSIDE!

Part I

Using the information about the solar system that the class has collected, you will now create a model of the solar system *outside*! A typical football field is about 92 meters long, and you will scale the solar system down to that size. Your group is responsible for making the poster with an actual scaled drawing of your celestial body (or a scaled 3-D model, optional). First, scale calculations must be made to get the appropriate dimensions to fit the model solar system on the football field or other open area at your school.

Assume that the Sun is 500 mm in diameter. How large would the planets be? Calculate the scaled diameters of the celestial bodies if the Sun were scaled down to 500 mm. Present your answer in millimeters. Show calculations on a separate paper and record the final answers in Table 1. Check the accuracy of your calculations with the rest of the class.

TABLE 1.

Celestial Body	Actual Diameter (km)	Scaled Diameter (mm)
Sun	1,392,000	
Mercury	4,878	
Venus	12,102	
Earth	12,758	
Mars	6,796	
Ceres	950	
Jupiter	142,980	
Saturn	120,560	
Uranus	51,120	
Neptune	49,530	
Pluto	2,300	
Eris	2,500	

If the distance from the Sun to Pluto was 92 m, where would the other planets fit in? Calculate the scaled distance of the celestial bodies from the Sun, based on a Sun–Pluto distance of 92 m. Present your answer in m. Show your calculations on a separate paper and record the final answers in Table 2 on page 92.

TABLE 2.

Celestial Body	Actual Distance From Sun (km)	Scaled Distance (m)
Sun	0	
Mercury	46,000,000	
Venus	108, 200, 000	
Earth	150, 000,000	
Mars	227,900,000	
Ceres	420,000,000	
Jupiter	778,500,000	
Saturn	1,352,500,000	
Uranus	2,872,400,000	
Neptune	4,495,060,000	
Pluto	5,869,000,000	
Eris	14,000,000,000	

Now, based on the scaled diameters calculated earlier (entered in Table 1 on page 91), sketch an accurately scaled color diagram of your celestial body. Use other information collected during the previous section to help you decide how to color it. Optional: Create a scaled 3-D model of your celestial body.

Once the posters (and/or models) are complete, it's time to head outside!
- Remember safety applies to all activities—even outside.
- Don't forget calculators, tape measures, meter sticks, and other materials listed on page 80.
- Find the edge of the area where you will recreate the solar system, and have the Sun group place their poster/scaled model there.
- From this point, using the scaled distances and tape measures, each group should place their poster/scaled model the appropriate distance from the Sun.
- Once the placements are completed, gather in a central location your designated by your teacher.
- After class discussion, complete Part II below.

Part II
1. What does an astronomical unit (AU) represent? What does one AU equal in miles? What does one AU equal in kilometers?

2. Why do you suppose scientists chose to measure distances in space with astronomical units?

3. Complete actual distances in astronomical units in the Table 3.

4. How do you suppose you could measure the distances of the solar system you made today if you did not have meter sticks or tape measures? Name several methods you could use to measure. (For example, you could pace or hop the distance between the Sun and each of the planets.)

5. Make up a unit. Choose one of your methods for measuring without meters, centimeters, and so on, and choose a name for the new unit of measurement that you created. How long is your unit in meters?

6. Using your newly created unit of measurement, complete the Table 3 for the distances from the Sun to each planet.

TABLE 3.

Body	Actual Distance From Sun (km)	Actual Distance in Astronomical Units (AU)	New Unit of Measurement _____
Sun	0		
Mercury	46,000,000		
Venus	108, 200, 000		
Earth	150, 000,000		
Mars	227,900,000		
Ceres	420,000,000		
Jupiter	778,500,000		
Saturn	1,352,500,000		
Uranus	2,872,400,000		
Neptune	4,495,060,000		
Pluto	5,869,000,000		
Eris	14,000,000,000		

93

Chapter 7
Time Flies When You're Learning About Scale!

Overview

Not many students would forget to say "Dinosaurs!" if you mention the Jurassic period, yet the word scale only conjures up ideas of measuring objects. Most students automatically think of measuring mass, volume, or distance, and not necessarily time. In this activity students explore geological time scale in the context of major events from the biological, physical, and Earth sciences, as well as from their own lives.

Objectives

- To diagram geologic time scale.
- To compare and contrast the age of major geological and evolutionary events.
- To summarize the events of geologic time scale using diagrams.

Process Skills

- Modeling
- Classifying
- Communicating
- Comparing and Contrasting

Activity Duration

Two 60-minute class periods

Background

Geological time is a very important scale concept that includes understanding where species "belong" in a linear timeline of Earth's history. Geological time scales include domains from geology to evolutionary biology and are embedded in the context of Earth's major geological events as well as in the emergence and remission of various flora and fauna. The absolute age of fossils may be determined by radioactive dating methods, but relative age may also be determined by the fossil locations in the rock layers of the Earth. Paleontologists compile absolute and relative age information to form a geologic time scale of prehistoric events and their impacts on biological organisms.

Current evidence indicates that the Earth is almost 5 billion years old. Scientists have divided geologic time scale into various units of time such as *eons*, *eras*, *periods*, *epochs*, and *stages*. Each time unit can be found nestled in a larger increment of time. For example, eons are made up of eras, and eras are divided into periods, and so forth. This activity allows students to explore the relationships among geological units of time, geological events, and when life began to develop and change on our planet.

Geologic time scale has important implications for learning about fossils and geological events as well as evolution. The Earth's history is emphasized in the National Standards at all grade levels (see the National Research Council's *National Science Education Standards*). In K–8, students learn how fossils provide information about the plants and animals that lived long ago, as well as major geological events that have affected the Earth's structure. For grades 9–12, the Standards emphasize (1) how the Earth and the rest of the solar system formed from a nebular cloud of dust and gas 4.6 billion years ago; (2) how geologic time can be estimated by observing rock sequences and using fossils to correlate the sequences at various locations; and (3) how the evolution of life caused dramatic changes in the composition of the Earth's atmosphere.

Geologic time is crowded with many events occurring simultaneously. It is a challenge for students to recall all the major geological and evolutionary events and to place them correctly within the proper eon, era, period, or epoch. Stressing the importance of a broad overview of time, and providing a few benchmarks, will help students to understand the big picture of how organisms and the environment developed and changed over the last 4.6 billion years. This activity is not a comprehensive list of all major events but emphasizes a few important ones: the age of the Earth (4.6 billion years old), oldest fossils of blue-green algae (3.3 billion years old), first reptiles (320 million years ago), first mammals (220 million years ago), and earliest human ancestor (3.5 million years ago). These examples provide students with anchor points in the Earth's history to help them develop more of a relative understanding of time. In addition to helping them acquire anchor points for geologic time, the overall purpose of this activity is to give students a sense of the relative scale of the age of the Earth, the age of life on Earth, and the age of many major geological and evolutionary events.

Materials

- Small square sheets of paper
- Metric rulers
- Meter stick
- Unlined paper (5–8 pieces per group)
- Crayons or colored pencils
- Student Data Sheets
- Large index cards
- Box of paper clips
- String or yarn (length of classroom)
- Four different-colored clothespins, tape, or sticky notes
- Encyclopedias
- Internet access

Engage

Assign the students to groups of two or three. Ask them to write about two important events from their lives and to write down the date that they occurred. Have them also write, on individual slips of paper, about the oldest thing or event that they can think of. (You could have history books or encyclopedias available to help them think of an old event.)

Have the students place the slips of paper in the center of their tables and mix them up. Each group should arrange the slips of paper into a timeline from oldest to most recent. Encourage the students to think about how they can describe a person's life span in decades. Have them draw the timeline and present it to the rest of the class. This activity promotes students' thinking about time as a scale and helps them to see that there can be an absolute age (day and year) as well as relative time (how the events are placed in chronological order with respect to one another).

As a class, brainstorm what the students already know about the different increments of time. For example, you can talk about the Earth's age in billions of years, geologic time periods (such as the Jurassic), and the appearance of the first fish, mammals, or plants. Record student answers on the board. See Figure 1 on p. 98 for an example of a geologic time scale.

Using a meter stick as a visual aid, ask the students to review the different ways the meter can be broken down into smaller sections (see the activity *It's Not All Relative*). For example, the smallest unit on the meter stick is millimeters (mm). The next-highest division is centimeters (cm), and so on. Next, review how many mm and cm make up a meter:

$$10 \text{ mm} = 1 \text{ cm}$$
$$100 \text{ cm} = 1 \text{ meter}$$
$$1,000 \text{ mm} = 1 \text{ meter}$$

Discuss how the Earth's history can be divided in much the same way as a meter stick, with the larger measurements of time divided into smaller and smaller increments. Have the groups identify, define, and explain the major terminology found in geological time scales, using textbooks, reference books, and the internet. A list of suggested terms can be found in the vocabulary box on p. 98.

97

VOCABULARY

absolute time	atmosphere	billion	carbon dating
eon	epoch	era	evolution
extinct	fossils	geologist	ice age
inhabit	mammal	paleontologist	Pangea
period	relative time	time scale	

FIGURE 1.
Geologic time scale.

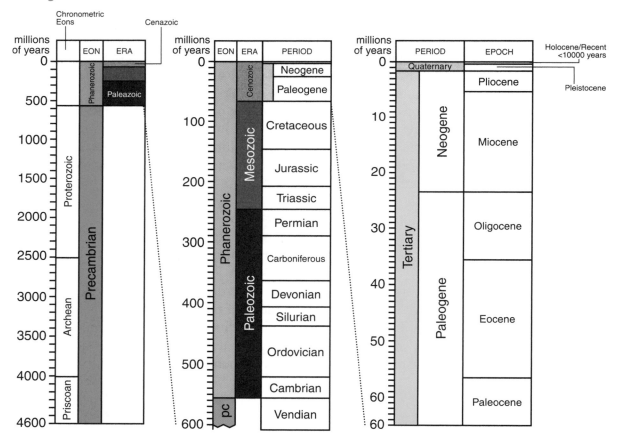

Source: Adapted from *www.talkorigins.org/faqs/timescale.html*.

Explore

Using the topics discussed as a class, have the students create a time scale using centimeters to represent the units of time in the age of the Earth. Give each group five pieces of unlined paper (8 ½ × 11 inches) and instruct the students to tape the paper together end to end (see Figure 2). (Large pieces of poster paper may be used, as long as the result is a meter or more in length.) After taping the pieces of paper together, arrange the paper on a table horizontally.

FIGURE 2.
Pieces of paper taped end to end and placed horizontally on table.

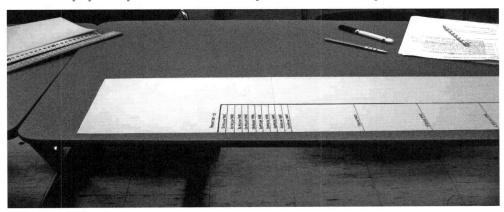

Using a small ruler, students should measure 20 cm from the left edge of the paper and 10 cm from the bottom of the paper and put a dot at the intersection of these two measurements. From this dot, draw a straight line down to bottom edge of paper and label this line "0." Using a meter stick, students should then draw a horizontal line to the right (1 m in length and parallel to the bottom edge), beginning at the dot on the 0 line. Without removing the meter stick, mark off the line (from left to right) in 1 cm increments all the way up to 10 cm (1 cm, 2 cm, 3 cm, . . . 10 cm). At that point, continue to make tick marks along the timeline in increments of 10 cm, all the way up to 1 m or 100 cm (10 cm, 20 cm, 30 cm, . . . 100 cm). Using a ruler, extend the tick marks to the bottom of the paper. Have the students label the 0 line *Present Day* and the 1 cm line *50 Million Years*. Students should label what units of time *each* tick mark represents. For example, let 3 cm equal 150 million years or 30 cm equal 10,000 million years or 1.5 billion years (see Figure 3 on p. 100).

FIGURE 3.
Student example of how to label each tick mark

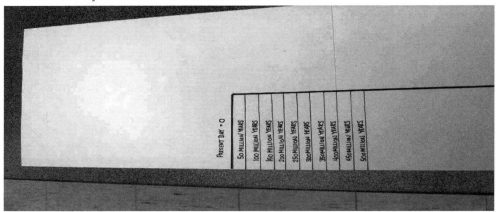

Note:

More advanced students can create their own proportional scale by making 1 cm equal the time increment of their choice.

Remind the students to indicate the amount of time represented by each line:

1 cm = 50 million years, 2 cm = 100 million years, 3 cm = 150 million years, and so on, until they reach 10 cm. Now indicate the amount of time represented by the remaining tick marks, continuing for the entire length of the meter line:

20 cm = 1,000 million years or 1 billion years
30 cm = 10,000 million years or 1.5 billion years
40 cm = 100,000 million years or 2 billion years

Have students label their timelines with the events provided in the Event Chart on page 101 (completing the chart as needed). To label the timeline, students should draw a vertical line up from the point in time where the event occurred and make colorful, creative drawings to represent the event. The images should be placed at the end of each vertical line. The vertical lines may be of varying lengths to accommodate the drawings.

Once the timeline has been labeled with events, have students label their timelines in terms of the Precambrian era, Paleozoic era, Mesozoic era, and Cenozoic era, using a color-coded key from information in their textbook (see Figure 4 on p. 101).

FIGURE 4.

Example of student work and color-coded key for eras.

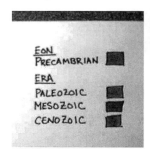 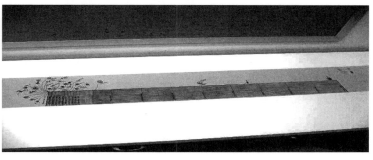

Event Chart

Event in Earth's History	Number of Years Ago
Event of your choice	
Event of your choice	
Your birthday	
Sharks first appeared	400 million
Year Vietnam War ended (1975)	34
Flowering plants appeared	150 million
Darwin wrote *On the Origin of Species*	149
Formation of Appalachian Mountains began	300 million
Ancient swamps began to form Earth's coal deposits	280 million
First invertebrates appeared	2.5 billion
First insects appeared	380 million
Formation of Sierra Nevada mountains began	4 million
First primates appeared	60 million
First mammals appeared	220 million
Extinction of the dinosaurs	65 million
Mount Vesuvius erupted, destroying Pompeii	1,929
First fish appeared	500 million
Pilgrims on the Mayflower arrived at Plymouth Rock	387
Most recent ice age ended	12 thousand
Trilobites appeared	540 million
First vertebrates appeared	450 million
Invention of the Model T automobile by Ford (1908)	100

(Continued on p. 102)

101

(Continued from p. 101)

Dinosaurs first appeared	230 million
Abraham Lincoln assassinated (1865)	143
Earliest human ancestors appeared	3.5 million
First reptiles appeared	320 million
First birds appeared	170 million
Man walked on the Moon (July 1969)	40
Grand Canyon carved by Colorado River	10 million
Blue-green algae and bacteria formed earliest fossils	3.3 billion
The movie *Jurassic Park* was released in theaters	15
Formation of the Earth	4.6 billion

Explain

After students complete the timeline, ask them to write descriptions of the events on the geologic time scale. As students share their timelines, they should begin to realize that much of the development of Earth's plants, animals, humans, and so on has occurred only recently in the whole of geological time.

Students can compare and contrast the geological time categories with the appearance and extinction of various organisms. Have students answer the questions at the end of Student Data Sheet and discuss student responses.

Extend

Have each student choose an extinct plant and animal. Using the internet, library books, and textbooks, the students should gather information about each of their chosen organisms. For example, *What did it look like? Where did it live? What did it eat? How long was the species on Earth? Why did it go extinct?*

On the top three lines of the index card, record the organism's common name, scientific name, and information about its occurrence on the geologic time scale. Underneath the name information, record the other information found about the organism. On the opposite side of the card, students should draw a color sketch of what paleontologists think the extinct plant and animal looked like. See the student sample below.

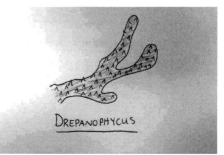

DREPANOPHYCUS

* PALEOZOIC ERA (Devonian Period)
* Leaves are unbranched and thorn-shaped.
* Eastern Canada, China, Russia
* Extinct in Devonian Age
* Competition caused it to go extinct

DREPANOPHYCUS

Using string (as in the activity *It's Not All Relative)*, place four different-colored clothespins, pieces of tape, or sticky notes to indicate the four eras on the time scale: Precambrian era, Paleozoic era, Mesozoic era, and Cenozoic era. Tell the students to place their index cards in the proper order (according to their organism's time of appearance in geologic time) on the string with paper clips. Allow the groups to examine the extinct organisms on the class timeline, and have the students share how paleontologists believed that the various organisms became extinct. Have the students discuss how the cards are arranged on the string and notice that the Cenozoic era has the most events. Encourage students to recall the ages of the Earth (4.6 billion years old), the oldest fossils of blue-green algae (3.3 billion years ago), the first reptiles (320 million years ago), the first mammals (220 million years ago), and the earliest human ancestor (3.5 million years ago).

Evaluate

Check for student understanding:

1. Compare and contrast the geologic time frames: eon, period, era, and epoch.
2. Which appeared first, animals or plants?
3. Which organisms on your timeline have been around the least amount of time?
4. Which organisms on your timeline have been around the most amount of time?
5. In which time era have most of Earth's events or occurrences taken place? Why do you think this is?
6. Which types of organisms are found in the oldest known fossils? How do you think the existence of these organisms could have allowed the existence of other types of organisms?

For more information about geologic time scale and other similar activities see the websites below.

Modeling geologic time scale:
- *www.geosociety.org/science/timescale/timescl.htm*
- *www.geology.wisc.edu/~museum/hughes/GeoTimeScale1.html*
- *www.csmate.colostate.edu/cltw/cohortpages/debacker/geologic.html*
- *http://serc.carleton.edu/quantskills/methods/quantlit/DeepTime.html*
- *http://orchard.sbschools.net/library/tasks/5thgrade/science/earthspace/geology/geologicaltime/activities.htm*
- *www.utexas.edu/tmm/education/lessonplans/time/index.html*
- *www.smithlifescience.com/GeologicTimeLine.htm*

103

- *www.accessexcellence.org/AE/AEPC/WWC/1991/geologic.html*
- *www.mysciencebox.org/timelines*

Interactive timeline:
- *www.fossils-facts-and-finds.com/geologic_time_line.html*
- *www.ucmp.berkeley.edu/fosrec/TimeScale.html*
- *www.cotf.edu/ete/modules/msese/earthsysflr/geotime.html*
- *www.uky.edu/KGS/education/geologicscale.htm*
- *www.palaeos.com/Timescale/default.htm*
- *www.enchantedlearning.com/subjects/Geologictime.html*

Geologic time scale as a clock:
- *www.3d-fossils.com/earth_sciences/paleontology/geological_time_scale_1.html*
- *www.uky.edu/KGS/education/clockstime.htm*

104

Name _____

Geological time is a very important scale concept that includes an understanding of where species "belong" in a linear timeline of Earth's history. Absolute and relative age information is compiled by scientists called *paleontologists* to form a geologic time scale of important events. You will construct your model of geologic time scale using a few major events in Earth's history.

Event in Earth's History	Number of Years Ago
Event of your choice	
Event of your choice	
Your birthday	
Sharks first appeared	400 million
Year Vietnam War ended (1975)	34
Flowering plants appeared	150 million
Darwin wrote *On the Origin of Species*	149
Formation of Appalachian Mountains began	300 million
Ancient swamps began to form Earth's coal deposits	280 million
First invertebrates appeared	2.5 billion
First insects appeared	380 million
Formation of Sierra Nevada mountains began	4 million
First primates appeared	60 million
First mammals appeared	220 million
Extinction of the dinosaurs	65 million
Mount Vesuvius erupted, destroying Pompeii	1,929
First fish appeared	500 million
Pilgrims on the Mayflower arrived at Plymouth Rock	387
Most recent ice age ended	12 thousand
Trilobites appeared	540 million
First vertebrates appeared	450 million
Invention of the Model T automobile by Ford (1908)	100
Dinosaurs first appeared	230 million
Abraham Lincoln assassinated (1865)	143
Earliest human ancestors appeared	3.5 million
First reptiles appeared	320 million
First birds appeared	170 million
Man walked on the Moon (July 1969)	40
Grand Canyon carved by Colorado River	10 million
Blue-green algae and bacteria formed earliest fossils	3.3 billion
The movie *Jurassic Park* was released in theaters	15
Formation of the Earth	4.6 billion

Student Data Sheet
Time Flies When You're Learning About Scale!

Procedure

1. Obtain five pieces of unlined paper, tape them end to end (short edges together), and place on table horizontally.
2. Using a small ruler, measure from the left end of the paper 20 cm and from the bottom of the paper 10 cm, and put a dot at the intersection of these two measurements.
3. From this dot, draw a straight line down to the bottom of the paper and label this line "0." Next, using a meter stick, draw a horizontal line (1 m in length) beginning at the dot on the 0 line toward the right end of the paper.
4. Without removing the meter stick, mark off the line (from left to right) in 1 cm increments all the way up to 10 cm (1 cm, 2 cm, 3 cm, . . . 10 cm).
5. At that point, continue to make tick marks along the timeline in increments of 10 cm all the way up to 1 m or 100 cm. (10 cm, 20 cm, 30 cm, . . . 100 cm).
6. Using a ruler, extend the tick marks to the bottom of the pages. Label what units of time *each* tick mark represents. Let 1 cm equal 50 million years. Label the 0 line *Present Day*. For example, let 3 cm equal 150 million years, or 30 cm equal 10,000 million years or 1.5 billion years.
7. To label the timeline, draw a vertical line up from the point in time where the event occurred. Make your timelines colorful by adding creative drawings to represent each event. The images should be placed at the end of each vertical line.
8. Label your entire timeline with the events provided in the event table above (completing the table as needed).
9. Using your textbook, label the Precambrian era, Paleozoic era, Mesozoic era, and Cenozoic era using a color-coded key. Draw the key on the top right corner of the paper.
10. Describe the arrangement of the events on your timeline below, and then answer the questions that follow.

Describe your timeline:

106

Support or reject the following statements based on your timeline:

1. Dinosaurs and mammals lived together at the same time.

2. Birds appeared before reptiles.

3. Insects appeared before flowering plants.

4. The Earth's coal deposits formed after the most recent ice age.

5. Primates were the first mammals to appear.

6. All mountains on Earth formed within 1 million years of each other.

7. Sharks were the first type of fish to appear.

8. Vertebrates were the first organisms on Earth.

Answer the following questions:

9. According to your timeline, what do the following increments of measurement equal in time?

      a. 1 cm =
      b. 6 cm =
      c. 10 cm =
      d. 18 cm =

10. How many eras make up the Earth's history?

11. Name the four eras and how long ago each began.

12. In which time era did the majority of the events occur?

13. How might Earth's history have been different if blue-green algae did not exist?

14. Name two biological or chemical processes that may have contributed to the abundance of life on Earth. Explain your answer.

Chapter 8
Billions of Us: Scale & Population

Overview

Population is increasingly important as both a scientific and a political subject. The world is getting more crowded. Providing students with the tools to understand population numbers is not only important for their basic understanding of their world, but it is also essential for their future navigation of social and political subjects ranging from energy use and the environment to globalization and the economy. How many people live in your city? Your state? Your country? Your world? How many people live in the United States versus China? This exercise helps students explore the magnitudes of populations and build familiarity with the scales of city, country, and world populations. A related exercise explores the connection between population and energy consumption by comparing the populations of various countries and their corresponding use of oil.

Objectives

- To use examples of different magnitudes to explore the sizes of things.
- To compare and contrast populations of the world, students' own city, and the world's largest cities and countries.

Process Skills

- Applying data
- Comparing and contrasting
- Manipulating ratios
- Modeling

Activity Duration

60 minutes per section

Background

Big numbers, small numbers, and scaling concepts are often presented to students in the abstract. Students typically learn to manipulate numbers mathematically and understand the powers of ten independently from concrete examples in their world.

However it is also important that students attach these mathematical tools—namely scale concepts and powers of ten—to familiar, real-world examples. Of particular interest to children are comparisons between the largest and smallest things (buildings, mountains, dinosaurs) and the fastest and slowest (animals, planes, spacecraft). Exploring a range of examples not only provides exercise for the understanding of large numbers and scale but also provides important content knowledge. Gaining a rough but accurate working knowledge of numbers such as the populations of the United States and the Earth, the age of the United States, and other historical and geological/evolutionary scales is valuable in developing mathematical skill. These exercises also provide students with the outlines of quantitative content knowledge that is crucial to their navigation of the scientific, social, and even political concepts that they will face in their education and adulthood.

109

Population: Knowing the Magnitude

One of the most important skills that scientists and technical professionals learn is how to mentally catalog magnitudes of important numbers. This does not mean that they memorize numbers but that they have a working understanding of the rough size of the numbers. In its purest form, this means knowing a number to the nearest significant digit. For example we all know the rough magnitude of the height and weight of the average human adult: roughly five feet and somewhere between 100 and 200 pounds. This is a very rough range, but we know that 10 feet and 1,000 pounds is wrong. Most of us have a hard time giving even this close an estimate of the population of our own city, state, country, or world. The exercise in this chapter help students gain an understanding of the scale of these different population categories. Emphasize that when making these important estimates, getting the answer exactly right is not the point. In fact it can distract us from the more important point: the magnitude of the number. We want to know roughly how large these numbers are (e.g., "around 10 million," not "13.3 million"; "around 500,000," not "517,000"). The extra precision is of little use in gaining an understanding of the scale of the number in question.

Materials

For each student:
- Student Data Sheets
- Drawing materials (pencil or pen, paper, ruler)
- Construction paper
- Scissors
- Small stackable objects of uniform size (pennies, Lego pieces, popsicle sticks)

Note: Each student or group should have access to several dozen of these pieces.

Preparation: If you do not have access to the internet for students to look up population statistics, have a few numbers on hand prior to this exercise: the population of the city (or cities) the students live in and the population of another well-known city in your state (perhaps the biggest city or another large city).

Engage

Distribute the Student Data Sheets and instruct the students to study the table in Part A, City Scales. The first exercise requires the students to enter the population of their city and another important city in their state. This can be done either by providing the statistics or by having the students research them on the internet, in class, or at home the night before the exercise. In Part B,

Paper Cities, the students are then required to cut out pieces of paper whose areas represent the populations of several of the world's largest cities. In the simplest case, the students can draw squares on sheets of paper to represent the populations, if scissor use is not convenient. The main goal for the students is to derive a scale by which to determine the appropriate size of each paper city. As suggested on the Student Data Sheet, it is prudent to start with the biggest city when determining an appropriate scaling. You want your biggest city to use up most of whatever sheets of paper you will be using. If you are using standard 8.5 × 11-inch sheets of paper, you will be able to make squares of roughly 20 × 20 cm.

- Starting with a standard 8.5 × 11-inch piece of notebook paper, cut out a 20 cm × 20 cm square, which will represent the population of the largest world city (Mumbai).

- This 20 cm × 20 cm square has an area of 400 cm^2.

- The largest city is Mumbai with a population of 13,000,000 people.

- So our scaling is 13,000,000 corresponds to 400 cm^2.
  - 13,000,000 people : 400 cm^2
  - So 1 cm^2 corresponds to 32,500 people; our scaling is (1 cm^2 / 32,500 people)
  - Paper city area in cm2 = population × (1 cm^2 / 32,500 people)

- Example: New York City, population 8,140,000.
  - Paper city area = (New York population)(scaling) = 8,140,000 (1 cm^2 / 32,500 people)
    = 250 cm^2

- If we are making a square city, the square root of this area will give us the length of the side of the paper city.
  - Length of side of paper city = (250 cm^2)$^{1/2}$
    = 15.8 cm

- After entering the information in the table in Part B, measure out a square 15.8 cm × 15.8 cm and cut it out. This square paper city will represent the population of New York City.

An example of the sizes of selected paper city areas, based on this scaling, is shown in Figure 1 on page 112. The small, unlabeled square represents Raleigh, North Carolina.

111

FIGURE 1.

Part B: Paper cities. Each square represents the population of the respective city. The small, unlabeled square in between Raleigh, North Carolina, and Los Angeles, California, is the small town of Hillsborough, North Carolina, population 5,450.

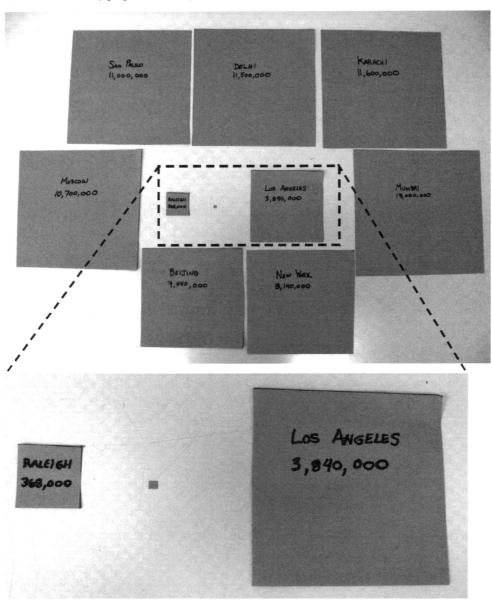

In Part C, Paper Countries, students will repeat the same type of exercise, but this time they will be cutting out square areas that represent the physical areas of each of the listed countries. Again they will need to determine a scaling that will allow them to make paper countries large enough to be able to compare the largest and smallest. Emphasize that in this exercise the paper countries are representing the actual physical size of the countries rather than population. The students then cut out little "tokens" from notebook or construction paper to represent chunks of population. They will have to determine for themselves an appropriate scale for the number of people each population token will represent. Note that the countries listed vary considerably in area and population. Initially you should have the students exclude the two smallest countries, as they would otherwise have to choose a scale for population tokens that would require dozens and dozens of tokens for the largest countries (which would be interesting but time-consuming). The same exclusion should initially be made for the oil consumption tokens. For a more challenging version of this exercise, have them include all of the countries listed.

For example, if all the countries are included, the population token should represent the population of the smallest country listed, in this case, Iceland, with roughly 300,000 people. If one population token equals 300,000 people, Iceland will have one, Ghana will have 76, and China 4,400! Though that is probably not practical, it is a revealing exercise just to calculate the number of population tokens that would be required. Help students understand that this means that China's population is almost 5,000 times larger than Iceland's.

The scalings that are recommended in Student Data Sheet will provide the results shown in the box below. Note that the population and oil numbers for Canada and Ghana will result in much less than one token. For all other countries the values have been rounded to the nearest token. You can either leave Canada and Ghana out, or come up with a way of representing a fraction of a token (see Figure 2 on p. 114).

Country	Paper Country Area (cm²)	Paper Country Length of Side (cm)	Population Tokens	Oil Tokens
China	380.0	19.6	13.0	7.0
India	131.0	11.5	11.0	2.0
EU	173.0	13.1	5.0	15.0
USA	393.0	19.8	3.0	21.0
Canada	399.0	20.0	0.3 (one-third)	2.0
Ghana	9.5	3.1	0.2 (one-fifth)	0.04

FIGURE 2.

Part C. Paper countries. The large paper squares represent the total land area of each country. The small paper squares represent the population of each country (each small square equals 100 million people). The stacked tokens represent oil consumption. Each token represents 1 million barrels per day.

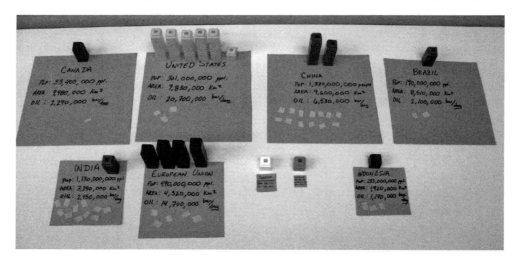

Explore and Extend

Have students conduct web research on the population of their state compared with, or contrasted to, those of neighboring states. Have them create a graph of the populations of the states. This kind of exercise may provide surprising results. Did you know that California has 35 million people? Does any state have less than a million people? What range of powers of ten do the populations of states cover?

Below are some examples of other statistics to research. Answers may vary.
- Do more people live in the greater Tokyo metropolitan area or in all of Canada?
- Do more people live in Atlanta, Georgia or in all of Alaska, Wyoming, and Montana combined?
- Do more people live in greater London or in the state of North Carolina?
- How many people live in Africa? Asia? Europe?
- Have students calculate the per capita usage of oil for each country listed in the exercise in Part C of the Student Data Sheet.

Evaluate

Check for student understanding:

Have students answer the questions at the end of the Student Data Sheet. These questions involve both quantitative comparisons between numbers and exploration of the range of powers of ten that different population contexts cover. Most of the questions can also serve as provocative starting points for class discussion on population, population density, and energy use in today's world and how each relates to the future.

Answers to Questions:

1. **How large are the populations of the largest cities in the world?**

   Answer: Around 10 million people.

2. **How many people live on the Earth?**

   Answer: Somewhere between 6 billion and 7 billion people (just knowing the world's population is several billion people is much better than not knowing it at all).

3. **How many people live in the most populated countries in the world? What are the countries?**

   Answer: Around 1 billion; China and India.

4. **How many people live in the United States?**

   Answer: Around 300 million.

5. **How many people live in your state?**

   Answer: *http://en.wikipedia.org/wiki/List_of_U.S._states_by_population*

115

How big is the biggest city in the world? How does it compare to the biggest city in the United States? How does it compare with your town?

Part A. City Scales

Take a look at the table below that lists the cities with the largest populations. Note that this ranking is for true city populations (population within the city limits*). The top five cities are ranked along with New York (#13), Beijing (#17), and Los Angeles (#42). Also included are two small North Carolina cities for comparison. In the two rows at the bottom, add your city and another city in your state. Find out the populations of those cities and enter in the population column.

World Ranking	City	Population in City Limits
1	Mumbai, India	13,000,000
2	Karachi, Pakistan	11,600,000
3	Delhi, India	11,500,000
4	Sao Paulo, Brazil	11,000,000
5	Moscow, Russia	10,700,000
13	New York City	8,140,000
17	Beijing, China	7,440,000
42	Los Angeles	3,840,000
?	Raleigh, NC	368,000
?	Hillsborough, NC	5,450
?	(your city)	
?	(another city in your state)	

*If entire metropolitan areas are included, the list is different and the populations are correspondingly larger. For example, the two largest metropolitan areas are currently Tokyo, with over 35 million people, and Mexico City, with over 19 million people. Source of population data: *http://en.wikipedia.org/wiki/List_of_cities_by_population#_note-WG*

Part B. Paper Cities

On a clean sheet (or several sheets) of notebook or construction paper, you will outline squares whose areas represent the population of several of the cities. Be sure to include your city as well as one of the big cities. Remember that the area of your square is the length times the width. Cut out each of your cities and label them.

Hint: You will need to choose a scaling to begin. You probably want to make the area of the biggest city correspond to the largest square you can make with your paper. That will set a scale (say 20 cm × 20 cm or 400 cm² corresponds to the population of Mumbai). Use three significant digits for your numbers.

- The population of Mumbai (13,100,000) corresponds to 400 cm²

- So 1 cm² = 32,800 people

- So what is the area of a paper city representing New York? Hillsborough, North Carolina?

City	Population	Area of Paper City	Width of Your Square City (cm)

Keep in mind that your scaling can be different. If you have big pieces of paper, or if you combine pieces, you can make your city squares bigger.

Part C. Paper Countries: Area, Population, Energy Consumption

In this exercise you will compare the actual physical area of countries, their populations, and their energy consumption, by making small models representing each variable.

Exercise

1. Country Area: Cut out square pieces of paper that represent the areas of each of the countries below. You will need to choose a scaling (see scaling hints below). The largest countries (the United States, Canada, China) should have areas close to the size of a full sheet of paper.

2. Country Population: We will represent the population of each country with population tokens. Cut out little square or circular pieces (perhaps ½ inch to 1 inch on a side) or 1 inch paper dolls to represent population. You will need at least 20 of these (probably more). One idea is to cut out little circles and draw stick figures on them to represent people. Each one of these population tokens will represent a certain number of people. A good place to start is to make each token worth 100 million people (100,000,000). Place the correct number of population tokens on each country's sheet. Spread them out so you can see each token. For example, if you choose 100 million people per population token, the European Union will have 5 (rounding 490 million up to 500 million).

3. Oil Consumption: Choose small, stackable objects such as pennies, small blocks, or Legos to represent oil consumption. These pieces should be uniform in size (all the same for every student). These will be your oil tokens and will represent a certain scale of oil consumption. A good starting point is to have each oil token represent 1 million barrels of oil per day. Determine how many oil tokens each country uses and stack them on the country.

4. Whole World: Make one sheet whose area represents the area of the whole world. You will probably need to attach sheets together with a stapler or tape to make the area large enough (keep the same scaling as you used in Part A). Also repeat steps B and C.

Rank	Country	Population	Area (sq km)	Oil Consumption (barrels /day)
1	China	1,320,000,000	9,600,000	6,530,000
2	India	1,130,000,000	3,290,000	2,450,000
3	European Union	490,000,000	4,320,000	14,700,000
4	United States	301,000,000	9,830,000	20,700,000
5	Indonesia	235,000,000	1,920,000	1,170,000
6	Brazil	190,000,000	8,510,000	2,100,000
38	Canada	33,400,000	9,980,000	2,290,000
50	Ghana	23,000,000	239,000	44,000
178	Iceland	301,000	103,000	20,600
	World	6,600,000,000	510,000,000 (total) 150,000,000 (land)	82,600,000

Source: All data in the table above from the Central Intelligence Agency's *World Factbook* and rounded to three significant digits: *www.cia.gov/library/publications/the-world-factbook/rankorder/2119rank.html*

Scaling Hints

As in the previous exercise, you will have to choose a scaling for each parameter (area, population, and oil consumption).

Example scaling:
- Area: 10,000,000 sq km : 400 sq cm (20 cm × 20 cm); 1 sq cm = 25,000 sq km
- Population: 100,000,000 people = 1 population piece
- Oil Consumption: 1 million barrels = 1 oil barrel piece (a penny, a Lego)

Population Questions

1. How much smaller is your town than the largest city in the world?

2. How many powers of ten do the populations of cities cover?

3. How many powers of ten do the populations of countries cover?

119

4. Which country has the highest population density? The lowest?

5. Which country uses the most oil per person? The least?

6. What fraction of the total world population lives in the United States? China? India?

7. For what fraction of total world oil consumption is the United States responsible? China?

ESTIMATION & MODELS

Chapter 9
Scale It!

Overview

When building a dollhouse or a model of a car or a cell, close attention to the details is crucial to making it look accurate and realistic. A consistent scaling factor for all details in the model is critical. In this activity students explore scaling through modeling objects of extreme sizes. They create both a scaled drawing of an object and a scaled 3-D model.

Objective
- To develop skills in scaling objects larger or smaller than actual sizes.
- To build an actual model of a scaled object.

Process Skills
- Observing
- Predicting
- Comparing and contrasting
- Calculating

Activity Duration
90 minutes
(Extension may take additional time.)

Background

What does it mean to scale something? Scaling involves taking an object and shrinking it or expanding it. City maps and model airplanes are familiar examples. Why do people make scaled models, maps, and drawings? If something is very large, such as the United States or the solar system, then the only way to visualize it within our range of perceptual experience is to scale it down in size. On the other hand, if dealing with an object so tiny we cannot see it with the naked eye, such as a virus or skin cell, we have to scale it up in size. Even objects that are not at extreme scales but are difficult to experience directly, such as a giant squid (13 meters), can be scaled for students to visualize.

Scientists, architects, engineers, and landscapers use scaled drawings and 3-D models daily. As noted in the activity *What Is Scale?* (Chapter 1), there are many different types of scales in the world. Architects have their own special types of scales, which they use to make scaled drawings and models of various sizes. They even have a special tools and triangular rulers to help them switch from one scale to another. For example, when a map or plan is made in which 1 foot is scaled to 3 inches, this is referred to as a *1:4 scale*, because the map distances are one-fourth of the true distances. When one foot is scaled to ¼ inch, it is referred to as a *1:48 scale*. Obviously a plan for a building cannot be the same size as the building! Among many other impracticalities, you would not be able to see the whole plan at once. Scaled maps and drawings help us see the general plan or structure in a useful, practical form. In creating a map or scaled drawing, a scaling factor or ratio must be chosen that prescribes the ratio of map distances to actual distances. Typically a colon notation is used for map scaling factors rather than a fraction notation, though both are correct.

123

Scaling factor → Distance on map: Actual distance

Scales can be written with or without units of measure—1 mm to 1 km or simply a ratio in colon notation—1: 1,000,000.

When written this way, they are called *ratios*. Scalings can also be represented as a fraction: 1/1,000,000. When written this way, we usually call them *proportions* or *fractions*. These different ways of representing a scaling factor are equivalent. It is a matter of choice, but to avoid confusion within this exercise, choose one and keep consistent.

In this activity students will explore extreme sizes of objects and create both a scaled drawing of an object and a 3-D model.

Materials

Each group will need:

- Graph paper or unlined paper
- Colored pencils
- Ruler
- Measuring tape
- Calculator
- Internet access
- Materials for building objects (e.g., cardboard, poster board, string, tape, glue)

Note: When deciding on objects to scale up or down, remember that square or rectangular objects are easier to rescale than other shapes. Students should note in their scaling that if any measurement or math errors occur, then their sketches and objects will have odd shapes. The key to accurate scaling of objects is precision in measurement.

Engage

Ask students to name the smallest and largest dog that come to mind. How many times larger is the large dog than the small dog? If you wanted to make a model of the small dog that is the actual size of the large dog, what would be the scaling factor? Keep in mind that you must be specific about what you mean by *larger*. In determining a scaling factor, you want to find the ratio of one dimension of the objects (the height, width, or length). Be careful not to confuse scaling of linear dimensions (length, width, or height) with scalings of area or volume (or mass). A very large dog may only be 7 times taller than a small dog but may weigh 100 times more. In the context of determining scaling for a map or a model, we are almost always talking about scaling the linear dimension of the object. This means picking its length, height, or width as the quantity that will be used to determine the scaling.

Give out the Student Data Sheet to the students and allow them to compare and contrast small and large objects. The students will determine how many times larger (or smaller) one object is than the other, as well as determine how it scales relative to objects of another size. Have students practice calculating size comparisons by dividing the larger size by the smaller size. Remind students to convert the sizes to common units before calculating. Help students recognize that comparisons can be made small to large or large to small, depending on the way the division problem is set up. For example, to compare the small to the large, divide the smaller number by the larger number (e.g., 25/100 = .25 or .25 times smaller) and vice versa for large to small (e.g., 100/25 = 4 or 4 times larger). Also, reinforce that when speaking or reading ratios aloud, the order of the comparison is very important.

For example, how many times taller is an average Great Dane dog (35 in) than a Chihuahua (5 in)?

35 in **divided** by 5 in **equals** 7, or 7 times taller

The scaling factor should be used in a consistent way.

On the Student Data Sheet, compare the following pairs: longleaf pine tree and redwood sequoia; pill bug and aquatic isopod; thread snake and anaconda; sunflower and daisy. The students should calculate how many times larger the organism in the right-hand box is compared to the organism in the left-hand box. Once the students have completed the table, they should answer the questions below it.

Show Calculations

Longleaf pine and redwood sequoia: 116 m divided by 35 m = 3.3 times larger
Pill bug and aquatic isopod: 350 mm divided by 13 mm = 27 times larger
Thread snake and anaconda snake: 1,000 cm divided by 11 cm = 91 times larger
Sunflower and daisy: 6 feet = 72 inches = 183 cm divided by 61 = 3.0 times bigger

If you wanted to make a model of the pill bug 20 feet long, what would be the scaling factor? Show your work. The convention for scaling factors is such that the first number refers to the model or map, and the second to the actual or true object being modeled.

125

Model or map: Real world

12.7 mm = 1.27 cm = 0.5 in = 0.04 ft → 20 divided by 0.04 = 500 times larger *or* 500:1

What would be the scale factor of a 1 foot miniature model of the anaconda?

1005 cm = 395.6 in = 32.9 ft → 33 times smaller *or* 1:33

Explore

Part A

Show students an architectural blueprint. Point out the scale used in the drawing. In this investigation, students create a scaled drawing of the classroom. (You may choose to have students draw other places, but having them all do the same thing for this part can ensure that all students understand how to create a scale.) First, the students should sketch the room, make actual measurements, and record the lengths of the sides of the room. Next, as a class, determine what scaling factor they will use for the drawings. For example, would a foot in the classroom equal a centimeter or a millimeter in their drawings?

Encourage the students to incorporate as many details as possible, including desks, chalkboard, books on a table, or a sink. Help them apply the scaling factor to these details to increase the precision of their drawings. Colored pencils can be used to capture details. The actual measurements should be recorded on the drawing as one would find in a blueprint. In addition, the students should remember to include the scaling factor legend on the corner of the drawing.

Once groups have completed their drawings, have the students put them up around the room to discuss similarities and differences. Were all the scaled drawings exactly the same? Were the measurements correct? Were the scaling factors accurate? Did some groups include more detail than others? Did that make a difference? What was difficult about making a scaled drawing? What would you do differently?

Part B

For this part of the activity, each group will construct a scaled drawing of an object, but this time each will use a different scaling factor. For example, you could have all the groups create a scaled drawing of a pencil, a piece of chalk, or an Erlenmeyer flask, each with a different scale that you assign. One group could use a scaling factor of 2 to 1, and another group could attempt 20 to 1. Once they are complete, have the students compare their drawings. Have the

126

students place them in the board in order, from largest to smallest scale. Make sure that they label the sketch with the appropriate scaling factor.

Explain

Creating scaled models and drawings is useful in various careers, such as architecture, drafting, engineering, and landscaping. But all of us use some type of scale every day. We use scales for determining the temperature, reading maps, planting gardens, cooking dinner, or building models. Understanding extreme sizes of objects and distances is also important in our understanding the diversity of life and materials on Earth. Comparing and contrasting sizes of things is the initial step in understanding why we must have scaling factors in the first place. We cannot always experience things directly, especially the very large and the very small. Sometimes we must scale objects up from the very tiny, as in the *Mega Virus* activity, and other times we must scale objects down, as in the activity *The Scale of the Solar System*. Building scale models can help students develop a conceptual sense of scale.

Students should be able to figure out how many times larger or smaller items are compared to each other and should know how to determine the scaling factor necessary to make an object a different size.

1. If you wanted to make a model of the pill bug 20 feet long, what would be the scale factor? Show your work.

2. What would be the scale factor of a 1-foot miniature model of an anaconda snake?

For more information on scale drawings, models, and questions:

- *www.mathsteacher.com.au/year8/ch06_ratios/06_scale/draw.htm*
- *www.engineersedge.com/drafting/drawing_scale.htm*
- *www.westone.wa.gov.au/toolbox8/furniture/toolbox/shared/resources_dr/techniques/conventions/scale.htm*
- *www.learner.org/channel/courses/learningmath/geometry/session8/part_a/index.html*
- *www.regentsprep.org/Regents/Math/math-topic.cfm?TopicCode=scale*
- *www.figurethis.org/challenges/c61/challenge.htm*

127

Extend

After the scaled drawing in Part B is complete, the students should use everyday items (paper, popsicle sticks, glue, tape, shoe boxes, clay) to make a 3-D model that is accurate to scale. The larger-scaling-factor 3-D models may have to be built outside, depending on what was assigned to each group. As the students share their drawings and models with the class, have them explain the procedure they used to decide on the scale, issues that arose during the construction of the model, and what they would do differently if they did it again.

You may choose to have the class work together on one large object (e.g., giant squid, height of the Washington Monument, length of the Titanic,). Find the actual size and dimensions of the object. Go outside and have the students use tape measures, string, or flags to map the dimensions of the object (width and length).

For other, similar activities in determining the size of large objects, see the Project WILD Aquatic K–12 Curriculum and Activity Guide, especially "A Whale of a Tail," about scaling the size of a whale:

www.projectwild.org/ProjectWILDK-12AquaticCurriculumandActivityGuide.htm

Evaluate

Check for student understanding:

1. What does it mean for something to be scaled?
2. Why do people make scaled models of objects?
3. Who uses different scales on a daily basis?
4. How many times smaller is the height of a hummingbird (3 in) compared with the height of an ostrich (7 ft)?
5. If you found a lizard that was 5 in long and you wanted to create a large model of it that would be 5 ft long, what is the scale factor for the giant lizard model?

128

Name _____

Compare and contrast each pair of organisms below. Calculate how many times larger the organism in the right-hand box is compared to the organism in the left-hand box. Remember to check the units of measure. Show all calculations beneath each pair.

Longleaf Pine	Coast Redwood Sequoia

35 m	116 m

Show calculations:

Pill Bug	Aquatic Pill Bug
	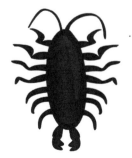
13 mm	350 mm

Show calculations:

Thread Snake	Anaconda

11 cm	1,000 cm

Show calculations:

Daisy	Sunflower

61 cm	6 ft

Show calculations:

130

1. If you wanted to make a model of the pill bug 20 feet long, what would be the scale factor? Show your work.

2. What would be the scale factor of a 1-foot miniature model of the anaconda?

131

Chapter 10
Mega Virus

Overview

The study of science at the extremes of size often involves creating and testing models of science phenomena. Scientists and engineers often build models at different sizes and scales. These models can be physical, such as a Styrofoam ball model of the solar system; virtual models such as animations; or mathematical models such as are used in predicting weather. In this investigation students create different-sized models of the common cold virus (adenovirus) and determine the scaling ratios for each model.

Objectives
- To develop skills in creating models.
- To apply proportional reasoning to determine spatial scale.

Process Skills
- Modeling
- Predicting
- Observing
- Analyzing data

Activity Duration
60 minutes total

Background

The study of science at the extremes of size often involves creating and testing models. Scientists and engineers build and test models of everything from machines and cells to hurricanes and population growth. These may be physical models, such as those that use balls to represent the solar system, mathematical models, or virtual models such as computer simulations. For phenomena that occur at very small or very large scales, models provide researchers the ability to test theories by tuning different variables and components within the model system. Often these sorts of tests are extremely difficult or impossible to perform on the real system. For example, wind tunnels are used to test the aerodynamics of airplanes, automobiles, or trains. Astrophysicists make models of black holes and supernovas on their computers to test the latest theories on how these phenomena actually work. Biochemists make models of proteins to predict enzymatic behavior or binding affinity to cell surfaces. Testing models helps researchers predict the behavior of phenomena at the extremes of scale. As often as not, building and testing models result in as many questions as answers. But a good question is the wellspring of good science. Models help us discover what we don't know and thereby point us in the right direction.

When they work with a model, it is important for students to have an understanding of the proportional relationships that exist between the size of the model and the actual object or process that is being simulated.

In this investigation students create several scale models of the common cold virus (adenovirus). Students quantitatively assess the differences in size between their model viruses and the actual virus, thereby defining different scales for their models.

Materials

Each group will need:
- Icosahedral patterns A and B (see p. 139)
- Masking tape
- Mounting adhesive clay
- Glue
- Origami or copy paper

Each class will need one or two sets:
- Icosahedral pattern C (an equilateral triangle with 50 cm sides; you will make this)
- Duct tape or other wide tape
- Sheets of cardboard or foam board

Engage

Show students a dollhouse object, such as a doll-sized chair, and ask them how much smaller the dollhouse chair is compared to a human-sized chair. Be precise in defining your scaling estimate. In this context, when we describe the scale we mean the linear scale, as opposed to the scale in volume or area. In the case of the dollhouse, we would take the ratio of the height (or width) of the doll-sized chair to that of a human-sized chair. So to determine the relative scale of a physical model, you measure some particular dimension (a side of a triangle, the height of a giraffe) and use that parameter to determine your scaling ratio. Introduce the idea of scale and brainstorm examples of scales that students typically encounter in their day-to-day activities. Examples of measurement scales include those on road maps and weather maps, as well as thermometers. An important point for students to consider is why measurements are scaled.

To engage students in thinking about the importance of scales for maps, pass out a series of road maps and ask the students to determine the scales. Remind them that the scale is noted on the edge of the map (e.g., a road atlas map of New York City shows that 0.9 of an inch of map equals 1 mile, and the map of New York State shows that 1.6 inches equals 20 miles). Ask students why the scales for a city map and a state map might be distinctly different. What would the state map look like if the scale of the state map was the same as that of the city map? Discuss with students the meaning of the scale. What does it mean to say 1 inch equals 10 miles? Remind the students about the concept of proportionality, and show them the ratio formula for the two map scales for New York, on the top of page 135.

134

Scale of New York City map = 0.9 inch map/1 mile of city (1: 70,400)

Scale of New York State map = 1.6 inches of map/20 miles (1: 792,000)

One of the goals is to help students develop a *sense of scale* or a conceptual sense for the numbers. Ask them to consider what it means to travel an inch across the city map, compared to an inch across the state map. How would time factor into travel planning using the map? (This can be complicated by traffic patterns for a city.) You may want to use Google Maps to demonstrate differences in scale, as you zoom in and out on different locations. Google has a measuring tool that students can use to look at distances in different units (e.g., feet and meters).

Invite the students to find other city and state maps and compare the scales.

Discuss scales as ratios of one quantity to another. Highlight what it means to say that a scale is 10:1 or 50:1. Note that the first number represents the map or model scale, and the second number represents the actual distance or object being modeled.

Explore

Part 1. Exploring Scale

Ask the students to consider Line 1 and Line 2, shown in Part 1 of the Student Data Sheet. Explain that the goal is to estimate how much longer the Line 2 is compared with Line 1 and determine the ratio of one line to the other. Students then draw a square that is 2 times larger than the small square shown on the page. Next students determine the ratio of the linear size of the big square to the small square.

Part 2. Scale Models of Viruses

In Part 2 students construct virus models at three different sizes (approximately 1 cm, 8 cm, and 1 m in diameter). Ask the students to try to imagine a nanometer-sized virus and then imagine what a virus would look like that was a million times bigger. In this investigation students construct models of the adenovirus (the virus that causes the common cold).

Model A. Students first create a hand-sized model of the icosahedral virus that is about 8 cm in diameter. Distribute copies of Model A and demonstrate how to fold and tape the edges of the model together. Guide the students through the process

135

FIGURE 1.
Models A and B.

of determining how much bigger Model A is than the adenovirus that causes the common cold. First, have students convert 8 cm to meters (8 cm = 0.08 m). Next, students convert the size of an adenovirus from nanometers to meters (80 nm = 0.00000008 or 8×10^{-8} m). Students should divide the size of Model A in meters by the size of the adenovirus in meters (0.08 / 0.000000008 = 1,000,000). Model A is 1,000,000 times larger than the adenovirus. The model scale is then (1,000,000: 1).

Model B. Next students create a model of an adenovirus that is only 1.0 cm in diameter. Fold and glue Model B to make this tiny model. If you fold the pattern along the lines, you can wrap the model around modeling clay to hold the pattern in place while you glue the edges. How many times bigger is this model than the adenovirus that causes the common cold?

Students should use the same process they used with Model A to calculate how much bigger Model B is than an adenovirus. The 1.0 cm Model B virus equals 0.01 m. The 80 nm adenovirus equals 0.00000008 or 8×10^{-8} meters. Dividing Model B by the size of an adenovirus shows that Model B is 125,000 times bigger than the adenovirus. Model scaling: (125,000: 1).

Model C: Mega Virus. Finally, students create a large model of an adenovirus that is a meter in diameter. If materials are limited, divide your class into two groups to construct the large model. You may want to precut the triangular sides of the icosahedral shape out of cardboard. Each side of the triangle is 50 cm in length. Students can lay the cardboard triangles on the floor to match the pattern used in Model A. Tape the edges of the pattern together with duct tape to assemble the icosahedral shape.

FIGURE 2.
Mega virus.

Next, students calculate how many times bigger the mega virus model is than the adenovirus. The size of the model (1 m) is divided by the size of the adenovirus (0.00000008 m). The mega virus is 12,500,000 times bigger than the actual adenovirus that infects the body. Scaling: 12,500,000: 1.

136

Explain

The adenovirus is the shape of an icosahedron, or 20-sided figure. There are 20 equilateral triangles that fit together. The icosahedron is one of the five platonic (convex regular polyhedron) solids. A variety of viruses take on the icosahedron shape, with the 20 repeated units that self-assemble when the virus replicates inside the cell. One theory is that having a place on the genome that only has to make one shape 20 times saves room on the genome.

FIGURE 3.

Scientists often create scaled models of objects and systems that they are studying. Having a good conceptual feel for the scale of the model compared with the actual object being studied is an important part of the process. By creating different-scaled models, students can develop a sense of the magnitude of the scaling.

Extend

Challenge your students to figure out how many times the mega virus (Model C) would have to be enlarged or reduced if it were the size of a car or as small as an atom.

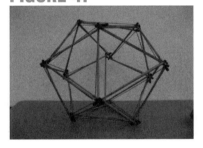

FIGURE 4.

Icosahedral forms are found in a variety of everyday objects and forms of art. Invite students to bring in examples of icosahedron shapes. Alternatively students can use a variety of different modeling and construction materials to make different sizes and types of icosahedral models (see Figures 3, 4, and 5).

FIGURE 5.

Challenge students to estimate differences in size for a variety of materials that they encounter in their daily lives. How much bigger is the Wienermobile than a hot dog that they buy in the store? How does a toy train engine compare to the size of a real train? Encourage students to think about images they encounter in the media and to consider the degree to which those images have been enlarged or reduced.

People have a natural fascination with miniature and magnified objects, such as giant pencils, tiny chairs, and even miniature

animals like toy dogs or miniature horses. Create a collection of images of objects of unusual sizes and encourage students to estimate and calculate the differences between the normal and abnormal sizes.

Evaluate

Check for student understanding:

Give students cardboard boxes of two different sizes, and ask them to predict and then calculate the number of times longer the larger box is than the smaller one. Using both miniature and oversized objects (such as action figures or toy cars), ask students to calculate the size differences.

Challenge Question

Ask students to come up with a way to create a model of an object that is too small to be imaged with an optical microscope. What strategies and techniques would they need to use to determine the size and shape of an object that is too small to be seen with a light microscope?

Resource

Conversion calculator: *www.worldwidemetric.com/metcal.htm*

FIGURE 6.
Boot used in advertising.

138

Icosahedral Pattern A

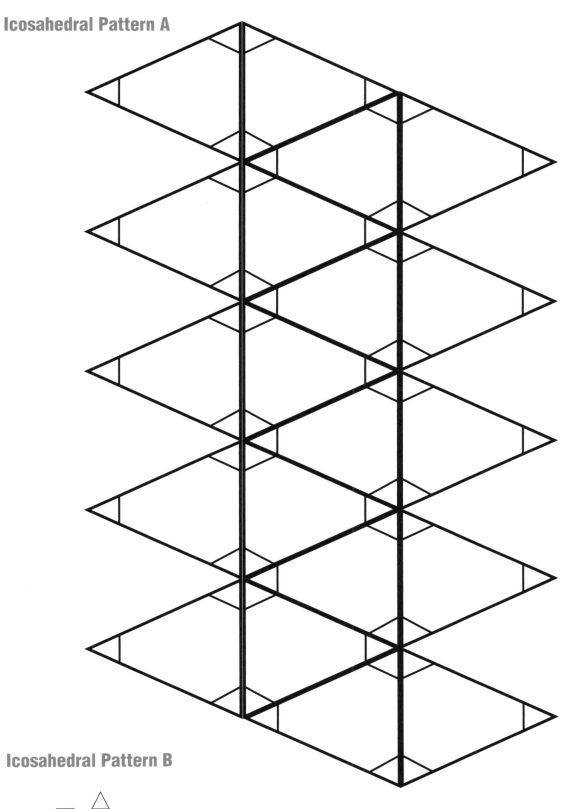

Icosahedral Pattern B

Student Data Sheet
Mega Virus

Name _____

Part 1. Exploring Scale

1. Examine the two lines below. How much longer is the
    second line compared with the first line?

    What is your estimation of the relationship of Line 2 to Line 1?

    _____   _____
    　　　Line 1   Line 2

    Line 2 is _____ times as long as Line 1.

    The ratio of Line 2 to Line 1 is _____ to 1.

2. Measure one of the sides of the square below. Draw a
    square each of whose sides is 2 times longer.

    The ratio of the length of a side of the big square to the length of a side
    of the small square is ___ to 1.

NATIONAL SCIENCE TEACHERS ASSOCIATION

Part 2. Scale Models of Viruses

Viruses are nanometer sized. A nanometer is a billionth of a meter. Imagine a meter cut into a billion parts. One of these tiny parts would be the size of virus (1×10^{-9}). The adenovirus causes the common cold. It is approximately 80 nanometers in size. You will create a model of a nanovirus.

The adenovirus is the shape of an icosahedron or 20-sided figure. It has 20 equilateral triangles that fit together. The icosahedron is one of the five platonic solids (convex regular polyhedrons with faces, edges, and angles that are all congruent). A variety of viruses take on the icosahedron shape, with the 20 repeated units that self-assemble when the virus takes over a cell and replicates itself. One theory is that the single identical units that compose the 20-sided virus capsid make the replication process more efficient.

Model A. First, assemble a model of the icosahedral virus that is approximately 8 cm in diameter. Cut out the virus capsid and fold and tape the edges to form the icosahedral shape (see Figure 1 showing Models A and B).

FIGURE 1.
Models A and B.

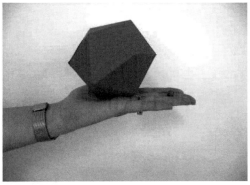

How much bigger is the 8 cm virus (Model A) than the adenovirus that causes the common cold?

8 centimeter Model A = _____ meters

80 nanometer adenovirus = _____ meters

$$\frac{\text{Model A size (_____) meters}}{\text{Adenovirus size (_____) meters}} = \underline{\hspace{1cm}} ?$$

Part 3. Changing Scale

Model B. Next create a model of an adenovirus that is only 1.0 centimeter in diameter (see Figure 2). Fold and glue Model B to make this tiny model. If you fold the pattern along the lines, you can wrap it around wall picture mounting clay to hold the pattern in place while you glue the edges. How many times bigger than the adenovirus that causes the common cold is this model?

FIGURE 2.
1cm virus.

How much bigger is the 1.0 cm virus than the adenovirus that causes the common cold?

1.0 centimeter Model B = _____ meters

80 nanometer adenovirus = _____ meters

$$\frac{\text{Model B size (_____) meters}}{\text{Adenovirus size (\qquad) meters}} = \_\_\_\_\_?$$

Part 4. Mega Virus

FIGURE 3.
Mega virus.

Model C: Mega Virus. Create a giant model of the virus that is a meter in diameter. Cut the triangular sides of the icosahedral shape out of cardboard. The sides of each triangle should be 50 cm in length. Lay the triangles out in the same configuration shown in Model A. Tape the edges of the pattern together with duct tape and use the same process you used to fold and assemble Model A. The virus model should fold together into a magnificent giant model (see Figure 3).

How many times bigger is the Model C mega virus model than the adenovirus that causes the common cold?

    Mega virus Model C = 1 meter
    80 nanometer adenovirus = _____meters
    Model C mega virus size 1 meter
    _____ = _____?
    Adenovirus size (   ) meters

Stand back and look at the differences in the sizes of the three viruses that you constructed. Each virus is increasingly larger than the one before it. How big would the model be if you made a mega mega virus that was 10 times larger than the mega virus that you made? Would it fit into your classroom?

Questions

1. What are the benefits for a researcher of making large models of viruses? What are the drawbacks or limitations?

2. If you were studying viruses, which of your three models would be the most useful in understanding the shape of the virus?

143

Chapter 11
Your World or Mine?
Different Perspectives

Overview

Is the glass half-empty or half-full? That depends on your perspective. Differences in vantage point or prior knowledge can lead to different interpretations or conclusions. Scientists also have various perspectives on new discoveries or the results of experiments. In this activity students will gain awareness of differing perspectives and consider how scientists must sometimes work together to navigate challenging concepts.

Objectives

- To develop skills in observation.
- To create models based on communication.
- To develop spatial visualization skills.

Process Skills

- Observing
- Predicting
- Comparing and contrasting
- Communicating

Activity Duration

90 minutes
(Extension may take additional time.)

Background

Perspective can have many meanings in various contexts, but it refers primarily to how the eye views an object or situation. *Merriam-Webster's* (2008) has four definitions for the term *perspective:* (a) the technique of representing the spatial relation of objects as they might appear to the eye; (b) the interrelation in which a subject or its parts are mentally viewed; (c) the capacity to view things in their true relations or relative importance; or (d) the appearance to the eye of objects in respect to their relative distance and positions. Different points of view or vantage points may lead to different perceptions or conclusions. Each of these is a significant factor in scientific research.

As we move away from the human scale into extreme scales of the very large (astronomical scale) and very small (micro- and nanoscale) it is easy lose perspective. When viewing a "human scale object" it is usually easy to obtain different perspectives by simply walking around it or even taking pictures from above. Telescopes and microscopes, although powerful in their magnification, actually limit one's perspective of an object. Optical microscopes give only one perspective. For example, they enable the observer to view the top of a bug at a higher power but not the bottom.

Now more than ever, it is critical that students understand the importance of perspective in science, as we begin to explore the extreme scales. In this activity students gain an awareness of differing perspectives and how scientists must work together to infer what is not completely known or understood.

145

Materials

Each group will need:
- Optical illusion example from the internet (see examples under "Engage," below)
- Graph paper or unlined paper
- Colored pencils
- Ruler
- Perspective Viewing Box (one per group of four students)
- Legos or some similar building manipulative (200 + various building pieces per group)
- Internet access (Google Earth)

FIGURE 1.

Note: The Perspective Viewing boxes should be made ahead of time. Once they are constructed, you can use them multiple times. For best results, have a box at least the size of a shoe box. Tape the sides and edges to prolong the life of the boxes. Cut an opening in each side about same distance from the top of the box (see Figure 1).

Have enough building blocks for each group to create a structure composed of 75–100 pieces, as well as enough additional pieces to reconstruct that structure. Groups may share extra pieces during the building process.

You can construct a model for each group ahead of time, or have each group make one and exchange with other groups. Just make sure that the students do not have an opportunity to study the models thoroughly beforehand because that would influence their *perspective* of the model.

Engage

Show the students an optical illusion that can be interpreted several different ways. An example is the vase/face illusion in which the figure is interpreted by some as two faces and by others as a vase. Various hidden figure illusions can be found at *http://en.wikipedia.org/wiki/Optical_illusion* or *www.eyetricks.com/illusions.htm*

Ask the students to discuss what they see and why they see different things. Ultimately, it comes down to a person's perspective. Viewing a 3-D object from different angles may produce drastically different conclusions as well.

This next portion of the activity can be completed either in the classroom or outside. Give each student drawing paper, colored pencils, and rulers, and ask them to pick an object such as a desk, hallway, tree, or water fountain and draw it from an unusual perspective. For example, a student could make a detailed sketch of an oak tree from the perspective of an ant at the base of the tree. What would it look like? Would the angles be different? Why is it different from this perspective than what one would normally see if one were standing in front of the tree? Share the drawings with the class.

Explore

In this investigation students look at a structure made of Lego blocks from different perspectives and attempt to reconstruct the shape. See Figure 2 for an example of a Lego structure. Divide the class into groups of four. Each group represents a team of scientists who will work together to gather information about a newly discovered object. Each scientist (student) has a different perspective and must work with the other scientists to determine the structure of the newly discovered object. Eventually they will make a 3-D model representing their findings.

FIGURE 2.

Each group of four students should obtain a Perspective Viewing Box. Ask the students to study the box and to notice that all four sides have an opening and a letter: A, B, C, or D. Assign each student in the group to one of the letters: Side A, Side B, Side C, or Side D. Explain that you will place a Lego model (representing the newly discovered object) in the box and that they should not open the box at any time or move the model around. They may only view the model through their assigned opening. (Taping the model to the bottom of the box may help the model keep its position.)

The students' task is to work together as a group to decide on the model's structure based solely on the **four different perspectives** in the group. Each student in turn must study the model from the perspective of his or her assigned opening (see Figure 3 on p. 148). Students may take notes and make sketches in color separately from other group members. After the students feel confident about their perspectives of the model, they should discuss with the rest of the group and try to decide what the unknown model looks like. Then, using the extra pieces, they should try to build the model. **At no time should any student look into other students' assigned openings.**

FIGURE 3.

After all the groups have finished their proposed model based on their discussion of the four perspectives, have each group individually present their newly constructed model, and then reveal the original model from the box. How do they compare? Were they correct? What was different? Were there times when the group members disagreed? How did you negotiate the model during those disagreements? What caused the four different perspectives? How does this compare to what scientists might do when making a new observation or discovery?

Explain

Perspective can have many meanings in various contexts, but it deals primarily with how the eye views an object or situation. Depending on prior knowledge and experiences, people may perceive the same thing in drastically different ways. Spatial ability is important in many everyday applications and occupations. Thus the answers to these questions may have important implications for teaching and learning, especially in science. For example, mechanical reasoning and success in scientific domains may be related to facility with spatial tasks, particularly mental rotation (Brownlow, McPheron, and Acks 2003). Visual-spatial thinking includes (a) vision—the process of using the eyes to identify, locate, and think about objects and orient ourselves in the world, and (b) imagery—the formation, inspection, transformation, and maintenance of images in the "mind's eye" in the absence of a visual stimulus (Mathewson 1999). Teachers can also explore with their students the differences among types of symmetry, visual rotation, and visual-spatial skills, all of which are important when taking perspectives into account.

For more information about perspective, particularly in drawing:
- *www.artic.edu/aic/education/sciarttech/2d1.html*
- *www.npg.org.uk/live/perspectivedef.asp*
- *http://en.wikipedia.org/wiki/Perspective_(graphical)*

Extend

Have students experience various perspectives of places around the world using the free download at *http://earth.google.com.* To get a more complete perspective, make sure to check the availability to view 3-D buildings and structures.

148

Ask:

- What shape does the Washington Monument have when as you are directly overhead? What about from the side?

- How does the north rim of the Grand Canyon compare with the south rim?

- How does Mount St. Helens volcano compare in size and shape with Mount Mazama?

- How does the Tower Bridge in London compare with the Brooklyn Bridge in New York?

- How does the Statue of Liberty compare in size with the Leaning Tower of Pisa?

- How does the width of the Mississippi River change as it flows from the northern to the southern United States?

Invite students to make up comparisons of various perspectives on their own to share with the rest of the class.

Evaluate

Check for student understanding:

1. What is perspective?
2. When people view an object, what causes different perspectives?
3. Draw a sketch of two perspectives of a table.
4. Are perspectives always symmetrical? Explain your answer.
5. Even when collaborating with classmates to determine the details of the Lego model, did you always know what the bottom and inside of the model looked like? Why or why not?
6. How does perspective play a role in how scientists view objects through a microscope or telescope?
7. Research the evolution of atomic models based on changes in theoretical perspective.
8. How have science and technology enabled construction of models of various objects such as DNA, cells, and the solar system?
9. How can perspective influence science?
10. Imagine that you are a scientist trying to develop a new kind of microscope. Make an argument about how new technologies developed in your lab could benefit society.

149

References

Brownlow, S., T. McPheron, and C. Acks. 2003. Science background and spatial abilities in men and women. *Journal of Science Education and Technology* 12(4): 371–380.

Merriam-Webster's Dictionary. 2008. Perspective. *www.merriam-webster.com/dictionary*

150

Chapter 12
Eye in the Sky:
An Introduction to GIS & Scale

Overview

New computer technologies allow us to examine scientific data at a variety of different scales from global to local. In this investigation students use Geographic Information Systems (GIS) as a tool to investigate different questions related to the environment. Questions on subjects ranging from changes in tree canopy to Africanized bee habitats or climate changes can be investigated with GIS.

Objectives

- To develop skills in observation.
- To develop a sense of scale.
- To develop skills in using technology in inquiry.

Process Skills

- Observing
- Predicting
- Comparing and contrasting
- Collecting data
- Analyzing data

Activity Duration

30 minutes

Background

Maps come in all shapes and sizes. You may have folded paper road maps in the car or printed maps from online sources. You may have seen the electronic maps produced for cars or cell phones. Some of these maps use Geographic Information Systems or GIS. GIS is a computer system that stores data digitally and allows information retrieval at the user's request. The user can select one or many layers of information that are overlaid on the map. If you are planning a road trip, you may want to know where gas stations and restaurants are located but have no interest in parks or libraries. You may also want to know how much rain an area gets or the average temperature range. With GIS you can select exactly the information you need and see it mapped to a location on the Earth's surface. A gas station or restaurant has a position on the Earth at a certain latitude and longitude. GIS allows you to layer the information you want to make informed decisions.

GIS information can come from measurements taken on the ground, such as rainfall data, or from pictures taken by planes or satellites. Information obtained from satellites and planes is often referred to as *digital aerial imagery* because it comes from digital pictures that cover large areas of the Earth's surface. Aerial data are referred to as *large-scale data* because the altitude of a plane or satellite allows a large portion of the Earth to be photographed at once. The scale of the data can be represented with a scale bar, scale graphic, or scale ratio. The scale bar will have a distance printed next to it indicating the distance it represents in the real world. A scale graphic looks like a bar graph with the tallest bars first. The bars represent the amount of surface covered on the ground. The tallest bar covers the most surface and is the smallest scale.

151

The best way to understand the concept is to look at the scale ratio. A scale ratio shows the scale written as a ratio of numbers, usually 1: some number. The larger the second number in the ratio, the smaller the scale of the map. For example, a scale ratio of 1:10 means a map feature is 1/10 or 0.1 of its actual size. A scale ratio of 1:100 means a map feature is 1/100 or 0.01 of its actual size. A ratio of 1:10 is the larger scale map and shows greater detail because 0.1 is greater than 0.01. The *resolution* of the image tells us how far we can zoom in on it before we see just blocks of color or pixels. A picture with 1-meter resolution shows little detail for anything smaller than 1 m. An image with 1-centimeter resolution will lose details when an object is smaller than 1 cm. Scale and resolution give us important information about aerial imagery maps.

Materials

Each group will need:
- Internet access
- Printed maps generated in the exercise
- Student copy of the background information

Engage

Ask the students to draw a map of the room ceiling by only looking up and not turning around. Discuss what the students are seeing and drawing. How could you get a better map of the ceiling? What if all the drawings were put together?

Repeat the exercise, but this time have students lie on the floor and look up. How does this change the map? How does this relate to the way satellites image the Earth?

Explore

Download and print a variety of digital aerial images with different resolutions. Each group of two students should have two images with different resolutions. Ask them to compare and contrast the two images for detail and clarity. Give each student a magnifying glass or hand lens. Ask them to identify and trace one of the individual dots or squares of which their picture is made. The square is the pixel size. The smaller the pixel size, the finer the resolution of the image.

Nightlights—Eye in the Sky

Essential Questions: What is a GIS? How can GIS and satellite imagery be used to investigate problems? How does the scale of satellite imagery affect the questions that researchers can ask and answer?

Steps

A. Discuss how GIS works and is used to investigate problems (see the introduction on pp. 151–152 for background information). Provide students with copies of the Student Data Sheet.

B. Show students how to the navigate using the National Map Viewer that can be found at *http://nmviewogc.cr.usgs.gov/viewer.htm*. Allow them to explore the map using their Student Data Sheet as a guide.

After the students have completed the investigation explore the discussion questions.

Discussion Questions

1. If you wanted to open a new business someplace in the United States, where would you locate it? Why?

2. If you wanted to locate a new observatory some place in the United States, where would you locate it? Why?

3. List three questions you could investigate if you only had the Nightlights map at the largest scale.

4. List three questions you could investigate if you only had the Nightlights map at a small scale.

5. What role does scale play in the types of questions that can be investigated and answered?

153

For more examples of satellite images:

- TerraServer-USA, *http://terraserver-usa.com*
- National Hurricane Center, *http://www.nhc.noaa.gov/satellite.shtml*
- GLobeXplorer-ImageAtlas, *www.globexplorer.com/ImageAtlas/view.do?group =ImageAtlas&lat=39.5276&lon=-97.142&zoom_level=1*
- Your local city and county government planning offices or GIS office.

Explain

GIS stands for Geographic Information System's and is a computer technology (software and hardware) that maps a variety of different data sets onto geographical maps. Almost any data that are tied to a location can be explored with GIS. GIS technologies are used for resource management as well as land use and development planning. The beauty of GIS is that it allows the user to examine relationships and trends, as well as create charts and maps of an array of data. The visual output that results from GIS can provide insight into large-scale phenomena.

A number of different types of databases can be used with GIS technology, including geographic features (river systems, mountains, or cities), satellite and aerial images, survey measurements, and other statistical data. One of the valuable aspects of GIS is the capability to combine different types of information and view them simultaneously to study spatial relationships. For example, you can look at rainfall in relation to human population spread out over a country. In this example, the data include rainfall, population densities, topographical map information, and other information such as elevation. By combining different sources of data we can make better-informed predictions and develop plans for using resources. In scientific research, GIS can be used to combine different types of data to understand a particular phenomenon or environment. For example, in marine biology, GIS may combine color images of the ocean surface taken with satellites, ocean current movement data, ocean depth data, fish or algae movement data, and ocean floor data to create a single visual model of the ocean system. The data could be used to predict changes in fish populations, to examine the movement of pollution, or to study the migrations of marine mammals.

Many of the topics in the National Science Education Standards (NRC 1996) can be examined with GIS, including populations, resources, environments, human activities and resource acquisition, weather, geology, and marine science.

154

Extend

Students can use various other exercises to explore GIS. Use the National Map Viewer to ask other questions such as:

- How does the tree canopy differ for three locations from 1992 to 2001?
- Where are the Superfund sites for the United States?
- What is the range of the Africanized honeybee?

Evaluate

Check for student understanding:

1. How does detail change as you zoom in or out on a location?
2. What are the limitations of looking at a large-scale model of GIS data?
3. What is GIS?
4. Why has GIS only become available in the last 30 years?

References

ESRI. 2008. What is GIS? *http://www.gis.com/whatisgis/index.html*

National Research Council (NRC). 1996. National Science Education Standards. Washington, DC: National Academy Press.

United States Geological Survey. 2008a. Geographic information systems. *http://erg.usgs.gov/isb/pubs/gis_poster*

United States Geological Survey. 2008b. National Map Viewer. *http://nmviewogc.cr.usgs.gov/viewer.htm*

155

Name _____

Essential Questions: What is GIS? How can GIS and satellite imagery be used to investigate problems? How does the scale of satellite imagery affect the questions researchers can ask and answer?

Steps

1. Navigate to the National Map Viewer—*http://nmviewogc.cr.usgs.gov/viewer.htm*

156

2. Notice the scale graphic in the upper right corner. What bar on the scale graphic is highlighted? _____

3. This means that the map is displayed in the largest scale possible. In the lower left corner of the map, there is a scale bar. On this view, the bar is equal to how many miles? _____

4. Notice the list of tools going down the left side of the map. We will use the second tool, Zoom In, which will change the scale of the map. Select the Zoom In tool by clicking on it once. Place the arrow in the middle of the map and click once. What happens? _____

_____

5. Which bar in the scale graphic is highlighted now? _____

6. What is the scale bar equal to? _____

7. Notice that on the right-hand side of the page there is a frame titled Layers. Scroll down and find the layer named Imagery. Click on the arrow to the left of Imagery to see the list of images available. Place a check in the Satellite box and the Nighttime Lights box. Click the Refresh Required button at the bottom of the Layers column. What does the map show?_____

8. What bar is highlighted in the scale graphic? _____

9. What is the value of the bottom scale bar?_____

10. Click on the second bar in the scale graphic. What happens? What is the value of the bottom scale bar? _____
_____

11. Scroll down the Layers column and click on Transportation. Uncheck the Roads layer. Click the Refresh Required button. Click the tallest, far left bar on the scale graphic. The entire United States should be visible. Now select the Zoom In tool. Put the pointer over a spot on the map that appears white. Click the spot once. What happens? What bar is highlighted on the scale graphic? What is the value of the scale bar?
_____

12. Continue to click the Zoom In tool on the same white area until you get squares of white, pink, red, and burgundy. Record the number of times you had to zoom in, the bar in the graphic that is highlighted, and the scale value. What do you think the different colors indicate?
_____

Discussion Questions

1. If you wanted to open a new business someplace in the United States, where would you locate it? Why?

2. If you wanted to locate a new observatory someplace in the United States, where would you locate it? Why?

3. If you only had the Nightlights map at the largest scale, list three questions you could investigate.

4. List three questions you could investigate if you only had the Nightlights map at a small scale.

5. What role does scale play in the types of questions that can be investigated and answered?

157

Chapter 13
Drops to the Ocean: A GIS Study of River Basins

Overview

Water is a critical element of life. It plays a crucial role at many scales from single cells to huge river systems. In this investigation students explore local, regional, and global river basins using GIS as a tool. The study begins with an examination of river basins on paper maps, followed by observations at different levels of detail revealed with interactive GIS maps. These exercises allow students to explore water systems across a range of scales.

Objectives

- To develop skills in observation.
- To predict drainage patterns for water across several model terrains.
- To use software to determine which scale is appropriate for local watershed and river basin identification and measurements.

Process Skills

- Observing
- Predicting
- Hypothesizing
- Comparing and contrasting
- Collecting data
- Analyzing data

Activity Duration

90 minutes

Background

Although we often don't think about where water goes or where it comes from, it is a resource that is critical to life on Earth. In this investigation students explore drainage basins. They follow the water from the point where it falls to Earth (or melts), through channels, watersheds, river basins, and finally to drainage basins.

Encourage the students to ponder the following question: *Where does the water go after it falls on your yard or street?* The creeks, streams, gullies, and drainage ditches in your neighborhood are part of the local *watershed*. Watersheds are small-scale, local drainage areas. Creeks and streams are fed by *precipitation* in the form of rain or snow, snowmelt, or storm water runoff. Precipitation that does not soak into the ground runs downhill until it reaches a creek, stream, gully, or drainage ditch. Those channels conduct the collected water and continue to move it downhill. Eventually several streams, creeks, or ditches meet and form a small river that becomes the watershed. Figure 1 shows a map of the paths of water in a typical watershed.

FIGURE 1.
Watershed.

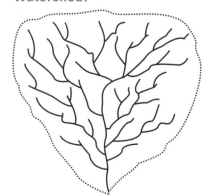

159

Just as small creeks and streams join to form a small river, small rivers join to make a larger river. This regional, larger-scale drainage area is a river basin. Often a large river basin is broken down into subbasins so that individual rivers and streams can be more easily identified. Figure 2 shows a map of several river basins that form a river shed.

The boundaries separating river basins are usually along land ridges of high elevation. The water falling on the boundary region will flow into one basin or another depending on the side of the boundary it falls on. The river draining the basin is in the region of lowest elevation.

FIGURE 2.
Mississippi River basin (in red).

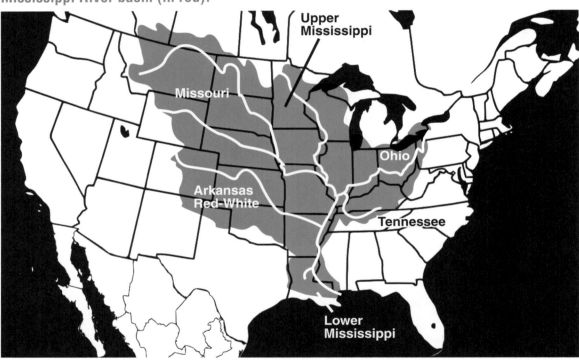

On a nationwide scale, we can trace the route that water takes by looking at drainage basins. Drainage basins combine the smaller river basins and link individual rivers into river systems. For example, the Red, Arkansas, Missouri, Illinois, Wabash, Ohio, and Tennessee rivers all join the Mississippi River to form the Mississippi Drainage Basin, which drains the majority of the central United States.

On a global scale, we can map drainage basins worldwide. The United Nations collects data on the amount of water available in each drainage basin. That information is used to map global river basins that drain into oceans and seas. The United Nations Environment Programme (UNEP) Major River Basins of the World map is found at *http://maps.grida.no/go/graphic/major_river_basins_of_the_world*.

Students can trace a water drop through watersheds, river basins, and drainage basins to the ocean, using different map scales. The investigations that follow explore the pathways of water using physical models, maps, and computer-based interactive maps.

Part A. Drainage Patterns and Terrain Inquiry

Materials Part A

- Aluminum foil (12 × 12 in. piece per student)
- Colored water
- Dropping pipettes
- Small plastic cup or can
- Internet access or copies of paper maps
- The National Map Viewer—*http://nmviewogc.cr.usgs.gov/viewer.htm*—is a source for downloading and printing state and regional maps that display major rivers. In addition, most states have river basin maps that can be found online. Conduct a web search on your state: "_____ river basin maps."

Engage

Ask students to draw a picture of the branching structure of a deciduous tree. Have them show their drawings and describe the similarities. Then ask the students to hypothesize how drainage basins or river systems are like the branching structures of trees. Brainstorm with the class as students locate and name examples of rivers on classroom maps (if available).

Explore

Part A. Modeling Drainage Basins: Scale, Watersheds, and River Basins

Give each student a 12 × 12 in. piece of aluminum foil, a beaker of colored water, a small plastic cup, and a dropping pipette.

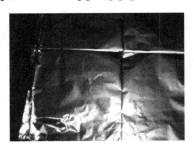

161

Instruct the students to fold the foil in half each way and then unfold it. Fold up the edges of the foil to form a tray. Ask the students to place three to four drops of colored water in the center of the tray, as well as in each of the four corners of the foil. Sketch the path the water takes.

Then ask the students to shape the foil into a single "hill" by placing a cup under the foil (see photo below). **Do not** flatten out the folds. Repeat the process of dropping the water on the foil and sketching the path.

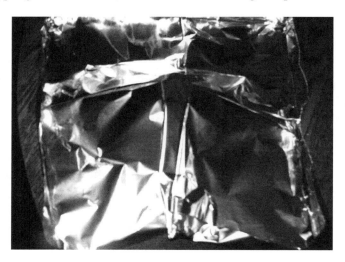

Next ask the students to gently ball up the foil. Direct them to unfold their aluminum foil but not to flatten it out. The foil should look like a mini mountain range, as in the photo below. Place one edge of the foil on a book, so that it is sitting at an angle. Fold up the edges of the foil to form a tray.

Using a disposable pipette, drop colored water at each corner and in the center of the foil. Sketch the path the water takes and discuss the similarities of the drainage patterns to the branching patterns of trees (Student Data Sheet 1).

Student observations may vary. The water will always run "downhill." The more rugged the terrain, the more of a branching pattern the water will take. The water will settle at the lowest point.

Part B. Worldwide Drainage Basins

Materials Part B

For each pair of students print the UNEP Major River Basins of the World Map located at *http://maps.grida.no/go/graphic/major_river_basins_of_the_world*, and the Physical Map of the World found at *www.lib.utexas.edu/maps/world_maps/world_physical_2007.pdf*.

- Give each pair of students a copy of the Physical Map of the World. Size the map to cover a legal-size piece of paper.
- Discuss with students where mountain ranges are found worldwide.
- Directly on the map, have the students sketch the path that water will take when it hits the surface. Remind them to ignore country borders.
- Now have the students compare their sketch to the UNEP Major River Basins of the World map. Their sketches should approximate the large global basins found on the UN basin map.
- Discuss with students what they notice about the relationship between mountain ranges and river basins. How does this relationship affect the overall size of a river basin?

163

Part C. Mississippi Drainage Basin
Materials Part C

The National Map Viewer, found at *http://nmviewogc.cr.usgs.gov/viewer.htm* is an example of a GIS mapping tool. On the left side of the map is a set of tools that allow the user to manipulate the map by zooming in and out, identifying, getting elevation, and measuring. On the right side of the map are the scale graphic, layers, and legend. The scale graphic is interactive; selecting a bar changes the scale of the map. A layer is a set of similar data that can be displayed on the map. The legend explains the color coding on the map and may be turned off or on.

Complete the following steps to examine the Mississippi River Basin:

- Launch the National Map Viewer: *http://nmviewogc.cr.usgs.gov/viewer.htm*
- On the Layer bar, scroll until you find the Hydrography Layer. Click on the arrow and check Streams and National Atlas Streams 7.5 m and Waterbodies and National Atlas Waterbodies 7.5 m.
- Click the Refresh Map button at the bottom of the Layer bar. Wait for the map to redraw.
- On the right side of the map, scroll down the Layer bar until you come to the Transportation Layer. Click on the arrow. Uncheck the Roads Layer.
- Look at the scale graphic. Which scale bar is highlighted in the upper-right corner? What is the scale ratio in the lower left corner?
- Use the Zoom In tool on the left side of the map to change the scale of the map. Get the tool and click once in the middle of the map. What is the new scale on the scale graphic and ratio? Click again and record both scales.
- Print the map showing the Mississippi River Valley rivers and water bodies. As before, sketch the direction you think water will flow in this region.
- Compare your sketch to the map of the Mississippi River Basin in the lesson. How are they similar? How are they different? What could cause discrepancies?
- Look carefully at the map. What do you notice about the area immediately to the west of the Mississippi River? What possible explanations are there for this landmass?
- If you are zoomed out completely, how many rivers appear to make up the Mississippi River Basin? If you zoom in three clicks, how many rivers are there? At what point do small creeks appear?
- What general statement can be made about the relationship between scale and accuracy?

Part D. Your State and Local Drainage Basin

Many states have river basin maps and management plans available through the internet. Have students complete a web search for their state and surrounding states. If interactive maps are available, they can complete the same mapping activities. Local GIS offices or city planning offices will also have data layers that include subbasins and local watersheds. Students can investigate the watershed in which they live or where the school is located. An example lesson from the North Carolina OneMap is included on page 171 as a sample.

Explain

Geographic Information Systems (GIS) provide ways to manage and use spatial data. Spatial data are data that are linked to a geographic location. The location may be on land, in the oceans, on the Moon, or even Mars. A powerful advantage of using GIS as a mapping tool is that GIS is interactive. The user can bring in the data she wants, color code it, and scale it so that it communicates most effectively. There are many sources for GIS data layers. These exercises made use of data from the United Nations, U.S. Geological Survey, and the Center for Geographic Information and Analysis. The lessons also made use of the ability of GIS to change scale. As you zoom in and out, the scale changes. When you are acting as a map creator and user, it is important to select an appropriate scale for the information you wish to communicate. Large-scale maps show great detail over a small area. Small-scale maps show little detail but cover a large area. Questions to ask yourself as you investigate a problem include these: *As the scale of the map changes, what features are lost and gained? What scale is appropriate for local watershed and river basin identification and measurements? How much information do I need displayed?* Unlike paper maps, GIS allows you to change scale quickly and effortlessly, add and delete data layers, and color code data so that it is easily understood. For these reasons GIS is one of the most important tools used in the study of hydrography.

Extend

- Have students obtain GPS data on positions of local streams and then locate them on a map. Determine the local watershed, river basin, and drainage basin in which the stream is located.
- For a more detailed basin map, have students complete a drainage basin map for the Mississippi River Basin by assigning groups the local river basins that make up the Mississippi River Basin. Draw each local basin to a set scale, and then put them all together.
- Research the river basins of neighboring states and countries.
- Research the water wars in the western United States and water rights legislation. Could those types of "wars" happen today? On a local scale,

what information would be needed to make wise decisions about water allotment? What is needed on a national or global scale to make decisions about water allotment?

- Have a debate or mock trial on a water allotment or use issue.

Evaluate

Check for student understanding:

1. How does terrain affect the flow of water? What happens to water flow as slope increases? What happens to water flow if there are no channels for the water to follow?
2. How does question 1 relate to erosion? How does it relate to the formation of the Grand Canyon?
3. Why is scale an important map attribute when one is addressing hydrography questions? What types of questions could be addressed using large-scale maps? What type could be addressed using small-scale maps?

166

Student Data Sheet 1
Modeling Drainage Basins:
Scale, Watersheds, and River Basins

Name _____

Objective
You will explore drainage patterns for water across several model terrains.

Materials
Aluminum foil, colored water, dropping pipette, small plastic cup or can.

Procedures
1. Get a 12 × 12 in. piece of aluminum foil, a beaker of colored water, a small plastic cup, and a dropping pipette.
2. Fold the foil in half each way and then unfold it. Fold up the edges of the foil to form a tray.
3. Place three to four drops of colored water in the center and at each of the four corners of the foil. Sketch the path the water takes.
4. Dump out the water remaining in the foil.
5. Shape the foil into a single "hill" by placing a cup under the foil. *Do not* flatten out the folds. Repeat the process of dropping the water on the foil and sketching the path.
6. Dump out the water remaining in the foil.
7. Gently ball up the foil.
8. Unfold the aluminum foil, but *do not* flatten it out. The foil should look like a mini mountain range. Place one edge of the foil on a book, so that it is sitting on an angle. Fold up the edges of the foil to form a tray.
9. Using a disposable pipette, drop colored water at each corner and in the center of the foil.
10. Sketch the path the water takes.

Sketch 1	Sketch 2	Sketch 3

Discussion
What are the similarities of the drainage patterns to the branching patterns of trees?

Name _____

Objective
You will explore global drainage basins and their relationships to terrain.

Materials
You will need the United Nations Environment Programme Major River Basins of the World Map located at *http://maps.grida.no/go/graphic/major_river_basins_of_the_world* and the Physical Map of the World found at *www.lib.utexas.edu/maps/world_maps/world_physical_2007.pdf*.

- Get a student copy of the Physical Map of the World.
- Where are mountain ranges found worldwide? Highlight the mountainous regions.
- Directly on the map, sketch the path that water will take when it hits the surface. Remember to ignore country borders. A border does not stop flowing water.
- Compare your sketch to the United Nations Environment Programme Major River Basins of the World map. How are they alike? How are they different?
- What do you notice about the relationship between mountain ranges and river basins? How does this relationship affect the overall size of a river basin?
- Are these two maps large scale or small scale? Under what conditions would you need to use a small-scale map for water basin studies? Under what conditions would you need a large-scale map?

168

Name _____

Objective
You will explore the rivers that make up the Mississippi River Drainage Basin using an interactive GIS map.

Materials
Internet access or copies of paper maps.

Background
The National Map Viewer, found at *http://nmviewogc.cr.usgs.gov/viewer.htm*, is an example of a GIS mapping tool. On the left side of the map is a set of tools that allow the user to manipulate the map by zooming in and out, identifying, getting elevation, and measuring. On the right side of the map are the scale graphic, layers, and legend. The scale graphic is interactive; selecting a bar changes the scale of the map. A layer is a set of similar data that can be displayed on the map. The legend explains the color coding on the map and may be turned off or on. To examine the Mississippi River Basin, complete the following steps:

Steps
1. Launch the National Map Viewer—*http://nmviewogc.cr.usgs.gov/viewer.htm*
2. On the Layer bar, scroll until you find the Hydrography Layer. Click on the arrow and check Streams and National Atlas Streams 7.5 m and Waterbodies and National Atlas Waterbodies 7.5 m.
3. Click the Refresh Map button at the bottom of the Layer bar. Wait for the map to redraw.
4. On the right side of the map, scroll down the Layer bar until you come to the Transportation Layer. Click on the arrow. Uncheck the Roads Layer.
5. Look at the scale graphic. Which scale bar is highlighted in the upper-right corner? What is the scale ratio in the lower left corner?
6. Use the Zoom In tool on the left side of the map to change the scale of the map. Get the tool and click once in the middle of the map. What is the new scale on the scale graphic and ratio? Click again and record both scales.
7. Print the map showing the Mississippi River Valley, the rivers and water bodies. As before, sketch the direction you think water will flow in this region.
8. Compare your sketch to the map of the Mississippi River Basin in the lesson. How are they similar? How are they different? What could cause discrepancies?

169

9. Look carefully at the map. What do you notice about the area immediately to the west of the Mississippi River? What possible explanations are there for this landmass?

10. If you are zoomed out completely, how many rivers appear to make up the Mississippi River Basin? If you zoom in three clicks, how many rivers are there? At what point do small creeks appear?

11. What general statement can be made about the relationship between scale and accuracy?

170

Name _____

Objective
You will explore the concept of scale using North Carolina river basins.

Materials
Internet access or copies of paper maps.
North Carolina OneMap—*www.nconemap.com*

Essential Questions
As the scale of the map changes, what features are lost and gained? What scale is appropriate for local watershed and river basin identification and measurements?

1. Begin with the NC OneMap viewer *www.nconemap.com*. Now click on the NC OneMap viewer under "Get Data." Notice that there is a group of tools on the left side of the page. Put your mouse over each tool and record what each tool is.

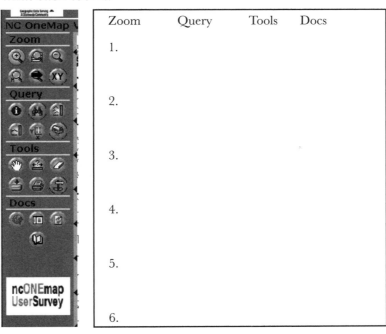

Zoom	Query	Tools	Docs
1.			
2.			
3.			
4.			
5.			
6.			

2. Notice that on the left side of the page there is a list headed "Layers." Layers are groups of related information that can be added to the map. Click on any of the pointers to the left of the layer. A drop-down menu appears with the specific information included in the layer. For a layer to appear on the map it must be checked.

3. Right above the layers list is the scale bar. Scale is given in a graphic representation and a scale ratio. You can click on a scale bar in the graphic to change the scale or zoom in and out. What is the initial scale ratio for the map?

    _____

4. Click on the "Boundaries" layer and uncheck the "NC OneMap Participants" layer. What happens?

    _____

5. Click on "Hydrography," and check "National Atlas Streams, National Atlas Water Bodies," and "NC OneMap-River Basins." Let the map refresh. What features are visible?

    _____

    What is the scale ratio? _____

6. Get the "Zoom In" tool (+). Click twice in the middle of North Carolina on the map. What features are visible now?

    _____

    What is the scale ratio?

    _____

Scale Information

Out   Scale ~ 1:7,020,504   In

Layers

- Location-Geodetic
- Structures
- Transportation
- Cadastral
- Boundaries
- Hydrography
- Utility-Telecom
- Economy
- Health
- Environment
- Socio-Demographic
- Bio-Habitat
- Geophysical
- Weather
- Land Cover
- Imagery-Basemap
- Elevation

7. Under "Tools" on the left column, click on the "Measure" tool (ruler). Measure the length of the two streams in southeast Guilford County that flow into Alamance County by clicking on the beginning of the stream and tracing its course. Each time you change direction, click. Read the total distance in the box at the top left on the map. Use "Clear Measure Tool" (eraser) to clear the measurement before you measure the second stream.

    Stream 1:_____
    Stream 2:_____

8. Zoom in one more time and repeat the same measurements. What is the new scale?

    Stream 1:_____

    Stream 2:_____

    Scale _____

172

How did your measurements change?_____

At which scale do you think your measurements are more accurate and why?
_____

9. Zoom in one more time. Be sure to place the Zoom In tool in the middle of Guilford County. What is the new scale?
_____

How did the appearance of the map change? _____

10. Under "Boundaries" turn off the "NC OneMap Municipality Names" layer and the "NC OneMap–Incorporated Municipalities" layer. Under "Hydrography" turn on "USGS RAD Streams." How has the map changed?
_____

If you had to make a decision about a local water issue, what scale and layers would you choose and why? If you had to make a decision about a statewide water issue, what scale and layers would you choose and why?
_____

11. Under "Layers," scroll to "Elevation" and turn on the "NOSA Shaded Relief" layer. Propose an explanation as to why there are more and smaller river basins in the western part of the state.

12. Examine the other layers included in NC OneMap. On your own, using the layers and tools of your choosing, investigate the following questions:
    a. How many river basins are in North Carolina?
    b. Where are the largest basins?
    c. What are the perimeters of the four largest river basins?
    d. Why do you think the river basin size differs from west to east?

13. What layers and tools did you use to investigate each question? What scale was appropriate to use to investigate each question and why? Keep track of the actual steps you used to investigate each question above and create a procedure log.

173

References

National Research Council (NRC). 1996. *National science education standards.* Washington, DC: National Academy Press.

North Carolina Department of Environment and Natural Resources. 2008. *River basins. www.ee.enr.state.nc.us/public/ecoaddress/riverbasinsmain.htm*

North Carolina Geographic Information Coordinating Council. 2008. *NC OneMap Viewer. www.nconemap.com*

United States Geological Survey. 2008a. *National Map Viewer. http://nmviewogc. cr.usgs.gov/viewer.htm*

United States Geological Survey. 2008b. *Hydrologic Unit Map. http://water.usgs. gov/GIS/regions.html*

Wikipedia. 2008. *Drainage basin. http://en.wikipedia.org/wiki/Drainage_basin*

Chapter 14
Zoom Zoom: Magnification

Overview

As science extends into the very large and the very small ends of the scale, the images of objects and materials lose recognizable contexts and can be very complex. New advances in microscopes and telescopes allow us to zoom in on very tiny and very distant objects and see amazing new worlds. This investigation involves students in thinking about the changes in scale that take place as we zoom in on very small and very large objects.

Objectives

- To develop skills in observing.
- To develop skills in applying proportional reasoning to the interpretation of magnified images.
- To become familiar with different levels of magnification.
- To develop an understanding of the relationship between level of detail and degree of magnification.

Process Skills

- Observing
- Measuring
- Communicating

Activity Duration

60 minutes

Background

When you see an image in the media of a virus or bacterium, it appears to be very large. Just how small, however, is a bacterium? What clues do the images give you to help you understand the size? Magnification opens an amazingly beautiful and complex world of the very large and the very small that we cannot see without binoculars, microscopes, and other tools.

In this investigation students are encouraged to think about the scale of the viewed object and how magnification changes their perspective. How do different degrees of magnification influence the amount of detail that we can see? What information do we lose when we zoom far into an object or organism? These are the questions that are explored in this lesson on magnification and scale.

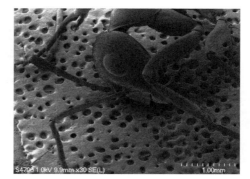

S4700 1.0kV 9.9mm x30 SE(L)   1.00mm

Materials

Each group will need:

- Hand lens
- Pocket microscope
- Digital handheld microscope
- Digital microscope
- Digital movie camera
- Feather, carpet fibers, leaf, and hair

Note: Different components of the investigation can be completed if some materials are not available.

Class materials needed:

- A set of electron micrograph images of unusual objects, such as insects, at different magnifications
- Computers and internet access for the extended investigations

Engage

Observing is one of the critical science process skills. Scientists make observations with their eyes, as well as with a variety of tools such as optical microscopes, scanning and transmission electron microscopes, and the new forms of probing microscopes (scanning tunneling microscopes and atomic force microscopes) that allow them to look at very small things. Other tools, such as telescopes (optical and radio), are used to look out at great distances to "see" stars and other objects in space. The development of increasingly sophisticated tools has opened new worlds for exploration.

Part 1. Zooming in on Lincoln

First show students this image from a Lincoln penny and ask them to identify the image. The students may suggest that it is a ghost, a painting, or a shadow. Tell them it is something that they have seen many times, though they may not have noticed the detail.

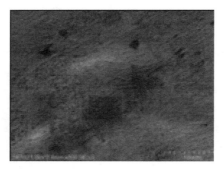

Show the next series of images, giving more hints until the students can identify that the image is that of President Lincoln in the Lincoln Memorial, found on the penny. This image of the penny is magnified 300 times with a scanning electron microscope.

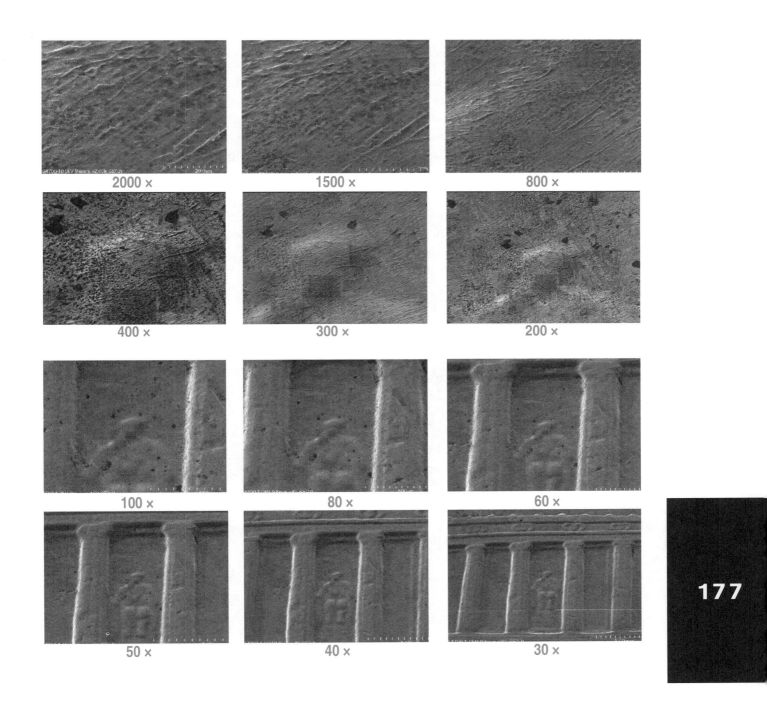

2000 × 1500 × 800 ×

400 × 300 × 200 ×

100 × 80 × 60 ×

50 × 40 × 30 ×

177

Explain that they will have the opportunity to look closely at different objects, such as the penny, to observe the details close-up.

Part 2. Insects Close-Up

Engage students by asking them to identify a set of electron micrograph images that depict beautiful and odd-looking materials. For example, show an image of a bee, mite, or beetle. Help the students locate clues in the image that they can use to identify the object. (Examples of close-up photos of insect faces in color can be found at *www5.pbrc.hawaii.edu/microangela*.) Many of the micrograph images available on the internet are very beautiful and engaging to students.

Explore

If possible have your students explore magnification beginning with low technology and moving through increasingly sophisticated technologies to end with computer imagery. If materials are limited, the series of investigations can be set up as laboratory stations and students can rotate from one station to the next.

Station A. Magnification and Zoom

Part 1. *Hand Lens*

To set the context for the use of increasingly complex magnification, pass out simple hand lenses (10× magnification; see Figure 1) to students and encourage them to look at newsprint, fabric, and their skin and fingernails. Students should make detailed drawings of a section of a feather, a carpet sample, a leaf, and a hair. After they have had a chance to use the lens to look at objects, briefly review how a convex lens works to magnify an image (see Figure 2).

FIGURE 1.
Hand lens.

FIGURE 2.
Convex lens magnification.

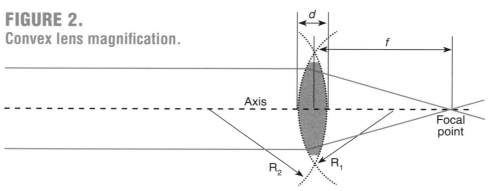

Positive (converging) lens

Part 2. *Lighted Pocket Microscope*

Add increased levels of magnification by exploring materials such as color newsprint photographs, bits of fabric, or different sand samples using a pocket microscope. Students are amazed to see the detail that emerges with simple 30× to 100× magnification. Allow the students to look at materials of their choosing before assigning them to view a set of common objects including a feather, carpet, leaf, and hair.

Part 3. *Digital Handheld Microscopes*

The new digital handheld microscopes (sold under different names, such as Scope on a Rope) are great tools for exploring everyday materials magnified at various levels. These microscopes are relatively inexpensive and come with different lenses that are easy to pop on and off, as well as a zooming lens. Museums and science centers have successfully created displays around these microscopes and have found the microscope to be both durable and very engaging to people of all ages. The advantage of the handheld form of microscope is that the user can move it around with ease to examine clothing, hair, freckles, and fingernails. The images can be projected onto a television, computer display, or laptop for viewing by the class. Capture images at increasing magnification (10×, 50×, 100×, 200×). Print copies of the magnified images and lay them in front of students, so that they can see the previous magnification as the new, increasingly magnified image appears. Encourage the students to look across the copies from low to high magnification as new lenses are added. Laying objects side by side helps students create visual bridges from one magnification level to the next.

Part 4. *Digital Microscopes*

Next use a digital optical microscope to show students the same images with increased magnification. If enough microscopes are available, the students can take their own images at different magnifications, or the images can be displayed for the class using a computer projector. If images are printed for the students to view individually, be sure to note the magnification level on the printed image. As the objects are increasingly magnified, point out the changes in the level of detail as details are both lost and gained. In some cases more detail is seen (as in a carpet fiber). But a point is typically reached in magnification at which many images become less detailed, as a single point or component becomes the focus of the image.

179

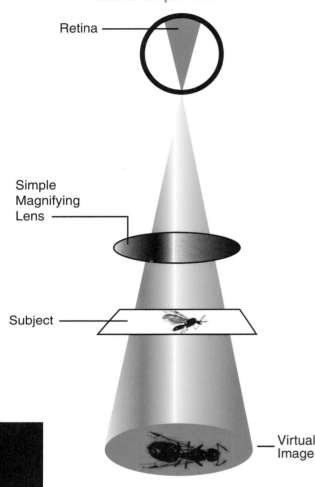

FIGURE 3.
Magnification
with a simple lens.

Retina

Simple
Magnifying
Lens

Subject

Virtual
Image

Part 5. *Movie Madness*

In the next investigation students use a digital camera to zoom in on an object outside the classroom and capture different magnifications in a movie. First, demonstrate to the students how to use the digital camera and how to alter the magnification. Instruct them to capture images of a single object at different magnifications, including 20×, 80×, and 400×. Then they should review the series of magnified images as a movie sequence. Encourage them to look carefully at how the image changes as the camera zooms in with increasing magnification.

Explain

Begin the discussion of magnification by reviewing how light bends through a convex lens. You may want to point out the wide variety of lenses that exist in common objects, including eyeglasses, cell phone cameras, binoculars, and telescopes. Help the students identify the magnification of each of the lenses and microscopes that they used in the investigation. Point out that a lens marked 10× magnifies the object 10 times.

Figure 3 illustrates how a simple magnifying lens works. The ant is being viewed with a single lens (other than the eye). Light reflected from the ant enters the lens in straight lines. The light from the ant is bent by the lens and is focused to create a virtual image of the ant on the retina. The ant appears to be magnified because we perceive the actual size of the ant to be larger than it is, as a result of the bending of the light.

Compound microscopes use two lenses to magnify an object (Figure 4, p. 181). The lens in the eyepiece is the same but the objective lenses can be moved to increase the magnification.

180

FIGURE 4.
Compound microscope.

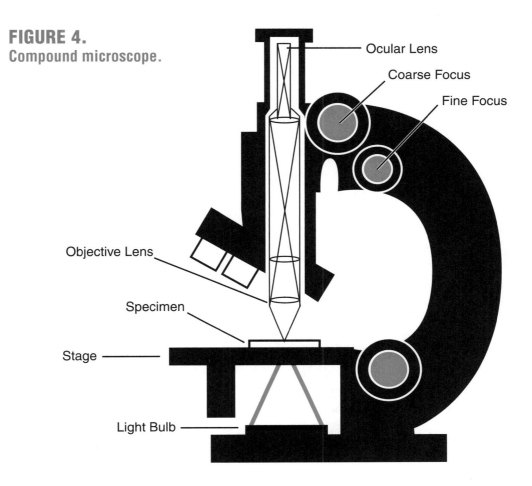

Ocular Lens

Coarse Focus

Fine Focus

Objective Lens

Specimen

Stage

Light Bulb

Image galleries for scanning electron micrographs:

- For diatoms to porcupine quills: *www.mos.org/sln/SEM/sem.html*
- Insects to hairs: *www.mse.iastate.edu/microscopy/tutorials.html*
- Wood to hotdogs: *www.egr.msu.edu/cmsc/esem/gallery/index.html*
- Aspirin to nerve cells: *www.wellcome.ac.uk/en/bia/gallery.html?image=24*
- Cells to embryos: *www.microscopyu.com/smallworld/gallery/index.html*
- Anatomy to algae: *www.ulb.ac.be/sciences/biodic/homepage2.html*

For additional information about microscopes and lenses:
- *http://science.howstuffworks.com/light-microscope1.htm*
- *http://micro.magnet.fsu.edu/primer/index.html*
- *www.mse.iastate.edu/microscopy/choice.html*
- *www.docstoc.com/docs/590164/Compound-Light-Microscope*

181

Extend

There are a number of excellent websites that allow students to zoom in on different objects in virtual environments. They provide additional examples of how images appear at different scales and can be useful in helping students develop a sense of scale when magnification and zooming are used.

Nanoreisen. The Nanoreisen website takes students on a journey that begins with people sitting at a café. Through increasing zooms, the focus changes to a mosquito on the arm of a man, to the proboscis entering the skin, and on into a cell. Students are able to control the speed of the journey and explore different areas within each zooming frame.
www.nanoreisen.com

Strange Matter. The Strange Matter website has an interactive slide that moves up and down through different sizes of images (from human scale to the atomic scale). Students can see examples of different objects at each size.
www.strangematterexhibit.com/structure.html

Cells Alive. In this simulation students view a straight pin, and then by clicking on a scale in increasing powers of ten, they see the pin and other objects on the pin at magnifications of 10×, 100×, 1,000×, and so on. The images shown are increasingly magnified, ending with a 20-nanometer-sized Rhinovirus.
www.cellsalive.com/howbig.htm

The Elegant Universe. This simulation allows students to increasingly magnify images that begin with a scene of an apple on a street and then zoom in on the apple at different powers of ten, passing the DNA and moving into the nucleus of a carbon atom, and on to a scale of 10^{-33} centimeters.
www.pbs.org/wgbh/nova/elegant/scale.html

Powers of Ten. This is the classic examination of the powers of ten. The website includes several interactive modules for students to move back and forward through the powers of ten. Students begin with the human scale and then move out into space, back to the human, and then inside the skin to the atomic level.
www.powersof10.com

Zoom Zoom: Magnification

Answer Sheet

Evaluate

Check for student understanding:

Below are magnified images of a common ant.

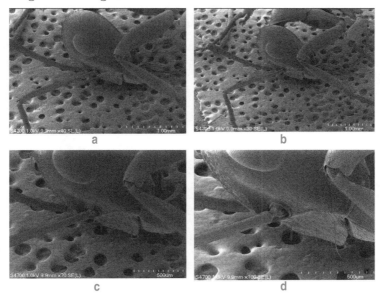

1. **Which of the ants shown above would be magnified 100×?**

   A. Image A

   B. Image B

   C. Image C

   D. Image D

2. **Which of the images of an ant shown above has been magnified 30×?**

   A. Image A

   B. Image B

   C. Image C

   D. Image D

3. **If a ladybug is 8 mm long and is magnified 20 times (20×), how big would the image of the bug be?**

   A. 80 mm

   B. 800 mm

   C. 160 mm

   D. 16 mm

Student Data Sheet
Zoom Zoom: Magnification

Name _____

In this investigation you will examine series of objects using a variety of different magnification tools. Carefully observe each object and make detailed drawings in the space provided below.

Materials:
- Hand lens
- Pocket microscope
- Digital handheld microscope
- Digital microscope
- Digital movie camera
- Feather, carpet fibers, leaf, and hair

Part 1. Hand Lens
What is the magnification of the hand lens? _____

Use the hand lens to carefully observe each object.
Draw a section of each magnified object in the space provided below:

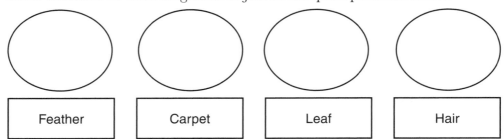

| Feather | Carpet | Leaf | Hair |

Part 2. Pocket Microscope
What is the magnification of the pocket microscope? _____

Use the pocket microscope to carefully observe each object.
Draw a section of each magnified object in the space provided below:

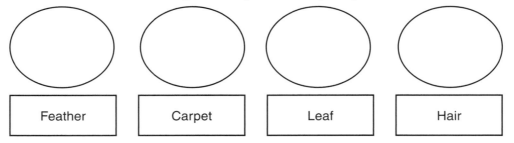

| Feather | Carpet | Leaf | Hair |

NATIONAL SCIENCE TEACHERS ASSOCIATION

Part 3. Handheld Microscope

What is the magnification of the handheld microscope? _____

Use the handheld microscope to carefully observe each object.
Draw a section of each magnified object in the space provided below:

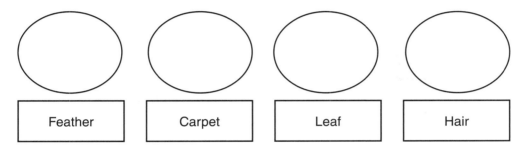

| Feather | Carpet | Leaf | Hair |

Part 4. Digital Microscope

What is the magnification of the digital microscope (use the highest magnification)? _____

Use the digital microscope to observe each object carefully. Draw a section of each magnified object in the space provided below:

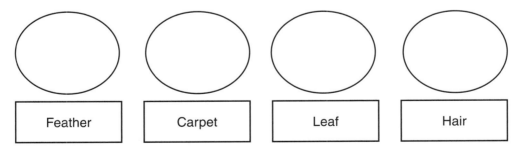

| Feather | Carpet | Leaf | Hair |

185

1. **Look across the different types of magnified images. How does the appearance of the feather change as you increase the magnification?**

2. **Which of the four objects looks the most unlike the original object when viewed under the microscope?**

Part 5. Movie Madness

Use a digital camera to observe an object outside the classroom. Try to capture images of a single object at different magnifications including 20×, 80×, and 400×.

1. **How does the appearance of the object change as the camera zooms in with increasing magnification?**

2. **Do you see more or less detail on the object?**

3. **If you saw only the last image, at the highest magnification, would you still know what the object was?**

186

SURFACE AREA-TO-VOLUME RELATIONSHIP

Chapter 15
That's Hot! The Effect of Size on Rate of Heat Loss

Overview

Through the use of common household items such as aluminum pans and thermometers, students will investigate how the size and shape of an object affect the rate of heat loss from the object to the environment This lesson is relevant to biology, as it relates to the size and shape of animals, their metabolism, and their ability to live in very cold or hot environments. A rate of heat loss that is too fast or too slow may affect the survival of an organism. By modeling different shapes and sizes of organisms using containers of various sizes, students explore how these variables affect the rate of heat loss.

Objectives
- To develop skills in observation.
- To use observations to make inferences about how size affects the rate of heat loss.

Process Skills
- Observing
- Predicting
- Comparing and contrasting
- Collecting data
- Analyzing data

Activity Duration
90 minutes
(Extension may take additional time.)

Background

Could a hamster live in Antarctica? Organisms that must regulate their body temperatures automatically release heat into the environment. Any loss or gain of heat occurs through the outermost surface of the animal (i.e., the skin). The requirement of organisms to strike a balance between the heat transferred to the environment through the skin and the heat generated within their bodies by their metabolism, is one way in which the size and shape of organisms are optimized and in some cases limited.

Even though metabolic mechanisms are similar among all types of organisms, the rate of metabolic regulation may vary greatly. A hamster's metabolic rate is significantly faster than the metabolic rate of a rhinoceros. One reason for the great difference is the larger surface area-to-volume ratios in the smaller mammal.

A warm-blooded animal's body (when healthy) is in thermal equilibrium, meaning that

189

its body temperature remains constant. For this to occur, the heat generated within the animal through metabolic processes must equal the amount of heat leaving the animal through its surface (skin). The heat generation happens within the bulk or volume of the animal, and the heat transfer to or from the environment happens at the surface. When the temperature of the environment (air) changes to extreme levels, the animal's metabolism adjusts such that the heat equation remains balanced.

As a very small mammal, the hamster has a surface area-to-volume ratio that is very large. This means that the surface effect of heat transfer to (or from) the environment is quite large relative to the capacity of the hamster's small body volume to generate heat to compensate. A hamster therefore has a relatively high metabolic rate, resulting in high heat generation to maintain this balance. An elephant or a whale, on the other hand, has an enormous volume. Its surface-to-volume ratio is low. The rate of heat loss is easily compensated by the bulk metabolic processes, and therefore metabolic rates of those animals are correspondingly slower. So the connection between metabolic rate and the body size of an animal comes down ultimately to the surface-to-volume ratio!

The importance of the size and shape of an object to the rate of heat transfer to the environment holds for all objects, not just living ones. For example, two different bodies of water (e.g., lakes and ponds) will lose heat at different rates depending on their size and shape. A pond that is very deep and narrow will lose heat more slowly than a pond of the same volume that is wide and shallow. In the design of engines or high-power electronic components that get very hot, heat transfer fins are often used to increase surface area and enhance air cooling. Surface-to-volume ratio and its relation to heat transfer and temperature regulation are important in living, nonliving, and technological contexts.

Materials

Each group will need:

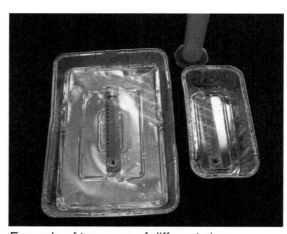

Example of two pans of different sizes.

- 2 thermometers
- 1 pan (9 × 4 × 3 in.)
- 1 pan (13 × 9 × 2 in.)
- Hot plate
- Two 500 ml flasks or beakers
- Pair of hot mitts
- Safety goggles
- Access to water
- Timer or stopwatch
- Graph paper
- Colored pencils

Note: Depending on the size of the class, groups may share hot plates. For younger students, the teacher may want to pour the hot water into the pans for each lab group.

For the Engage portion of this activity, the labels of continents and cards with animals should be prepared before the first day of the activity.

Engage

Make a label on card stock for each of the seven continents. Before class begins, place the labels around the room. As the students enter the classroom, hand each student an index card with a name and picture of an animal. Ask them to tape the card underneath the continent on which they think the animal lives. Have the students discuss why they placed the animals in those locations. Have them brainstorm why certain animals live on certain continents.

Seven Main Continents	Examples of Organisms
Asia	Panda, elephant, small-clawed otter
Africa	Elephant, cheetah, meerkat, giraffe, zebra
North America	Prairie dog, cougar, wolf, bison
South America	Jaguar, chinchilla, Brazilian tapir
Antarctica	Penguin, seal, Arctic tern
Europe	Norwegian lemming
Australia	Koala, kangaroo, platypus

African elephant

Asian elephant

191

After discussion of where and why certain species of animals have adapted to their climates, show the class pictures of Asian elephants and African elephants. Have the students compare and contrast the characteristics of the two. The students will eventually notice that the ears of the two elephants are different in size. The ears of the African elephant are much bigger and may reach a length of about 5 feet from top to bottom. The huge ears of the African elephant function not only for hearing but also for ventilation, visual communication, and heat transfer. The size difference in the ears of the two elephants can be linked partly to their climates. African elephants live near the equator, where it is warmer; they have bigger ears (increased surface area) to aid in heat loss. Note that the large, flat ear is perfectly optimized for heat transfer. Like a piece of paper, it has a huge surface-to-volume ratio compared with the rest of the body of the animal. Asian elephants live farther north, in cooler climates; they have smaller ears (smaller surface area) to reduce heat loss.

Note: Older students could also research the various scientific rules that apply to climate, body size, and heat loss, such as Allen's rule (organisms from colder climates have shorter limbs than similar animals from warmer climates), Bergmann's rule (the body mass increases with latitude for a particular species), and Gloger's rule (darker-pigmented forms of an organism tend to be found in more humid climates, such as equatorial environments). There are several other rules that may apply not necessarily to heat loss but to scaling issues in general.

Explore

Now explain to the students that they will investigate how the size and shape of an object may affect the rate of heat loss. In lab groups, have the students discuss whether or not the shape and size of the container should have an effect on the heat loss of water in the container and why. Then have them formulate a hypothesis based on this discussion. They should record their hypotheses on the Student Data Sheet.

In their lab groups, the students will investigate how the size and shape of two different containers affect the rate of heat loss. Older students should boil 1,000 ml of water. (The teacher may want to boil and pour the water for younger students.) Before the water is at a rapid boil, carefully pour 500 ml of water into the large container and the other 500 ml of water into the small container. Gently place a thermometer face up in bottom of each container. Warn the students that the water is very hot and that care should be taken when handling pans, thermometers, and water.

The students should *immediately* take the *initial* temperature of the water in each container and record the data in the table provided on their Student Data Sheet. The students should then take a reading on the thermometers one

192

minute after the water has been poured into the pans and then continue to measure the temperature every minute for five minutes. After the five-minute data collection, have the students calculate the change in temperature using the following formula:

$$\Delta T = (\textbf{Final Temperature} - \textbf{Initial Temperature})$$

Have the students also determine the overall rate of temperature loss or "cooling rate." This is simply the number of degrees per minute that were lost for each pan:

$$\textbf{Cooling Rate} = \Delta T / \Delta \textbf{time}$$
$$= (\textbf{Final Temperature} - \textbf{Initial Temperature}) / (\textbf{Final Time} - \textbf{Initial Time})$$

Since the initial time in this exercise is zero minutes, the above equation simplifies to:

$$(\textbf{Final Temperature} - \textbf{Initial Temperature}) / (\textbf{Final Time})$$

The cooling rate is expressed as "degrees per minute" or (°F/min.). In this case, since the water is cooling, the rate will be negative (since ΔT is negative).

Each group should then plot their data on graph paper using colored pencils. Students should use one color for the data collected from the large pan and another color for data collected from the small pan. Once all groups have completed the graph, have the students discuss their answers to the Conclusion questions on their Student Data Sheets and be ready to report their findings to the rest of the class (see the example of a student graph below). Note that the overall cooling rate that the students calculate is simply the slope of these graphs.

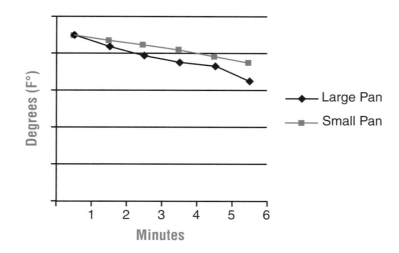

Explain

As each lab group reports their results to rest of class, record the similarities and differences between groups on the overhead or blackboard. Ask the students to analyze the results of the entire class. If there are groups with findings different from those of the majority of the class, have the students brainstorm why some groups may have different results. They may suggest different types of error, including human error, broken equipment, unequal amounts of water, too much time between recording temperatures, and so on. At this point, you may also review the importance of a controlled experiment and various ways of improving the investigation.

Both pans had the same volume of water and very close initial temperatures. The large pan had more surface area exposed to the air and so has a higher rate of heat loss. Not only is more water surface exposed to air, but more is also exposed to the pan (which is metal and a great thermal conductor). The smaller pan had less surface area exposed to the air, resulting in a slower rate of heat loss. This investigation models how smaller animals (with higher surface area-to-volume ratios) lose heat faster than larger animals (with smaller surface area-to-volume ratios).

Extend

Since this investigation explored only the difference in surface area while keeping the volume constant, have the students design a similar investigation that looks at differences in surface area *and* volume. In their lab groups (or as a class), have the students decide what materials they will need to complete this investigation, as well as the procedure and safety precautions necessary to carry out the experiment. Complete the experiment and discuss the results.

Evaluate

Check for student understanding:

1. What are surface area-to-volume ratios? Give an example.
2. How does the surface area-to-volume ratio affect the rate of heat loss of a pond?
3. How does the size of an organism affect the rate of heat loss?
4. What are some adaptations of animals to deal with hot and cold climates?

For other activities or information about heat loss:

- *www.courseworkhelp.co.uk/GCSE/Science/11.htm*
- *www.faqs.org/docs/Newtonian/Newtonian_44.htm*

Name _____

Problem
Do the shape and size of the container have an effect on heat loss of water in the container? Which container will cool more quickly?

Hypothesis
_____

_____

 SAFTEY PRECAUTIONS
*Remember to wear goggles and be careful not to touch the hot water, hot glassware, or hot plate.

Procedure
1. Let 1,000 ml of water come to a slight boil. Using hot mitts, carefully pour 500 ml of water into the large container and the other 500 ml of water into the small container.
2. Gently place a thermometer face up in the bottom of each container without touching the water!
3. Take the initial temperature of the water in each container and record in the data table.
4. Take a reading on the thermometers one minute after the water has been poured into the pans. Record the temperature in the data table below. Do not remove the thermometers from the water.
5. Continue to measure the temperature every minute for five minutes. Remember to record the temperatures in the data table.
6. Calculate the change in temperature using the formula under the data table.
7. Determine the overall rate of temperature loss using the formula under the data table.
8. Using graph paper and colored pencils, plot your data on a line graph.

195

Data Table

Time (Minute)	Temp. of Water in Large Pan (Celsius)	Temp. of Water in Small Pan (Celsius)
Initial		
1		
2		
3		
4		
5		
$\Delta T = T_f - T_i$		
Cooling Rate		

ΔT = (Final Temperature − Initial Temperature)

Cooling Rate = $\Delta T / \Delta$time
= (Final Temperature − Initial Temperature)/(Final Time − Initial Time)

Since your initial time is 0 min., this simplifies to
= (Final Temperature − Initial Temperature)/(Final Time)

196

Student Data Sheet
That's Hot!

Conclusion

1. Examine the data for the five time periods.
   Was your hypothesis supported or refuted?

   _____

2. Write a few sentences summarizing the answer to the
   problem statement according to your data.

   _____

   _____

   _____

   _____

   _____

3. How could you improve this investigation?

   _____

   _____

   _____

   _____

4. Apply the results of this investigation to similar processes
   found in living organisms.

   _____

   _____

   _____

   _____

Chapter 16
SWEET! Exploring Surface Area of Sugar Molecules

Overview

Two forces that are very familiar to us in our daily lives are gravity and adhesion. The force of gravity on an object, which we commonly refer to as the object's weight, is proportional to the volume of the object. Adhesion or stickiness, on the other hand, is a surface effect. As objects become smaller, the surface-to-volume ratio increases, changing the relative strengths of these two common forces. At very small scales, such as the micro- (cells) or nanoscales (molecules), the stickiness property completely dominates. This activity demonstrates a crossover point from the dominance of gravity for big objects (sugar cubes) to the dominance of adhesion for smaller objects (powdered sugar grains).

Objectives

- To develop skills in observation.
- To use observations to make inferences about the physical properties of sugar molecules.

Process Skills

- Observing
- Predicting
- Hypothesizing
- Comparing and contrasting
- Collecting data
- Analyzing data

Activity Duration

60 minutes

Background

The scale of a problem affects the types of forces that are most important. For example, some small organisms such as insects and lizards can walk upside down on a ceiling, a feat larger animals cannot accomplish. Because of the small size of these wall-climbing animals, the adhesion between their feet and the ceiling dominates the competing pull of gravity. All living things have size limits, mainly due to physical structures or processes that function properly only at particular scales.

These geometrical considerations are crucial even at the cellular level. The size of a living cell is limited by its surface area-to-volume ratio, which determines the relative rates of nutrient uptake and waste removal. As a cell (or any object) gets bigger, its volume increases more rapidly than its surface area. If the cell becomes too large, the nutrient requirements of the processes within the cell's volume outstrip the ability of the surface to absorb nutrients at a sufficient rate. Conversely, the waste produced by those same processes within the volume of the cell cannot be expelled by the surface quickly enough. This jeopardizes the life of the cell. If too large, the cell must either divide or die if it cannot get enough nutrients or get rid of unnecessary wastes suitably.

At very small scales, this competition between adhesive forces and gravitational forces is even more

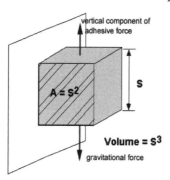

199

unbalanced. At the nanometer scale, where molecules exist, intermolecular forces that are the origin of "stickiness" completely dominate weight and inertia. Chemical and intermolecular interactions such as hydrogen bonds, van der Waals bonds, and hydrophobic bonds are the dominant influences on the life of molecules. Gravitational forces that dominate at the macroscale are effectively nonexistent. (*Note:* Gravity is always there; it's just that its influence is a billion times smaller than the other forces.) At very small scales, the world appears to be a very, very sticky place, and gravity is not very important. At our human scale, and especially at larger scales like that of the Sun, planets, Moon, and stars, gravity becomes the dominant force. It all comes down to surface-to-volume ratio.

So whether an object "sticks" to another depends on the strength of the adhesion relative to other forces—most importantly, the object's weight. If the adhesive force is greater than the gravitational force, then an object sticks. This is directly related to the size of the object. When an object gets smaller, the surface area-to-volume ratio increases, and gravitational forces are therefore less dominant.

Materials

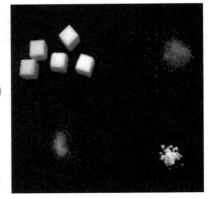

Each group will need:

- 4 plastic containers with lids (shoe box size)
- 1 box of powdered sugar
- 1 small bag of granulated sugar
- 1 box of raw sugar
- 1 box of sugar cubes
- 4 station labels (one for each type of sugar)

Note: Fill each container half-full with one type of sugar. Place the containers at four different locations or tables in the classroom and label with the type of sugar. See example below.

Have paper towels on each table for students to wipe their hands between stations. It's best if their hands are not wet when doing this activity.

Engage

Once the students are in lab groups, they first answer the questions, *What is surface area?* and *What is volume?* With their lab group, have them write down what they already know about surface area and volume. Have them discuss their responses with the rest of the class. Write their responses on chart paper or the blackboard.

Ask them to answer the following questions: *What is gravity? What is weight? How is weight related to volume?* With their lab groups, have them write down what they already know about gravity, as well as the answers to the questions. Have them discuss their responses with the rest of the class. Write the student responses on chart paper or the blackboard.

As a class, brainstorm how surface area and volume determine the effect of gravity and adhesion on an object.

Explore

Explain to the students that they will investigate how sugar crystals of different sizes are affected by gravity and adhesive forces. Have them write a hypothesis about how the grain size of sugar (cubes, granulated, raw, or powdered) may or may not affect how well it sticks to their hands. Record the hypothesis on the Student Data Sheet.

Each lab group should rotate to each Sweet! station. All the students should wipe their hands with paper towels to make sure they are dry. With their fingers stretched out and palm down, the students should place a hand in the sugar. They should then slowly remove their hand from the container and turn it over to observe the sugar stuck to their palm.

On a scale from 0 to 4, they should determine how much sugar was sticking to their hand and record it in the data table on the Student Data Sheet. Have lab groups compare their data results and write whether their hypotheses were supported or refuted.

This investigation applies a rough estimation using the values 0 to 4. You may ask students how they could design a test or a new apparatus to measure more accurately the amount of sugar that adheres to the hand.

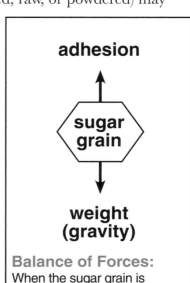

adhesion

sugar grain

weight (gravity)

Balance of Forces: When the sugar grain is stuck to the hand, there is a balance between the adhesion forces and the weight. When the weight is larger than the adhesion, the grain falls.

201

Explain

As groups share their conclusions to this investigation, write the types of responses on chart paper or the blackboard. Most groups will find that the powdered sugar sticks to their hands much better than any of the other size sugar crystals. This finding is a result of the higher surface area-to-volume ratio of the powdered sugar, which causes it to stick or adhere better than the other types. Because the powdered sugar has the highest surface area-to-volume ratio, gravity is proportionally smaller, compared to adhesive forces, for the tiny powdered sugar grains; they stick instead of falling off. The opposite case is that of the sugar cubes, whose surface area-to-volume ratio is much smaller, and gravitational force, or weight, dominates adhesion. Use a diagram like the one in the box on page 201 to describe the orientation and balance of forces (adhesion versus weight).

Note: Keep in mind that the adhesion force between the hand and the sugar cube is actually larger than that for the hand and the powdered sugar grain. The sugar cube is larger and therefore touches a larger area of your hand. However, the weight is much, much larger and therefore dominates. This is a fine point, with which it may or may not be appropriate to challenge the students, but it should be kept in mind in talking correctly about the problem.

Extend

Allow the students time to think about how the surface area-to-volume ratio affects the balance of gravity and adhesion on an object. Have the student groups design another experiment to test the results of this relationship using other objects such as salt or soil. Share the results of their new investigation and discuss how the results are similar to and different from those of the Sweet! sugar exploration.

For more advanced students

Research the different forces that affect objects ranging from the nanoscale to macroscale, such as chemical bonds (covalent, ionic, and metallic bonds), intermolecular forces (van der Waals, hydrogen bonds, hydrophobic bonds), electrostatic interactions, capillary forces, and so on. Give students the challenge of trying to determine what forces are involved in the ability of a water strider insect to "walk on water."

Evaluate

Check for student understanding:

1. What is surface area?
2. What is volume?
3. What is meant by surface area-to-volume ratio? Give an example.
4. What is gravity?
5. What is weight?
6. If a golf ball and a piece of notebook paper were dropped at the same time and from the same height, which do you predict would hit the ground first? Explain your answer.

For other references that use sugar grain size to investigate rates of dissolving, rates of reaction, or adhesion see:

- *http://invsee.asu.edu/nmodules/sizescalemod/unit4/unit4.htm*
- *www.newton.dep.anl.gov/askasci/phy00/phy00848.htm*
- *www.iserv.net/~chargers/chem/secagrain.htm*
- *www.slate.com/id/2184485*
- *www.primaryresources.co.uk/science/pdfs/6chanmat.pdf*

203

Name _____

Brainstorm with your lab group:

a. What is surface area?

b. What is volume?

c. What is surface area-to-volume ratio?

d. What is gravity?

Problem

Does the grain size of sugar affect how well the sugar sticks to your hand?

Write a hypothesis predicting how the grain size of sugar (cubes, granulated, raw, or powdered) may or may not affect how well it sticks to your hand. Predict which of the four types of sugar will stick the most and least (rank them from most to least).

S4700 5.0kV 13.1mm x30 SE(U)   1.00mm

Hypothesis

_____

_____

Procedure

1. Go to each Sweet! station. Wipe your hand with a paper towel before each station to make sure it is clean and dry.

204

2. With your fingers stretched out and palm facedown, put your hand on the sugar. Then turn your hand over and observe how much sugar is stuck to your palm. On a scale from 0 to 4, determine how much sugar was stuck to your hand.

0	1	2	3	4
None	Few grains	A lot	Almost covered	Completely covered

3. Record all results in the data table.

Data Table

Type of Sugar	Scale	Comments
Powdered sugar		
Granulated sugar		
Raw sugar		
Cubed sugar		

Conclusion

1. Was your hypothesis supported or refuted?

2. What do your results indicate? Explain.

205

LIMITS TO SIZE

Chapter 17
Captivating Cubes: Investigating Surface Area-to-Volume Ratio

Overview
In this two-part activity, students investigate how surface area-to-volume ratios change with cube size. Students apply those calculations to explore how surface area-to-volume relationships limit the size of cells. Extensions of these activities probe the role that surface area-to-volume relationships play in science contexts.

PART A
Surface Area-to-Volume Relationships

Background
Issues related to surface area-to-volume ratios occur widely throughout all science domains. This relationship can limit the size of an organism or affect the rate of a chemical reaction. From gecko feet to elephant ears, surface area-to-volume relationships play key roles in the structure and functions of organisms. Before students can understand how surface area-to-volume ratios can be applied in science contexts, they must first understand what surface area and volume are individually and then, subsequently, understand them as a ratio.

Surface area and volume can most easily be explained using cubes as models. The total surface of the cube equals the combined area of all of the faces of the cube. One side of the cube is essentially a square; therefore, to find the area of one side of the cube students would use the formula *length × width (L × W)*. Since they are finding the entire surface area of a cube, the students must take into account that the cube has six sides. The formula for finding the entire surface area of a cube is then *length × width × 6* (number of sides). The students should also be aware of how to write the units correctly. If you are using centimeters (cm) to calculate surface area, the answer should be written as cm^2.

For example:
Surface Area Equation: *Length × width × 6 (no. of sides of a cube) = surface area*

Surface Area = 3 cm × 3 cm × 6 = 54 cm^2

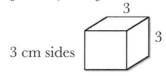

3 cm sides

Objectives
- To calculate and compare surface area-to-volume ratios of cubes of different sizes.
- To predict how limits to size are determined by surface area-to-volume relationships.

Process Skills
- Observing
- Predicting
- Comparing and contrasting
- Collecting data
- Analyzing data

Activity Duration
90 minutes for each part of the activity

209

Volume measures the total three-dimensional space inside the cube. To find the volume of a cube, the students would use the formula *length × width × height (L × W × H)*. If they are measuring in centimeters (cm), the answer should be presented in cm^3 units.

For example: 3 cm × 3 cm × 3 cm = 27 cm^3

To determine the surface area-to-volume ratio of the cube in the example above, simplify the number of units of surface area for each unit of volume. The surface area was 54 cm^2 and the volume was 27 cm^3, so therefore the ratio is 2 to 1.

There are several cautions that should be understood when presenting the ratio in this way. First, the units are ignored. Formally, it is a ratio of two quantities that have different dimensionality. The ratio above, if written correctly (in a formal sense), would be (2/1 cm) or 2/cm. Another caution is that the ratio is dependent on the units being used. Because surface and volume have different dimensionality, when we calculate their ratio, the units we are using will affect the answer. If the above example were done using inches, the ratio would not be 2 to 1.

For advanced students, encourage using symbols until the last step in a calculation. For example, when determining the surface-to-volume ratio of a cube, calculate the surface area, *A*, and volume, *V*, using the symbols representing length, *L*, width, *W*, and height, *H*. For a cube, *L* = *W* = *H*. So we'll call length, width, and height *L*.

Surface area:
$$A = 6 \times L \times W = 6 \times L^2$$

Volume:
$$V = L \times W \times H = L^3$$

Surface area-to-volume ratio:
$$A/V = (6 \times L^2 / L^3) = 6 / L$$

Now the calculation is simple. The ratio is simply 6 divided by the length of a side. In the example above, the length of the side is 3 cm. So the ratio *A/V* is 6/3 cm or 2/cm (or 2, ignoring units). Note that this answer would be different using a different unit (such as millimeters or inches). The crucial thing to understand is that when comparing a very large cube to a very small cube, the surface-to-volume ratio will always have the same trend, regardless of the choice of units: A small object has a higher surface-to-volume ratio than a larger one. The equation *A/V* = *6/L* expresses this in mathematical form. The smaller *L* is, the larger the ratio *A/V*.

Materials

Each group will need:

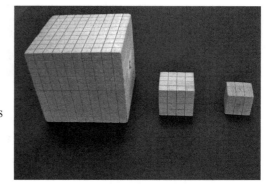

- Chart paper
- Felt-tipped marker
- Wood or plastic cubes of various sizes
- Rulers
- Graph paper
- Modeling clay
- Graduated cylinder
- Beaker

Engage

Arrange the students into groups of two or three and give each group a piece of chart paper and a marker. Ask each group to brainstorm everything they already know about surface area, volume, and surface area-to-volume ratios. Encourage them to use definitions, phrases, formulas, and sketches. Once they have finished, discuss what each group came up with, and compare and contrast with other groups.

Explore

In groups, have the students calculate surface areas, volumes, and surface area-to-volume ratios of various sized cubes using metric rulers and record their information in the data table in Student Data Sheet 1. Give the students cubes ranging in length from at least 1 cm to 10 cm, so that they can see a pattern of how size affects the ratios. After completion of the table, the students should answer the concluding questions and discuss their findings with the class.

Explain

Using the formulas in the Background section, students should calculate the surface area, the volume, and then the surface area-to-volume ratio of each cube. They should begin to recognize the pattern in which the surface area-to-volume ratio changes as cube size increases. As a cube increases in size, the surface area-to-volume ratio gets smaller.

   The table on the next page contains example answers, depending on what size cubes you have available for your students.

211

Size of Cube	Total Surface Area (cm²)	Volume of Cube Cell (cm³)	Total Surface Area-to-Volume Ratio	Simplified Ratio (divide each number by the volume)
Formula	L × W × 6	L × W × H	SA/Vol	
1	1 × 1 × 6 = 6	1 × 1 × 1 = 1	6 SA / 1 Vol	6 : 1
3	3 × 3 × 6 = 54	3 × 3 × 3 = 27	54 SA / 27 Vol	2 : 1
5	5 × 5 × 6 = 150	5 × 5 × 5 = 125	150 SA / 125 Vol	1.2 : 1

For more information and practice on how surface area relates to volume:

- *www.cod.edu/people/faculty/chenpe/sa-ratio.html*
- *www.shodor.org/interactivate/activities/SurfaceAreaAndVolume*

Extend

Give each lab group a chunk of clay, graduated cylinder, beaker, graph paper, and rulers. Tell each group to make three cubes of different sizes out of the clay, calculate surface area-to-volume ratios, and record their findings. Tell the groups that they can use any of the given materials to figure out surface area and volume. For example, the students can use the displacement method to determine volume.

Once the groups have finished their calculations, have them swap their clay cubes with another group and repeat their investigation with the new cubes. Have them double-check their findings against findings of other groups. Record all surface area-to-volume ratios on the blackboard or chart paper, and then put them in the order of greatest surface area-to-volume ratio to least. Place all the clay cubes on a table in that order. Compare and contrast the cube sizes with the ratios, and ask the students to determine a pattern.

Note:
- Various sized beakers and graduated cylinders should be provided to accommodate larger cubes.
- 1 milliliter equals 1 centimeter cubed.
- It is important to point out to the students that the absolute value of these ratios depends on the unit you are using. But the proportional change in surface area-to-volume ratio will be independent of the choice of units.

Ask advanced students to calculate the surface area-to-volume ratios for other three-dimensional objects such as pyramids, cylinders, or spheres. Do these objects show the same patterns of surface area-to-volume ratios as cubes?

Evaluate

Check for understanding:

1. **a.** What is surface area, and how do you calculate it?
   b. When would you use surface area in everyday life?
2. **a.** What is volume, and how do you calculate it?
   b. When do you use volume measurements in everyday life?
3. What is surface area-to-volume ratio, and how does it change as a cube increases in size?
4. As a cube increases in size, which increases faster: surface area or volume?
5. In your own words, describe how surface area-to-volume relationships could limit the size of an organism.

Name _____

Part A. Calculating Surface Area-to-Volume Ratios

Size of Cube	Total Surface Area (cm²)	Volume of Cube Cell (cm³)	Total Surface Area-to-Volume Ratio	Simplified Ratio (divide each number by the volume)
Formula	L × W × 6	L × W × H	SA/Vol	
			____SA / ____ Vol	____ : 1
			____SA / ____ Vol	____ : 1
			____SA / ____ Vol	____ : 1

Summarize:

What patterns or trends do you notice about the sizes of the cubes and the surface area-to-volume ratios?

1. **What is surface area, and how do you calculate it?**

2. **What is volume, and how do you calculate it?**

3. **What is surface area-to-volume ratio, and how does it change as a cube increases in size?**

4. **As a cube increases in size, which increases faster: surface area or volume?**

5. **Describe how surface area-to-volume relationships could limit the size of an organism.**

214

PART B
Surface Area-to-Volume Relationships and Limits to Size

Background

What makes a giant creature so large? Is it large because is has extra-large cells, or is it made of more cells than a creature of average size? Cells are microscopic building blocks of living things that play a role in how organisms grow larger, acquire nourishment, and get rid of wastes. All of these cell processes are influenced by surface area-to-volume relationships. Surface area-to-volume ratio is one of the reasons organisms are limited in size. A cell has size limits because at some point it would get too large to acquire enough nourishment or rid itself of toxic wastes. The surface area must be large enough to allow sufficient nutrients to enter the cell and to get to the organelles. If the cell grows to the point where the requirements of the cell's volume overcome the capacity of the surface to provide nutrient intake and waste outflow, then the cell must either divide or die.

The cell membrane acts as a barrier from the surrounding environment and as a gateway for the movement of nutrients and wastes through diffusion and active transport. The total surface area of the cell determines the maximum rate at which the cell can obtain nutrients or release waste. The volume of the cell determines the amount of nutrient uptake needed, as well as the waste disposal requirements. In this investigation students explore the relationship between surface area and volume and the effect that relationship has on living cells. Students consider which surface area and volume ratios are most beneficial to cells by calculating diffusion rates of various sized agar cells.

Materials

Each group will need:
- Goggles and apron
- 1 cm^3, 2 cm^3, 3 cm^3 agar cubes prepared with phenolphthalein
- 250 ml beaker or cup
- Ruler
- Plastic knife and spoon
- 0.4% NaOH (enough diffusion medium to cover all three cubes in a cup)

Note: Prelab preparation must take place before the activity begins:

- Make agar with phenolphthalein with distilled water over slow boil.
  - Follow the directions on the agar container to make 2,000 ml of 2% agar solution. Stir until powdered agar is fully dissolved.

As the agar is cooling, add one gram of phenolphthalein per liter of solution. Continue to stir until all is dissolved. If the agar turns a shade of pink, add a dilute acid (dropwise) to the solution until it appears colorless.

- Pour the agar into trays about 3 cm deep and let solidify (at least 30 minutes).
- Use enough trays to be able to cut sufficient 1 cm^3, 2 cm^3, and 3 cm^3 agar cubes for each group to have one of each size.
- Use 50 ml of 0.4% NaOH solution as the diffusion medium (per group).
- Kits with materials to be used for similar diffusion activities can be found at: *www.wardsci.com* *www.carolina.com/home.do*

Other materials can be substituted for this activity:

- Potato cubes may also be used. Cut potatoes into cubes of various sizes and drop into iodine potassium-iodide (IKI) solution. The solution will diffuse into the cubes.

Procedures

Engage

Review with the students what they know about surface area-to-volume relationships. Recall how surface area-to-volume relationships affect living organisms (e.g., the size of elephant ears). Have them consider different sized organisms and what climate they live in (Engage activity from the *That's Hot* investigation). Next, ask the students to consider the possibility of a "1 inch" man and whether or not he could ever exist. Would the "1 inch" man have special challenges staying warm or getting food throughout his body? Ask the students to think about applications of the surface area-to-volume relationships to cells.

For more information: Read about Allen's rule, which states that endotherms from colder climates usually have shorter limbs than the equivalent animals from warmer climates. Go to *www.backyardnature.net/ecorules.htm*

Explore

In lab groups, students will explore how surface area-to-volume relationships limit the size of cells in living organisms. Using agar cubes of various sizes, they will investigate how as cells increase in size they reach a point at which the surface area can no longer support the processes (such as diffusion, nutrient absorption, and waste disposal) within the volume of the cell. The cubes will

216

be dropped into a diffusion medium (NaOH) and eventually sliced open to investigate how diffusion affected cubes of various sizes (i.e., cells). (Remember to complete prelab preparation prior to this portion of activity.) Follow the student procedures on Student Data Sheet 2, and emphasize safety precautions! All students must use gloves and goggles during this portion of the activity.

Explain

In lab groups, students will explore how surface area-to-volume relationships limit the size of cells in living organisms. The answers to the activity can be found in the table below. The students will see that as the cells represented by agar cubes increase in size, so do the surface area and volume. As the cells increase in size, the volume increases at a faster rate than the surface area. A smaller cell (agar cube) has a larger surface area-to-volume ratio (more surface area units compared to volume units). The smaller surface area-to-volume ratios cannot support typical cell functions of taking in nutrients or excreting wastes, and so therefore the cell will have to either divide or die.

Size of Cube	Total Surface Area (cm^2)	Volume of Cube Cell (cm^3)	Total Surface Area-to-Volume Ratio	Simplified Ratio (divide each number by the volume)
Formula	L × W × 6	L × W × H	SA/Vol	
1	1 × 1 × 6 = 6	1 × 1 × 1 = 1	6 SA / 1 Vol	6 : 1
2	2 × 2 × 6 = 24	2 × 2 × 2 = 8	24 SA / 8 Vol	3 : 1
3	3 × 3 × 6 = 54	3 × 3 × 3 = 27	54 SA / 27 Vol	2 : 1

Extend

Once students have a grasp of how surface area-to-volume ratios affect living organisms, have them investigate other examples of this relationship using chemical reactions.

For more information:
- Marble chip and hydrochloric acid reaction:
  www.crocodile-clips.com/absorb/AC4/sample/LR1502.html
- Magnesium strips and hydrochloric acid:
  www.sep.alquds.edu/chemistry/scripts/Teacher/exp_6.htm
- Some simple experiments:
  www.rogers.k12.ar.us/users/ehutches/reactionratelab.html

Evaluate

Check for understanding:

1. What cell structure represents the surface area of a cell?
2. What is found in the "volume" portion of a cell?
3. What cell processes are most likely to be affected by surface area-to-volume ratios?
4. What happens to a cell when the volume grows too large to be maintained by the surface area?

218

Name _____

PART B
Surface Area-to-Volume Relationships and Limits to Size

Cells are the building blocks of living things. Can cells continue to grow larger and larger? No matter what the size of an organism, cells are microscopic in size. Cells need water and nutrients. But how do they get water and nutrients, and how do they get rid of waste? One way is through diffusion. Diffusion is a way that small particles move into and out of cells. These substances cross the cell membrane from areas of higher concentration to areas of lower concentration without requiring energy from the cell.

The cell membrane represents the surface area of the cell. What if the cell doubled in size? Would it have a greater volume and surface area? What effect would the changing size have on diffusion and the amount of nutrients the cell would need? If a cell doubled in size, it would require more nutrients and would have to excrete more waste. This investigation will allow you to observe the changing relationship of surface area to volume for a growing cell. To investigate this relationship we will use agar cubes as *models* of cells.

To track the rate of diffusion, a special solution will be used. The special solution diffuses into the agar cubes at an equal rate for each cube, but because of differing volumes, the results will not appear the same. Let's see what happens when we submerge different-sized cubes in this solution!

 SAFETY PRECAUTIONS
Use goggles and gloves when handling the agar cubes.

Procedure: Part 1

1. Obtain three agar cubes (one of each size—1 cm³, 2 cm³, and 3 cm³). Think of the cubes as large models of microscopic cells.
2. Place the cubes in the beaker and pour in enough diffusion medium to cover them. Make sure you wear goggles and gloves and BE VERY CAREFUL!
3. Allow the cubes to soak in the diffusion medium for the next 10 minutes. During this time, be sure to occasionally swirl the solution, but be careful not to scratch or cut the surface of the cubes.
4. While you are waiting for results in Part 1, answer the questions on the next page.

Questions

1. If the solution represents nutrients, which of your three model cells do you think would be getting the nutrients at the most efficient rate? Explain.

    _____

    _____

2. Do you think that the cell with the greatest total surface area will get the most nutrients into and out of the cell? Explain.

    _____

    _____

3a. Calculate the total surface area, volume, and surface area-to-volume ratio of each of your three models and record in the table below:

Cube	Total Surface Area (cm²)	Volume of Cube Cell (cm³)	Total Surface Area-to-Volume Ratio	Simplified Ratio (divide each number by the volume)
Formula	L × W × 6	L × W × H	SA/Vol	
1 cm³			____SA / ____ Vol	____ : 1
2 cm³				
3 cm³				

3b. Which cell has the greatest surface area?

    _____

3c. Which cell has the greatest surface area-to-volume ratio?

    _____

4. Do these calculations change your answer to question 2? Why or why not?

NATIONAL SCIENCE TEACHERS ASSOCIATION

Procedure: Part 2

1. At the end of 10 minutes, take your beaker to the sink. Carefully pour off the solution and rinse the agar cubes with water. Using plastic spoons, remove the agar cubes from the beaker, place them on a paper towel, and gently blot them dry.

2. Using a plastic knife, cut the cubes in half, and examine and compare their inside appearance. Using the mm ruler, measure the depth of the colored zones in each cube and record your data. Sketch each cube to show the color changes.

3. After you have made your observations and recorded your data, be sure to clean up your lab area and properly dispose of your agar cubes as directed by your teacher.

DATA TABLE

Cube	Depth of Color Change (mm)	Rate of Diffusion (mm/min)	Sketch of Color Change
1 cm cube			
2 cm cube			
3 cm cube			

221

Discussion

1. Anything that the cell takes in (such as oxygen, water, or food) or lets out (such as carbon dioxide) must go through the cell membrane. Which calculation (surface area or volume) best represents how much cell membrane the models have?

2. As the cell grows larger and gets more cell content, will it need more or less cell membrane to survive? Why?

3. How do your observations and calculations relate to the question of why cells are usually very small?

222

Chapter 18
Eggsactly

Overview

In this two-part activity, students make inferences about the relationships between egg size, incubation time, and bird size from data sets collected from hundreds of species of birds. Students will also investigate how an egg can exchange oxygen and carbon dioxide through pores in the eggshell. A four-day experiment allows students to explore the process of osmosis in the membrane of a chicken egg.

Objectives
- To develop skills in observation.
- To use observations to make inferences about data.

Process Skills
- Observing
- Predicting
- Hypothesizing
- Comparing and contrasting
- Collecting data
- Graphing data
- Analyzing data

Activity Duration
Part A. 60 minutes
Part B. Four-day data collection

PART A
Egg Shape and Size

Background

Schmidt-Nielsen (1984) described a bird egg as a mechanical structure strong enough to hold the chick securely during development, yet weak enough to allow it to break out. The shell must also let in oxygen and let out carbon dioxide, yet be sufficiently impermeable to water to keep the contents from drying out. The shape and structure of an egg are determined by many factors, such as development, environment, and species. These relationships have been studied extensively. Eggs are made of various substances, such as protein, water, and lipids, and have a hard outer shell containing pores. The pores appear to be irregular in size and shape (page 233) and facilitate gas exchange for the survival of the chick.

As with many structures, there are limits to size for the egg. There have been experiments on the strength of eggshells, but ultimately the chick's survival is dependent on gas exchange efficiency. The largest egg that exists today belongs to the ostrich, and the smallest, as you might guess, belongs to the hummingbird. The now-extinct elephant bird has the record for the largest egg. Its giant egg weighed about 10 kg, ten times as much as an ostrich egg and 30,000 times as much as a hummingbird egg. A typical hen egg weighs about 65 grams, and after incubation of

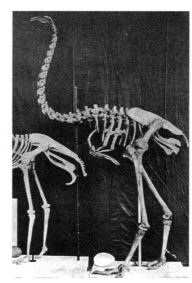

about 21 days a chick will hatch. During that time, the egg will give off as much as 4.5 liters of carbon dioxide, take in 6 liters of oxygen, and lose some of its total weight through water loss (Schmidt-Nielsen 1984). The rates of gas exchange and water loss are critical variables in the survival of the chick and limit the size of the egg.

In this activity students explore egg data collected by many different scientists (see the complete reference list on p. 229). Some of their experiments compared the altitude of the bird's habitat with the number of pores in an eggshell; factors, such as gas exchange, that determine the survival of an ostrich egg; the size of eggs versus bird body weight; and the relationships of eggs to clutch size. Relationships among various characteristics of eggs, such as thickness of shell, number of pores, incubation time, water loss, hatchability, and egg mass are investigated. Students will also model diffusion and osmosis, the necessary processes behind the survival of an egg.

Materials

Each group will need:

- Student Data Sheet 1
- Data tables and questions (Student Data Sheet 2)
- Graph paper
- Internet access or books on bird eggs

1. Elephant bird *(Aepyornis maximus)*; 2. Moa *(Dinornithiformes)*; 3. Ostrich *(Struthio camelus)*
4. Mute swan *(Cygnus olor)*; 5. Common guillemot *(Uria aalge)*; 6. Domestic chicken *(Gallus gallus)*;
7. Little owl *(Athene noctua)*; 8. Goldcrest *(Regulus regulus)*

Eggsactly
Answer Sheet

Engage

Give each pair of students an Egg Brainstorm Sheet (Student Data Sheet 1, p. 230). Have them investigate what they already know about eggs and eggshells, as they discuss the answers to the questions. When Student Data Sheet 1 is complete, discuss all the answers as a class. Have the students check their answers using books about eggs or the internet.

Explore

After the brainstorming session, give each student the set of data tables describing various characteristics of eggs (Student Data Sheet 2). This activity helps the students explore various parameters, such as eggshell thickness and number of pores (p. 231), which may affect factors such as hatchability or water loss. A typical hen egg has about 10,000 pores (Schmidt-Nielsen 1990). The data tables are divided into Parts A through F. If time is limited, you can put students into groups and have each group analyze a different data table. Parts A through C require the students to study the data tables, make graphs, analyze, and make conclusions about each egg characteristic. Graphs may be made on regular graph paper or on the computer. Graphs in Parts D through F need to be studied, compared, and contrasted before conclusions are made. The goal of this portion of the activity is for students not only to get practice making and analyzing graphs, but also to learn to take information from various sources to make "big picture" conclusions from the data analysis.

The data have been compiled and adapted from several sources, which can be found in the reference list on page 229.

Explain

After the students have completed the graphing, data analyses, and conclusions, compare their graphs and conclusions to examples of student explanations in Parts A to F.

Part A

Have the students study the data table containing information about the relationship between egg weight (percentage of bird body weight) and bird body weight and then make a *line graph*. Then have them analyze the graph and write conclusion statements about what they infer from the data.

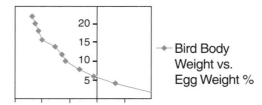

Source: Adapted from the data discussed in Schmidt-Nielsen.1984. *Scaling: Why is animal size so important?* Figure 4.2, p. 37.

Student explanation: An inverse relationship is revealed, showing that as body weight increases, egg weight (percentage of body weight) decreases.

Part B

Students should study the data table containing information about the relationship between egg weight (percentage of bird body weight) and incubation time, and then make a *line graph.*

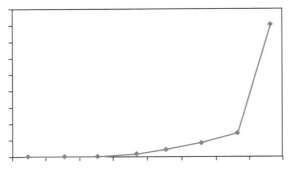

Source: Adapted from the data discussed in Schmidt-Nielsen 1984,
Scaling: Why is animal size so important? Figure 4.2, p. 37.

Student explanation: As egg weight (percentage of body weight) increases, the incubation time increases—an example of a direct relationship.

Part C

Students should study the data table about water loss at different altitudes and then make a line graph. Have students write a conclusion about the relationships that their line graph shows.

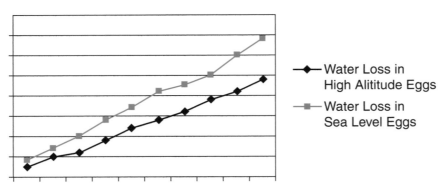

Source: Adapted from Rahn et al. 1977, with permission from authors.

Student explanation: Water loss occurs steadily over time. At lower altitudes, the rate of water loss is faster than it is at higher altitudes.

Eggsactly

Answer Sheet

Part D

Students should study the two graphs dealing with the effect of the number of pores in an eggshell and write a conclusion paragraph describing the data.

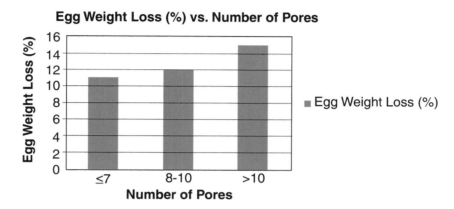

Egg Weight Loss (%) vs. Number of Pores

Source: Adapted from Gonzalez et al. 1999 with permission of the Poultry Science Assn., Inc.

Student explanation: Eggs lose weight as they lose water vapor and other gases over time. The more pores the eggs have, the greater the weight loss.

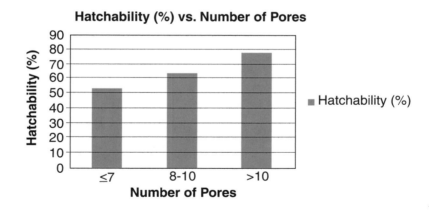

Hatchability (%) vs. Number of Pores

Source: Adapted from Gonzalez et al. 1999 with permission of the Poultry Science Assn., Inc.

Student explanation: The percentage of eggs that hatch is referred to as *hatchability.* The more pores, the greater the chance that the eggs will reach maturity and hatch.

Eggsactly

Part E

Students should study the set of two graphs dealing with the effect of eggshell thickness and write a conclusion paragraph describing the data.

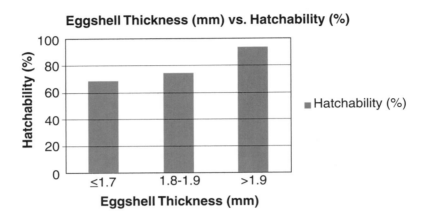

Eggshell Thickness (mm) vs. Hatchability (%)

Source: Adapted from Gonzalez et al. 1999 with permission of the Poultry Science Assn., Inc.

Student explanation: Thinner eggshells increase the proportion of eggs that reach maturity and hatch.

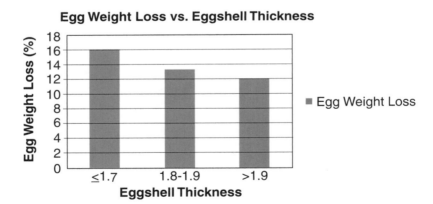

Egg Weight Loss vs. Eggshell Thickness

Source: Adapted from Gonzalez et al. 1999 with permission of the Poultry Science Assn., Inc.

Student explanation: The thinner the eggshell, the more weight loss an egg will experience.

Part F

Students should study the graph dealing with eggshell thickness and its relationship to egg volume. Have students write a conclusion paragraph describing the data.

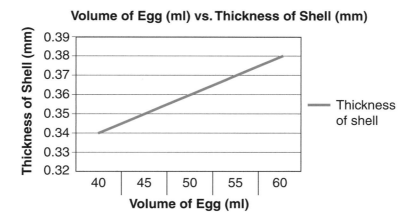

Volume of Egg (ml) vs. Thickness of Shell (mm)

Source: Adapted with permission from Romanoff and Romanoff. 1949, p. 151.

Student explanation: There is a direct relationship between the volume of the egg and the thickness of the eggshell: The larger the volume of the egg, the thicker the eggshell.

For more information and practice on how egg size is related to bird size and survival rates, refer to the works in the reference list.

References

Barta, Z., and T. Szekely. 1997. The optimal shape of avian eggs. *Functional Ecology* 11(5): 656–662.

Burley, R., and D. Vadehra. 1989. *The avian egg: Chemistry and biology.* New York: John Wiley.

Deeming, D. 2002. *Avian incubation.* Oxford, UK: Oxford University Press.

Gonzalez, A., D. Satterlee, F. Moharer, and G. Cadd. 1999. Factors affecting ostrich egg hatchability. *Poultry Science* 78: 1257–1262.

Rahn, H., C. Carey, K. Balmas, B. Bhatia, and C. Paganelli. 1977. Reduction of pore area of the avian eggshell as an adaptation to altitude. *Proceedings of the National Academy of Sciences of the United States of America* 74 (7): 3095–3098.

Romanoff, A. L., and A. J. Romanoff. 1949. *The avian egg.* New York: John Wiley.

Schmidt-Nielsen, K. 1984. Scaling: *Why is animal size so important?* New York: Cambridge University Press.

Schmidt-Nielsen, K. 1990. *Animal physiology:* Adaptation and environment.

229

New York: Cambridge University Press.

Seymour, R. 1979. Dinosaur eggs: Gas conductance through the shell, water loss during incubation, and clutch size. *Paleobiology* 5 (1): 1–11.

Weatherhead, P., and K. Teather. 1994. Sexual size dimorphism and egg-size allometry in birds. *Evolution* 48 (3): 671–678.

Extend

For further exploration, have students investigate other animals that lay eggs besides birds, such as insects, fish, reptiles, and amphibians. Encourage the students to research the platypus and echidna, two mammals that lay eggs.

Put slips of paper with the names of different non-avian egg-laying organisms into a bag or box. Mix up the slips and be sure to include two egg-laying mammals. Have each student (or pair of students) choose a slip, and ask them to become *eggsperts* about that particular organism's eggs. The student should research (in the library or on the internet) everything about his or her organism's type of eggs, egg-laying mode, and other characteristics.

Possible questions or facts to consider:

1. Considering shape, size, water loss, number of pores, and structure of the eggs of other types of organisms, how do they compare with chicken eggs?
2. How do shape and structure allow nutrients to enter the egg? Do all eggs need oxygen?
3. What is the duration of incubation?
4. How long do parents care for the eggs prior to hatching? After hatching?
5. What feeds on that type of egg?
6. Diagrams of internal structures or pictures of the eggs.
7. Facts about the egg-laying situation:
   - The male seahorse actually hatches the young.
   - The temperature of eggs in reptiles may affect the gender of the young.
8. More advanced students may want to explore the differences among oviparous, viviparous, and ovoviviparous.

For more information about different types of eggs:

- *www.eggsedu.org.uk/primary/ks1/ks1_whichanimaleggs.html*
- *http://en.wikipedia.org/wiki/Egg_(biology)*
- *www.manteno.k12.il.us/llacosse/egg.html*
- *www.thesolutionsite.com/lpnew_bin/UI_Metadata/public/22652*
- *www.exoticpetvet.net/reptile/rerepro.html*
- *www.wnrmag.com/stories/1996/apr96/frog.htm*

230

- *http://imnh.isu.edu/DIGITALATLAS/bio/amph/main/ameggid.html*
- *http://en.wikipedia.org/wiki/Egg_*(biology)
- *www.ucmp.berkeley.edu/mammal/monotreme.html*
- *www.backyardnature.net/ins_egg.htm*

Evaluate

Check for student understanding:

1. What is an egg?
2. What nutrients are needed for the egg to survive?
3. What is diffusion?
4. Describe the eggshell structure, and discuss how it facilitates diffusion.
5. What factors contribute to the survival of an egg?

231

Name _____

Discuss with a partner what you already know about eggs.
Answer the questions below:

What is an egg?

Name three different types of animals that lay eggs:

What is the smallest bird egg?

What is the largest bird egg?

What are eggs made of?

Do eggs breathe?   **Explain your answer:**

232

Name _____

Through several different experiments, scientists have studied birds and compiled information about the factors and characteristics of the bird egg and its structure. The amazing structure of the egg allows for the survival of a young chick by facilitating the movement of gases into and out of the egg. Study the data and graphs and explore the relationships among number of pores in the shell, weight of egg, incubation time, thickness of shell, and other factors. **Make graphs and answer questions when necessary to form your conclusions about these relationships.**

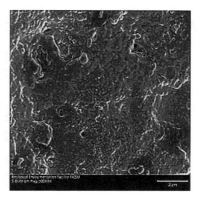

Scanning Electron Micrograph of Eggshell Pores.

Part A

Study the data table below containing information about the relationship between egg weight (percentage of bird body weight) and bird body weight and then make a line graph.

Analyze your graph and write a paragraph describing the data.

Body Weight of Bird (grams/Kg)	Egg Weight (% of body weight)
0.005	22
0.006	20
0.008	18
0.010	16
0.030	14
0.060	12
0.080	10
0.250	8
0.800	6
5.000	4
90.000	2

Part B

Study the data table (below) containing information about the relationship between egg weight (percentage of bird body weight) and incubation time, and then construct a line graph. Analyze your graph and write a paragraph describing the data.

Incubation Time (Days)	Body Weight (Kg)
10	0.005
20	0.6
30	2.0
40	10.0
50	60.0
60	100.0
70	200.0
80	800.0

Part C

Study the data table (below) about water loss at different altitudes and then make a line graph. Analyze your graph and write a paragraph describing the data.

Number of Days	Water Loss % High Altitude	Water Loss % Sea Level
1	0.25	0.4
2	0.5	0.7
3	0.6	1.0
4	0.9	1.4
5	1.2	1.7
6	1.4	2.1
7	1.6	2.3
8	1.9	2.5
9	2.1	3.0
10	2.4	3.4

Part D

Study the two graphs (below) dealing with the effect of the number of pores in an eggshell and write a conclusion paragraph describing the data.

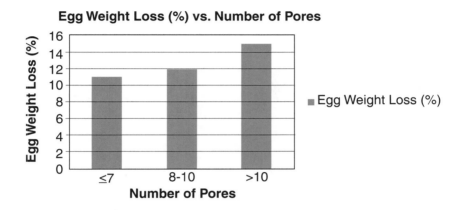

Egg Weight Loss (%) vs. Number of Pores

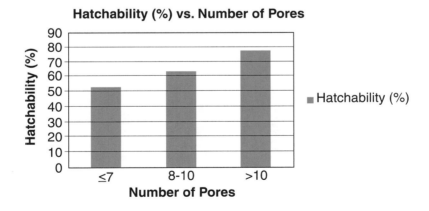

Hatchability (%) vs. Number of Pores

Part E

Examine the two graphs (below) dealing with the effect of eggshell thickness and write a conclusion paragraph describing the data.

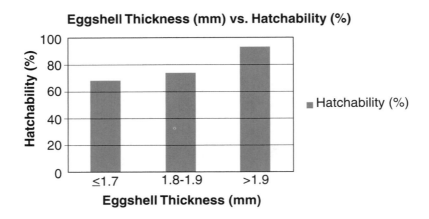

Eggshell Thickness (mm) vs. Hatchability (%)

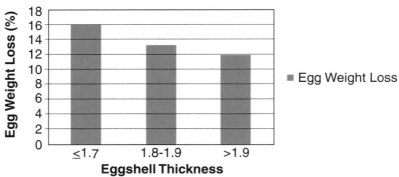

Egg Weight Loss vs. Eggshell Thickness

236

Student Data Sheet 2
Eggsactly

Part F

Study the graph (below) dealing with the eggshell thickness and its relationships to egg volume and write a paragraph describing the data

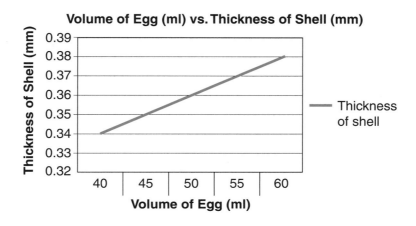

Volume of Egg (ml) vs. Thickness of Shell (mm)

Thickness of Shell (mm)

Volume of Egg (ml)

Thickness of shell

Questions

1. **If you had to design an egg, describe it in terms of number of pores, thickness, and volume. What would be the most successful combo?**

2. **What would you choose at sea level? Why?**

237

PART B
Osmosis in Eggs

Background
Just as humans need to take in nutrients and excrete waste products, so do each and every one of our cells. Some materials move in and out of our cells through the process of diffusion, moving from areas of high concentration to areas of low concentration. This process occurs naturally and without our cells having to use any energy. One important nutrient our cells need is water. Water can also move into and out of our cells. The membrane "selects" or allows certain particles to pass, while other particles may not pass because of size or other factors, until the cell reaches homeostasis. Part A explored how gases get into and out of eggshells through the pores. Eggs are also excellent models that demonstrate how osmosis occurs in our cells. Osmosis is the movement of water along a concentration gradient (flowing from high to low concentration). In other words, water will flow from an area where there are many water molecules to an area where there are not as many. This process occurs in our cells (or an egg) across a selectively permeable membrane until concentrations are balanced on both sides of the membrane or equilibrium is reached.

Depending on what type of solution a cell (or egg) is placed into, the egg may gain or lose water. When the solution outside the membrane is in equilibrium with the solution inside the membrane, it is referred to as an isotonic solution. If the solution that the egg is placed in has a lower number of dissolved particles (low solute concentration), then the water will diffuse into the membrane, causing the egg to bloat. This type of solution is referred to as a hypotonic solution. If a cell (or egg) is placed in a high-concentration solution, the water will diffuse out of the membrane and shriveling will result. This type of solution is referred to as a hypertonic solution. In this activity students will investigate osmosis in eggs over a four-day period.

Materials
Each group will need:

- Egg
- 500 ml beaker or clear plastic cup
- Large graduated cylinder
- White vinegar (250 ml)
- Aluminum foil
- Rubber band
- Corn syrup (250 ml)

238

- Distilled water (250 ml)
- Triple beam balance
- Student Data Sheet 3
- Graph paper
- Food coloring (any dark colors)

Note: Food coloring may be added to the water surrounding the egg in the beaker on the third day, just for a little added color to emphasize how particles move through pores in egg membrane.

Engage

Have a beaker of water sitting on top of on an overhead projector. Project the image of the beaker of water on a screen. Ask the students what would happen if you slowly put five drops of food coloring into the water. If you have not already discussed diffusion, give them a brief overview of how particles in water and air tend to move from an area of high concentration to an area of low concentration until equilibrium is reached. The food coloring drops are highly concentrated, and once in water they will disperse out until equilibrium is reached. Explain to the students that this process happens naturally without any help from you. You could ask the students to think of ways to speed up the process, and they may say "stir the water" or "heat the water."

Now that the students are aware that particles naturally mix with each other, as well as with water molecules, and can move and disperse, explain that substances in organisms' bodies must also disperse and move around. Just as we need to take nutrients into our bodies and excrete waste products, so do each and every one of our cells. One important nutrient that our cells need is water.

Eggs are good models of a cell because of their protective membranes, which allow particles (gases such as oxygen and carbon dioxide, as well as water vapor) to come and go. In Part A students learned that eggs need to take in oxygen and expel carbon dioxide. A certain amount of water loss must also take place for the eggs to survive to hatchability. The next section of the activity will address the movement of substances into and out of eggs.

Explore

To investigate how substances move into and out of an egg through the processes of diffusion and osmosis, students collect and analyze data over a four-day period. Have students form groups of four. Explain to them that this activity will extend over four days. They must set up different solutions for their eggs each day. Because eggs are fragile, students must take extra care not to drop or puncture their eggs.

239

DAY 1

Students obtain a 500 ml beaker and 250 ml of white vinegar. It is very important that the students follow the procedure set out on Student Data Sheet 3 to ensure that they collect all of the necessary data. The students take the mass of their eggs and make observations and record them in the data table. Pour 250 ml of vinegar into a beaker and slowly add the egg. Each group should cover the top of its beaker with aluminum foil and put a rubber band around the outside. Remind each group to label its beaker.

DAY 2

Students slowly remove the egg from the vinegar (letting the vinegar drain off as much as possible) and record its mass. Be sure to tell the students to record the volume of the remaining vinegar before they pour it out and to record observations of the egg and liquid on the data table. Ask them to describe what happened to the eggshell. The vinegar will have dissolved the hard portion of the eggshell, leaving only the egg membrane around the yolk. What has happened to the egg membrane? Is it soggy or bloated? Now the students rinse and dry the beaker and pour 250 ml of corn syrup into it. Carefully place the egg into the corn syrup and cover the beaker.

DAY 3

Students slowly remove the egg from the syrup (let syrup drain off) and record its mass. Be sure to tell the students to record the volume of the remaining syrup before they pour it out and to record observations of the egg and liquid on the data table. Rinse and dry the beaker and pour 250 ml of distilled water into the beaker. Carefully place the egg into the water and cover the beaker. See an example of an egg on day 3 in the photo on the right.

DAY 4

Students slowly remove the egg from the water and record its mass. Be sure to tell the students to record the volume of the remaining water before they pour it out and to record their observations of the egg and liquid on the data table. Students should discuss their findings with their group and answer the analysis questions at the conclusion of the activity.

Example of an egg on day 3, after the water has moved out of the egg and caused it to shrivel.

Explain

Over the course of four days, the solutions into which the eggs were placed caused the direction of the water flow to change. The direction of the water is determined by the diffusion of water along its concentration gradient. When the solution outside the membrane is in equilibrium with that inside the membrane, it is referred to as *an isotonic solution*. If the solution that the egg is placed in has a lower number of dissolved particles (more water), then the water will diffuse into the membrane, causing the egg to bloat. This type of solution is referred to as a *hypotonic solution*. If the solution that the egg is placed in has a higher number of dissolved particles (higher concentration of solute), then the water will diffuse out of the membrane, causing the egg to shrivel. This type of solution is referred to as *a hypertonic solution*. Discussing the types of solution may be more appropriate for older students. See the sample student data in the table below.

TABLE 1.
Sample Student Data

Day	Egg Mass (grams)	Liquid Volume (ml)	Observations
1	75	250	Egg average size, white eggshell
2	95	225	Eggshell gone, membrane intact, bloated
3	65	275	Egg shriveled and saggy
4	115	180	Egg bloated and smooth

Extend

Review with the students what they learned from both sections of this activity. Eggs come in different sizes, and their shells have various numbers of pores to allow gases to come and go through the process of diffusion. The membrane around the egg yolk also has pores that allow certain particles to come and go through the process of osmosis.

Have the students predict what they think would happen if they repeated Part B (egg osmosis) with eggs of different sizes, such as an ostrich egg (1,497 grams), turkey egg (100 grams), or quail egg (10 grams). See sample data on page 242:

241

Day	Turkey Egg Mass (grams)	Liquid Volume (ml)	Brown Hen Egg Mass (grams)	Liquid Volume (ml)	Japanese Quail Egg Mass (grams)	Liquid Volume (ml)	Bobwhite Quail Egg Mass (grams)	Liquid Volume (ml)
1	88.8	300	54.5	200	9.7	100	9.3	60
2	102.1	250	68.3	150	13	80	11.8	50
3	68.2	350	43.2	250	8.7	110	7.6	70
4	109.3	250	78.2	150	16.2	75	11.7	55

For more information using eggs as a model of osmosis:

- Cocanour, B., and A. Bruce. 1985. Osmosis and the marvelous membrane. *Journal of College Science Teaching* 15 (2): 127–130.
- *www.texashste.com/documents/curriculum/eggsperiment.pdf*
- *www.biologycorner.com/worksheets/observing_osmosis.html*
- *http://science-class.net/Biology/Osmosis.htm*
- *www.usoe.k12.ut.us/curr/science/sciber00/7th/cells/sciber/osmosis1.htm*
- *www.ratlab.co.uk/eggosmosis.htm*

Evaluate

Check for student understanding:

1. What is osmosis?
2. Why is an egg a good model for a cell?
3. What does it mean to be "selectively permeable"?
4. What determines which direction the water will flow inside the egg?
5. Name three different kinds of osmotic solutions and describe each.

Name _____

Osmosis in Eggs

Just as humans need to take in nutrients and excrete waste products, so do each and every one of our cells. Eggs are excellent models for the process of osmosis in cells. Osmosis is the movement of water along a concentration gradient (flowing from high to low concentration). In other words, water will flow from an area where there are many water molecules to an area where there are not as many. This process occurs in our cells (or an egg) across a selectively permeable membrane until solute concentrations balance on both sides of the membrane or equilibrium is reached.

Procedure

DAY 1

- Obtain a 500 ml beaker and 250 ml of white vinegar.
- Take the mass of the egg, make observations, and record in the data table.
- Pour 250 ml of vinegar into a beaker and slowly add the egg.
- Cover the top of the beaker with aluminum foil and put a rubber band around the outside. Label the foil over the beaker.

DAY 2

- Slowly remove the egg from the vinegar (letting the vinegar drain off as much as possible) and record its mass.
- **Take the volume of the remaining vinegar before pouring it out and record observations of the egg and liquid on the data table.**
- Rinse and dry the beaker and pour 250 ml of corn syrup into the beaker. Carefully place the egg into the corn syrup and cover the beaker.

DAY 3

- Slowly remove the egg from the syrup (let syrup drain off) and record its mass.
- **Take the volume of the remaining syrup before pouring it out and record observations of the egg and liquid on the data table.**
- Rinse and dry the beaker and pour 250 ml of distilled water into the beaker. Carefully place the egg into the water and cover the beaker.

243

DAY 4

- Slowly remove the egg from the water and record its mass.
- **Take the volume of the remaining water before pouring it out and record observations of the egg and liquid on the data table.**
- Discuss findings with your group and answer the analysis questions on the next page.

Data Table

Day	Egg Mass (grams)	Liquid Volume (ml)	Observations
1			
2			
3			
4			

Student Data Sheet 3
Eggsactly

Graphical Analysis

- Make a line graph to show changes in the volume of the liquid over the four-day data collection. Remember to include a title and label the axes.
- Make a bar graph to show how the egg's mass changed as the type of solution changed.
- Write a description of the relationship underneath each of the graphs.

Analysis Questions

1. **What was the purpose of putting the egg in vinegar?**

2. **Which direction did water molecules move when the egg was placed in syrup?**

3. **What did the egg look like after 24 hours of being immersed in syrup?**

4. **Which direction did water molecules move when the egg was placed in water? Draw a diagram to accompany your answer.**

245

5. **What did the egg look like after 24 hours of being immersed in water?**

6. What causes the water to move back and forth across the egg membrane?

7. Why is an egg a good model of how osmosis occurs in cells?

8. Can humans drink salt water? Why or why not?

9. What is the purpose of spraying vegetables with water at the grocery store?

10. Define the terms *isotonic*, *hypotonic*, and *hypertonic*. Relate these terms to the solutions used during this lab.

Chapter 19
Attack of the Giant Bug

Overview
Could a bug ever be the size of a Volkswagen Beetle? Could a dragonfly be larger than a seagull? Movies often portray huge creatures that roam the Earth and sometimes terrorize humans. Could these scenarios actually happen, and if so, how? This activity explores the scale of common arthropods such as spiders and insects by demonstrating that living things have limits to their size.

Objectives
- To develop skills in observation.
- To use observations to make inferences about limits to the size of organisms.

Process Skills
- Observing
- Predicting
- Hypothesizing
- Comparing and contrasting

Activity Duration
90 minutes

Background
All living organisms have size limits. For example, an organism's support structure and modes of movement depend on size (think of an elephant and an ant). Organisms' support structures (both endoskeletons and exoskeletons) must be optimized in an engineering sense: They must be strong and substantial enough to support and protect the organism but not so large and bulky that the organism collapses under the weight of the support structure! This consideration is one reason that there is a limit to the size of each type of organism.

The environment in which an organism lives on Earth, aquatic versus terrestrial, may also play a role in the type and size of these skeletons. The buoyancy of aquatic environments helps support the skeleton, and therefore aquatic animals may be much larger. Gas exchange can also limit size. Terrestrial life poses a continual conflict between the need for oxygen and the need for water because conditions that favor the entry of oxygen also favor the loss of water (Schmidt-Nielsen 1990). An insect's hard outer shell is a solution to this challenge.

The majority of insects obtain oxygen by diffusion through pores and tubes in their exoskeletons. Once again, the issue of limits to size presents a problem. If the insects become too large, diffusion cannot get enough oxygen into the organism. Why then have scientists found fossils of insects and other arthropods of gigantic proportions? Scientists have found evidence that Earth's earlier atmosphere had more oxygen. Recent geological models indicate a significant increase in atmospheric oxygen 300 million years ago (Carboniferous) and a subsequent drop during the Triassic. These changes in atmospheric oxygen have been thought to cause the appearance and extinction of giant insects (Klok and Harrison 2008). In this activity students will model limits to size in arthropods (such as insects) by attempting to build the biggest bug that can also support the most weight.

247

Materials

Each group will need:

- Small plastic bag or container to hold building materials
- 75–100 straws
- Roll of tape
- Box of small paper clips
- Construction paper (5 sheets)
- Colored pencils
- Washers (at least 50) or some type of weights
- Blank paper
- Scissors
- Internet access
- Reference books about insects, arthropods, and trees (extension activity)
- Two or three video clips of movies with large insects (such as *Harry Potter and the Chamber of Secrets* or *Mothra*)

Examples of washers that could be used for weights.

Notes: In the interest of fair competition, the bag or container for each student group should contain the same amount of materials. Completing *Captivating Cubes* (chapter 17) prior to this activity may help the students with the concept of diffusion.

Optional: Prizes may be given to the groups that build the largest bug and the bug that can support the most weight. A criterion can also be devised to measure the best combination of height and weight-carrying capacity.

Engage

First show the students two or three video clips from movies that feature some type of giant insect or spider. Ask the students to observe the characteristics of these large organisms, for example, *How do they move? What color are they? How large are they in meters? (In feet?) Could they exist? Why or why not?*

Next lead the students to discuss the characteristics of insects and spiders as a class:

- Exoskeleton made of hard material (chitin)
- Jointed appendages
- Number of appendages
- Two versus three body segments
- The mechanism in which a spider or insect "grows" in size
- How spiders and insects breathe

Could the creatures in the video clips really exist? Have the students write a few sentences answering this question in as much detail as possible. Generate a list on the board of the kinds of answers, such as "too big," "too heavy," "couldn't move," and so on. Encourage the students to think about the facts that the exoskeleton is on the outside of the bug's body and that the weight has to be held up and moved around at the same time. What happens when you move around at a fast pace? You eventually start to breathe faster. How do spiders and insects breathe? How would they breathe if they were as large as the movie creatures?

Allow the students to come to the conclusion that living organisms have limits to their size for various reasons. Insects and spiders must be able to carry and support the weight of their exoskeletons, as well as get oxygen into their bodies through diffusion. If these creatures were as large as cars, their legs would buckle under their own weight, and they would not get sufficient oxygen deep within their bodies.

Explore

Bug Olympics Competition

Give each group of two or three students a large bag or container of Bug Olympics materials and the Student Data Sheet, stating the rules and regulations for how to construct their insects.

Objective

To build the tallest insect that can also hold the most weight.

Rules and Regulations

- Every group has the same amount of building materials.
- Building materials consist of only straws, paper clips, tape, washers, and construction paper.
- Scissors may be used to cut the building materials.
- All insects must be anatomically correct (three pairs of legs, three body segments, antennae).
- Length of antennae will not be counted in overall height of insect.
- Insect legs must remain six separate appendages and cannot be taped to the table for added support.
- Be sure to have a place on the insect for the weights to be placed.
- Name your insect.
- Time limit: 10 minutes to discuss and sketch on blank paper a design of the insect and 30 minutes to construct the insect.

249

Once time has been called, all students must stop building and return all unused materials to their containers. Have the students come forward with their insects by group. Have one student put the name of the group's bug on the chalkboard or overhead. Using a ruler or meter stick, have the students measure the height and width of their insects in centimeters and record. Then add weights or washers to the back of the bug one by one, as the class counts, until the bug falls over or buckles.

Tally the number of weights that the insect can hold before falling over or buckling under the weight, and record it beside the name of the insect on the blackboard. As each group writes their information on the board or overhead, each student should record it on the Judges' Table on the Student Data Sheet. After all the groups have competed in the Bug Olympics, judge which bug was the tallest and withstood the most weight without falling over or buckling. Discuss the outcome of the competition with the class and have the students complete the questions on the Student Data Sheet.

Explain

Living organisms have limits to their size. The body's materials and architecture are factors that determine its size limits. Both types of skeleton, endoskeleton and exoskeleton, must be able to support the organism. As the prefixes suggest, endoskeletons are found on the inside of an organ-

ism (like our human skeletons), and exoskeletons are support structures on the outside of an organism such as an insect. However, the organism must be able to handle the weight of these structures as size increases, and that is one reason there are limits to size. Bones must be able to support the weight of an animal. As an animal gets larger, the diameter of the bones must increase disproportionately (Schmidt-Nielsen 1990). That is why large, heavy land animals, such as elephants and rhinoceroses, have relatively thick, stocky bones, compared to humans, deer, or mice.

Some scientists have studied the relationship between supportive tissue mass (muscles and skeleton) and total body mass. Anderson, Rahn, and Prange (1979) concluded that supportive tissue makes up a larger fraction of the total mass in organisms with external skeletons than in those with internal skeletons. In addition, they found a significant correlation between spiders' exoskeletal mass and their overall body mass. Different support structures scale optimally to resist various types of stress, such as elastic buckling, bending, or torsion (Prange 1977). There are differences in skeleton structure and scaling between terrestrial and aquatic species. Terrestrial life poses a continual conflict between the need for oxygen and the need for water because conditions that favor the entry of oxygen also favor the loss of water (Schmidt-Nielsen 1990). Insects' hard outer shells are an answer to this issue.

In all three types of arthropods (insects, crustaceans, and arachnids), breathing is associated with diffusion of oxygen into the organism. Many insects breath through tracheae, which are tiny tubes connected to pores in the exoskeleton; aquatic arthropods have gills; and arachnids have book lungs. But no matter what the mechanism, diffusion plays a role. Completing *Captivating Cubes* before this activity could facilitate students' understanding of diffusion and how the surface area-to-volume relation may propose limits to size. Huge arthropods have adapted interesting solutions to the problems posed by their size. In a study of tracheal tubes in four beetle species, X-rays showed that the larger beetle species devote a disproportionately greater fraction of their bodies to tracheal tubes than do smaller species (Argonne National Laboratory 2007). Owen (2007) describes scientists' discovery of a large scorpion (2.5 meters long) that existed 390 million years ago and a 2 meter long millipede.

For more information about arthropods and exoskeletons refer to the works in the reference list.

References

Anderson, J., H. Rahn, and H. Prange. 1979. Scaling of supportive tissue mass. *Quarterly Review of Biology 54 (2): 139–148.*

Argonne National Laboratory. 2007. X-ray images help explain limits to insect body size. Media Center. *www.anl.gov/Media_Center/News/2007/news070809.html.*

Klok, C., and J. Harrison. 2008. Atmospheric hypoxia limits selection for large body size in insects. Nature Precedings. *http://precedings.nature.com.*

Owen, J. 2007. Giant sea scorpion discovered: Was bigger than a man. *http://news.nationalgeographic.com/news/2007/11/071121-giant-scorpion.html.*

Prange, H. 1977. The scaling and mechanics of arthropod exoskeletons. *In Scale effects in animal locomotion,* ed. T. J. Pedley, 169–181. New York: Academic Press.

Schmidt-Nielsen, K. 1990. *Animal physiology: Adaptation and environment.* New York: Cambridge University Press.

251

Extend

To explore further the limits to size in organisms, have the students research the tallest, oldest, and largest plants and trees (such as the California redwoods and sequoias).

1. What are the main parts of a tree? (Compare and contrast the terms as you define.)
   a. Leaves
   b. Bark (What are the layers?)
   c. Buds
   d. Roots
   e. Canopy
   f. Xylem
   g. Phloem

2. How does water travel from the soil to the tree canopy?
3. What is transpiration?
4. What is turgor pressure?
5. What type of environment is needed for a tree to grow?
6. How do adhesion and cohesion apply to how a tree moves water from the soil against gravity?

For more information about limits to tree size:

Koch, G, S. Sillet, G. Jennings, and S. Davis. 2004. The limits to tree height. *Nature* 428: 851–854.

Enquist, B., G. West, E. Charnov, and J. Brown. 1999. Allometric scaling of production and life-history variation in vascular plants. *Nature* 401: 907–911.

Woodruff, D., B. Bond, and F. Meinzer. 2004. Does turgor limit growth in tall trees? *Plant Cell Environment* 27: 229–236.

EVALUATE

Check for student understanding:

1. What is an arthropod?
2. Name two limits to the size of arthropods.
3. How do bugs get oxygen?
4. Why do you suppose aquatic arthropods can be larger than terrestrial ones?
5. How could large ancient bugs found in fossils have existed?
6. What does the relationship of surface area to volume have to do with the sizes of organisms?

Name _____

Bug Olympics Competition

Objective

To build the tallest insect that can also hold the most weight.

Rules and Regulations

- Every group has same amount of building materials.
- Building materials consist of only straws, paper clips, tape, and construction paper.
- Scissors may be used to cut the building materials.
- All insects must be anatomically correct (three pairs of legs, three body segments, antennae).
- Length of antennae will not be counted in the overall height of the insect.
- Insect legs must remain six separate appendages and cannot be taped to the table for support.
- Be sure to have a place on the insect for the weights to be placed.
- Name your insect.
- Time limit: 10 minutes to discuss and sketch on blank paper a design of the insect and 30 minutes to construct the insect.

Judges' Table

Name of Insect	Height (cm)	Width (cm)	Number of Washers	RANK

253

Questions

1. What is an arthropod?

2. What are the two types of skeletons found in organisms? Give examples.

3. Name two limits to the size of arthropods.

4. What are three differences between insects and spiders?

5. How do bugs obtain oxygen?

6. Why do you suppose aquatic arthropods can be larger than terrestrial arthropods?

7. How could the large ancient bugs found in fossils have existed?

8. What does the relationship of surface area to volume have to do with the sizes of organisms?

Optional: ** If you were to build your bug again, what would you do differently and why?

254

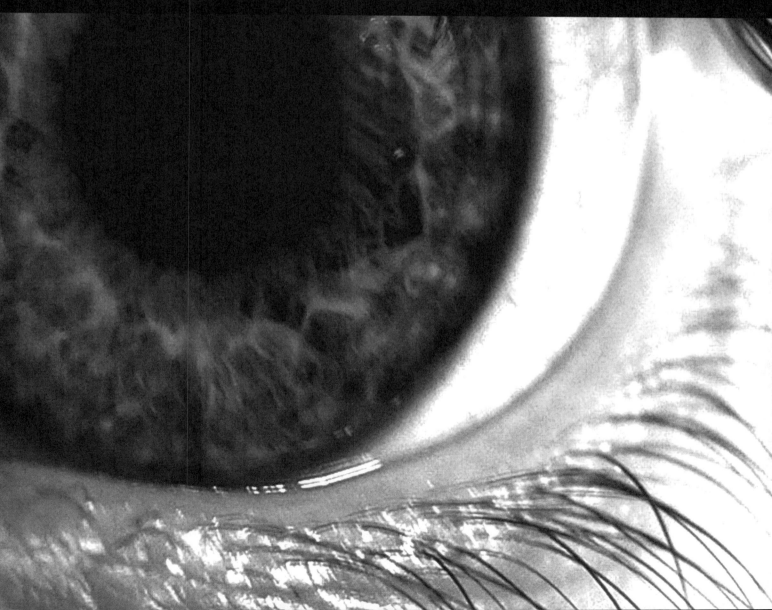

BEHAVIORS & SCALE

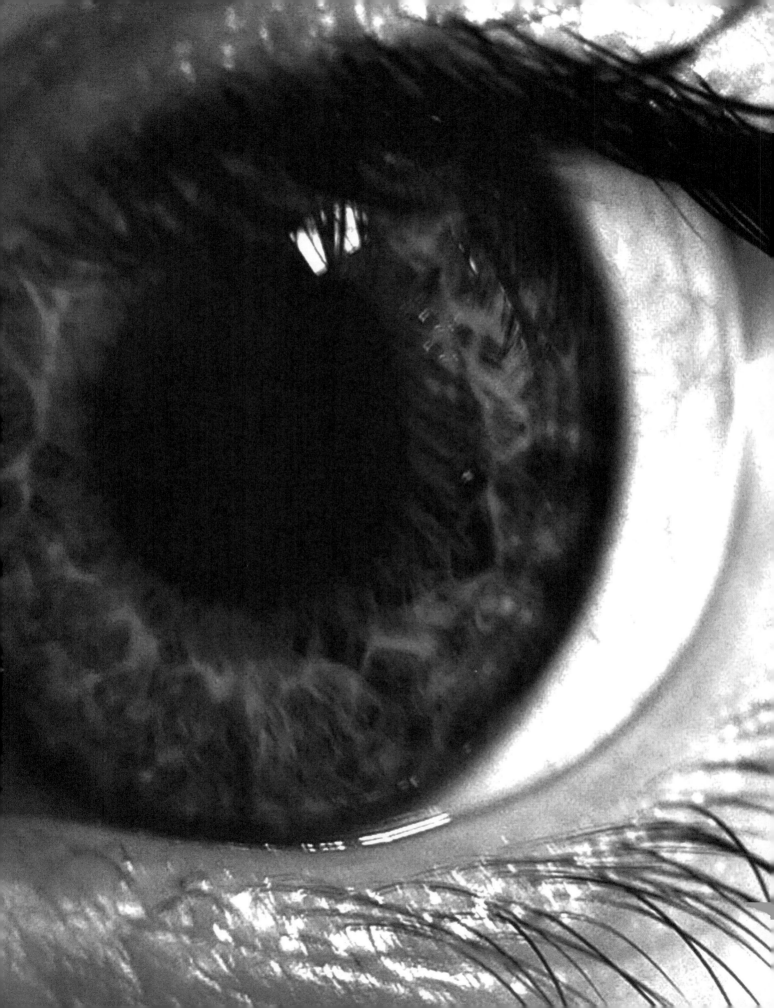

Chapter 20
Flying Foam: The Scale of Forces

Overview

The forces that are important for very large objects can be quite different than the forces that are important for very small objects. A planet is essentially unaffected by all but the gravitational force, whereas a molecule experiences mostly chemical bonding forces and is almost completely unaffected by gravity. In the human-scale world, we also see differences in how large and small objects are affected by forces. Why is an ant able to walk upside down on a ceiling but an elephant cannot? This exercise introduces students to the concept of scale-dependent properties as they explore how the size of objects changes their behavior.

Note: This activity is adapted from previous work by the authors, *Nanoscale science: Activities for grades 6–12*, M. G. Jones et al., NSTA Press, 2007.

Objective

To describe scale-dependent properties.

Process Skills

- Observing
- Measuring
- Predicting

Activity Duration

60 minutes

Background

The objects in the world around us are bound by the laws of physics to obey certain rules. They are affected by a variety of forces: fundamental forces such as gravity and electromagnetic interactions, as well as mechanical interactions such as friction and air resistance. As objects get larger or smaller, they still must obey all of these rules, but some rules may become more important than others. In this example, students explore how the effect of wind resistance is profoundly influenced by an object's size. The investigation is a concrete example of a switch in dominance between two competing properties (inertia and wind resistance) with the changing size of an object. In addition, this investigation provides a clear example of the importance of the scaling of the surface-to-volume ratio as objects get smaller or larger.

Materials

Each group will need:

- A set of four or five Styrofoam balls ½, 1, 2, 3, and 4 inches in diameter. The particular diameters are not important, as long as there are some at 1 inch and below (the smaller the better), some above 3 inches, and some in between.

259

- Ruler
- Balance
- Open area to throw balls across the room. This is preferably done indoors to avoid the effects of wind outside. School hallways or gyms are ideal locations.

ENGAGE

Divide students into groups of two or three and provide each group with a set of Styrofoam balls. Have the students determine the density of each ball. The density of the balls should be consistent (within 10% to 20%). Density can be determined by measuring the mass of each ball and dividing by the volume. This verifies that although the balls are of different sizes, they are otherwise the same (same material, same density). Density of Styrofoam should fall in the range of 0.01 g/cm^3 to 0.03 g/cm^3. Record all information in the data table in Student Data Sheet 1.

Helpful Hint: The density of the Styrofoam used to test this exercise was roughly 0.03 g/cm^3.

The students will then move to a clear area in which to throw the balls horizontally. They should predict which ball will travel the farthest. **After their predictions, ask the students to observe whether they see obvious deceleration due to wind resistance.** This will be most obvious with the smallest ball, especially if it is smaller than 1 inch. Most strikingly, they will not be able to throw the smallest ball very far. The students should make observations to determine where they see the most pronounced indication of wind resistance. One way to contrast clearly the behavior of each ball is to put two or more balls of different sizes in the hand together and throw them simultaneously (probably best underhand). In this case, all the balls start out with the same initial velocity, and the contrast of the effects of air resistance is most obvious. Keep in mind that in the absence of air resistance (i.e., in a vacuum), all balls should travel just as far (and fast) given the same initial throw.

Explain

The mass of an object is proportional to its volume (mass equals density multiplied by volume). The force of gravity on an object, or its *weight*, is proportional to mass and therefore proportional to its volume. Mass is also a measure of an object's *inertia*: its resistance to changing velocity under external forces. Drag forces (wind resistance) on a ball or any object flying through the air are proportional to the *surface area* of the object. So when a ball is thrown through

260

the air, there are two competing effects: The drag force, which is proportional to the object's area, is slowing the object down, and the inertia, which is proportional to volume, resists changes in velocity. How quickly an object slows down (its deceleration) is given simply by the ratio of the drag force to the inertia (mass).

Deceleration = Drag force/ Inertia = (C × Area × Velocity)/ (Density × Volume)

Surface Area of a Sphere:
$$A = 4 \pi r^2$$

Volume of a Sphere:
$$V = (4/3) \pi r^3$$

C is a coefficient that depends on the fluid the object is moving through and the particular shape of the object. For this exercise, all Styrofoam balls are roughly the same shape (spherical) and are moving through the same fluid (air), so this coefficient will be the same for all. It should also be noted that drag forces become proportional to the square of the velocity at higher velocities (for a car moving at 60 mph or a skydiver in free fall for example).

Styrofoam happens to be of the correct density such that we can observe a crossover from the dominance of inertia (for larger balls 3 or 4 inches in diameter) to the dominance of viscous drag, or air resistance (for balls of well below 1 inch in diameter). For very small pieces of Styrofoam (< ¼ inch) we will see a complete dominance of viscous drag.

Extend

Have students complete Student Data Sheet 2 for an extension activity. The deceleration of an object thrown at a particular velocity will be proportional to the ratio of area to volume (for objects made of a given material, the smaller the object, the larger the deceleration). The ratio of deceleration of ball 1 to ball 2 will be the inverse ratio of their respective radii.

Deceleration Ball 1/Deceleration Ball 2 = Radius Ball 2/ Radius Ball 1

Put simply, what we see in this exercise is that the laws of physics that are most important to a particular system depend on the size of that system. This is especially true when one important property or force depends on volume (such as mass or inertia) and another property depends on surface area (such as wind resistance).

Evaluate

Check for student understanding:

1. Define mass, volume, and density.
2. What is wind resistance?
3. How do mass, volume, and density affect how far an object can be thrown?
4. What causes an object to decelerate?
5. What is the relationship among deceleration of an object, air resistance, and mass of an object?
6. How do you think mass and wind resistance affect an airplane? An ocean liner?
7. An ocean liner and a kayak are moving through the water next to each other at the same speed. The ocean liner turns off its engines and the kayaker stops paddling at the same time. Who goes farther through the water before stopping? Why?

262

Name _____

Problem
How far can you throw Styrofoam balls of different sizes? How fast can you throw them? Is there a difference in behavior between big and small balls? Why?

Prediction
I predict that I will be able to throw the _____ ball the farthest.
I predict that I will be able to throw the _____ ball the fastest.

Materials
Styrofoam balls (½, 1, 2, 3, and 4 inches in diameter)

Calculations
- Determine the mass, volume, and density.
- Record your calculations in the Data Table.

Prediction
Predict which ball will travel the farthest.

Process
Toss each ball three times and record the distance traveled. Discuss your results with your group in light of your prediction.

Data Table

Ball Size	Mass	Volume	Density	Prediction (Which will go farthest?)	Toss 1 Distance	Toss 2 Distance	Toss 3 Distance
½ inch ball							
1 inch ball							
2 inch ball							
3 inch ball							
4 inch ball							

263

Conclusions

1. Which was the largest ball on which you saw a clear effect of wind resistance?

2. Is the reason that the small ball slows down more (has larger deceleration) that it experiences greater wind resistance?

3. How would this exercise be different if we used objects of the same sizes but made of stone? Would you see the effect of wind resistance? Why?

264

Name _____

Challenge Problem

You have two Styrofoam balls, one 5 inches in diameter and the other 1 inch in diameter. Answer the following questions about them:

1. **What is the ratio of the masses of the two balls (mass of large ball over mass of small ball)?**

2. **If you throw them both at the same speed, which ball experiences higher air resistance? Why? What is the ratio of air resistance experienced by the large ball to that experienced by the small ball?**

3. **Which decelerates more? Why? What is the ratio of deceleration of the large ball to that of the small ball?**

Hints
- Air resistance is proportional to the surface area of an object.
- Deceleration of an object is proportional to the ratio of the air resistance to the mass of the object.

265

Chapter 21
Stick With It

Objectives

- To visualize differences in surface area-to-volume relationships and electrostatic forces.
- To predict how the behavior of materials differs across different scales.

Process Skills

- Observing
- Predicting
- Comparing and contrasting
- Collecting data
- Analyzing data

Activity Duration

40 minutes

Background

One of the challenges that scientists face when doing research at the extreme ends of scale is that materials may behave differently than they do at human scales. At the smallest of scales, counterintuitive properties emerge. Not only do properties such as mass, volume, and surface area change, but properties such as color, conductivity, magnetization, and hardness also change as an object becomes small and approaches the nanometer scale. For example, the color of semiconductor quantum dots can be changed continuously by altering nothing but the size of the particle.

At the nanoscale, properties of objects are dramatically different from those at the macroscale. These properties include *bumpiness;* things tend to be *bumpy* rather than *smooth*. *Bumpiness* not only refers to geometrical bumpiness but also includes bumpiness in the magnetic, electronic, optical, and mechanical properties. *Stickiness* takes over at the nanoscale, and everything sticks together; gravity is irrelevant. At this scale relevant forces include the van der Waals forces, hydrogen bonding, hydrophobic bonding, and so on. For very tiny objects at the nanoscale, *shakiness* dominates; everything shivers and shakes and nothing stands still.

This lesson examines how the behavior of materials changes with changes in size. In this investigation students use different sizes of Styrofoam to explore how size affects the degree to which it sticks to plastic. It is recommended that students complete *Captivating Cubes* and *Sweet!* activities, which explore surface area-to-volume relationships, before turning to this investigation.

267

Materials

Each group will need:

- Plastic transparency film or other plastic sheeting
- Graph paper
- Styrofoam block (one 25 cm block per group)
- Plastic knife, dissecting kit, or similar tool

Engage

Imagine taking a crystal such as a ruby, cutting it in half, and seeing the color of the entire rock dramatically change—from red to blue. This process occurs at the nanoscale (a billionth of a meter) when quantum dots change size. Ask your students to think about how this can occur.

Quantum dots are nanometer-sized particles composed of metal or semi-conductor materials that exhibit the unusual characteristic of changing color as the material changes size. The larger the dot, the redder the light that is emitted. The smaller the dot, the shorter the wavelength of light, and the more the color moves into the blue range. Simply by changing the size of the quantum dot, a rainbow of colors can be produced. It is important to note that the material itself is the same—the only change is in the size of the material.

Researchers are investigating quantum dots as possible new indicators for drugs or pollutants. Invite students to think of new ways that quantum dots could be used to solve an existing problem or to make an existing technology more efficient.

Explore

At very large or very small scales, materials often behave in unexpected ways. This activity explores the behavior of Styrofoam when the size changes.

Using a small bag of tiny Styrofoam beads (beanbag chairs are a good source of small beads), demonstrate the electrostatic attraction of the beads to the plastic by opening the bag and dumping out the beads on an overhead projector. Point out the number of beads that stick to the plastic bag and do not fall out when the bag is turned upside down. Ask students to discuss in their groups why this happens. After the groups share their ideas, ask if slightly larger Styrofoam bits would show the same behavior. *What experiences have you had with sticky Styrofoam packing materials?* Ask the students to consider whether or not there is a particle size large enough that all of the particles would fall out of the bag.

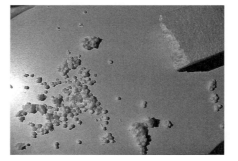

NATIONAL SCIENCE TEACHERS ASSOCIATION

Is there a relationship between the size of Styrofoam samples and the degree to which it adheres to plastic? Challenge each group to design a set of experiments to determine whether the size of the Styrofoam particles will predict whether or not they stick to plastic. Provide each group with a set of materials they can use to design their experiment (plastic sheeting, paper, graph paper, rulers, Styrofoam blocks, and a tool for cutting and manipulating the Styrofoam).

Remind the students to record their procedures and to create data tables to record their results. Ask them to discuss all the different ideas before deciding on one set of procedures for their experiment. (You may want to designate a recorder, discussion leader, presenter, and materials manager for each group.)

Students can either independently design the experiment to test whether or not there is a relationship between the behavior of the Styrofoam material and the size of the sample, or they can complete the investigation as described below. Inexpensive Styrofoam packing material can easily be broken into chunks. The ideal type of Styrofoam is the type that is composed of round pellets that are easily teased apart.

- *Samples 1 and 2: Large and small single beads.* Instruct the students to use a plastic knife or dissecting knife to tease the Styrofoam block into individual beads. Separate large and small single beads into different piles for individual tests. A sample of 10 to 20 beads works well. Place each sample of 10 beads on a slightly folded sheet of paper for transfer to the plastic testing sheet. Rub a piece of silk or small sample of fur back and forth across a transparency sheet to promote an electrostatic charge. Dump the sample of small beads on the film. Gently grasp opposing sides of the film and turn the film vertical. Record the number of beads that adhere to the plastic sheet. Scrape off the beads and start the process over with the large beads (see Table 1, p. 270).

- *Sample 3: Two-bead pieces.* For sample 3, tease samples of two beads from the Styrofoam block. Once a group has obtained at least 10 samples of two-bead pieces, test the samples on the transparency film. Be sure to remind the students to use the silk or fur to charge the plastic sheet after each trial.

- *Sample 4: Three-bead pieces.* Using the same process as with the other samples, students should tease apart Styrofoam samples composed of three beads stuck together. At least 10 three-bead clumps are needed. Students should record the number of three-bead pieces that adhere to the plastic sheeting.

- *Sample 5: Four-bead pieces.* Repeat the process with samples of four-bead pieces.

269

TABLE 1.
Sample Electrostatic Tests

Pretest Sample (Horizontal)				
1 Bead, Small	1 Bead, Large	2-Bead Clusters	3-Bead Clusters	4-Bead Clusters
10 beads	10 beads	10 clusters of 2 beads	10 clusters of 3 beads	10 clusters of 4 beads
Posttest Sample (After Vertical Test)—Number Remaing				
7 beads	5 beads	3 clusters of 2 beads	1 cluster of 3 beads	0 clusters of 4 beads

Explain

Ask the students, *Why did the Styrofoam adhere to the plastic?* After groups share their ideas, explain that when different types of materials come in close contact (as with the silk rubbing against the plastic sheeting), negatively charged electrons move from one material to another. This movement of electrons can result in one material having an excess of electrons, and as a consequence the material is negatively charged. The material that loses electrons becomes positively charged. The charged material has what is called *static electricity*. When the negatively charged material encounters a positively charged material, there is an attraction, and the materials may cling together. If a large amount of charge accumulates, a spark may result when two differently charged materials come into contact with each other.

In the experiments the students conducted, the plastic becomes negatively charged when the silk is rubbed on it. Silk tends to give off its electrons when rubbed, and these negative charges adhere to the plastic. This is known as *the triboelectric effect* (*tribo* means *rub* in Greek). The negative charges on the plastic attract the Styrofoam particles. The Styrofoam does not necessarily need a net positive charge for the attraction to occur. Because every particle has both positive and negative charges within it, the positive and negative charges in the Styrofoam tend to align themselves such that the positive charges are closer (in a sense) to the negatively charged surface. The particles are in this way *polarized* and attracted to the negative charge.

What makes this experiment a challenge is that there are both gravitational and electrostatic forces acting on the Styrofoam samples. In addition, there is a surface area-to-volume effect that influences the stickiness of the particles. The charge is held on the surface of the Styrofoam sample, and on small particles there is a larger surface area-to-volume ratio, so there is more charge per volume compared with a larger sample.

The electrostatic forces are greater than the gravitational forces for the very small particles. As the samples become increasingly large, the gravitational force has a greater influence than the electrostatic force, and the samples fall off when the plastic is held vertically.

For more information:

Quantum Dots
- *www.llnl.gov/str/Lee.html*
- *http://en.wikipedia.org/wiki/Quantum_dot*

Electrostatic Forces
- *http://library.thinkquest.org/CR0211620/static.html*
- *www.sciencemadesimple.com/static.html*
- *http://science.howstuffworks.com/vdg1.htm*
- *www.teachersource.com*

Extend

Explore the same process by charging a comb with fur or silk and then testing the electrostatic attraction of the comb on different sizes of paper, using very small to larger paper strips.

Another investigation that explores the influence of two different forces on a sample can be done with magnets. Students can compare the effects of magnetism and gravity on samples of different sizes. There is a point at which the gravitational pull on the mass of the sample will exceed the magnetic pull, and the object will fall off the magnet. This phenomenon can be explored by hanging a magnet from a wire and then attaching paper clips in a chain to the magnet. There is a point at which the gravitational pull on the mass of the paper clip chain will exceed the magnetic pull on the paper clip chain.

271

Further Extensions

Encourage students to research new inventions that take advantage the differences that exist in the behaviors of materials at very small scales. For example, engineers have created a robot that can climb the walls by using electro-adhesion (static electricity). For further information see *http://gizmodo. com/392110/robot-climbs-walls-with-static-electricity.*

Other researchers are studying how lizards use van der Waals forces to stick to walls and ceilings. Gecko lizards have very tiny, hairlike projections, known as *setae*, on their toes. These tiny setae have millions of tiny hairs that provide enough adhesive force for geckos to climb virtually anything because of van der Waals forces. These forces become significant only at very small scales, and that is why the small size of the setae is vital for a gecko's climbing ability. Scientists have nanofabricated artificial setal tips from different materials and observed the strong adhesive properties due to their size and shape, potentially leading to the manufacture of the first dry adhesive microstructures (Autumn et al. 2002).

Evaluate

Check for student understanding:

1. What does it mean to say that something has a large surface area to volume?
2. Which has a greater surface area-to-volume ratio: a large pea or a small pea?
3. What is static electricity?
4. Why do things with static charge tend to cling to other things?
5. A huge explosion occurred in the silo of a giant flour factory. The explosion occurred when the flour was being poured into the silo. What process could have occurred that would have caused the explosion?

Reference

Autumn, K., M. Sitti, Y. Liang, A. Peattie, W. Hansen, S. Sponberg, T. Kenny, R. Fearing, J. Israelachvili, and R. Full. 2002. Evidence for van der Waals adhesion in gecko setae. *Proceedings of the National Academy of Sciences of the United States of America* 99: 12252–12256.

272

Chapter 22
Fractals: Self-Similar at Different Scales

Overview

Lines, circles, squares, triangles—these geometrical objects belong to an ancient system of geometry that dates back more than 2,000 years to the Greek mathematician Euclid. Euclidian geometry is an effective tool for describing and measuring most of the shapes of objects in the world. However, a relatively new system of geometry, called fractal geometry, describes objects found in the natural world that have more complex shapes. These shapes seem to defy geometrical categorization. The shapes of coastlines, the branching of trees, or the leaf patterns of ferns are examples of fractal structures. Fractal geometry enables researchers to analyze complex shapes of natural objects and compare one system to another. It helps us define structure in new and useful ways. Moreover, if an object in a geological or biological context has fractal geometry, it informs how that system was formed or grew. So the fractal analysis provides clues about how things in the world are made. Fractals are fun, and once you learn the rules for making a fractal, you can make up your own!

Objectives

- Investigate the properties of fractals.
- Define fractal geometry.
- Develop skills in creating fractals.
- Calculate the fractal dimension of an object.

Process Skills

- Observing
- Inferring
- Predicting
- Analyzing data

Activity Duration

1 hour

Background

The new system is called *fractal geometry*, and its basic form can be easily described to middle school and high school students. One of the hallmarks of a fractal structure is that it shows *self-similarity*. *Self-similarity* simply means that the object has geometrical features that reappear at different scales. Simply put, as you change scale, or zoom in, the pattern of the fractal object looks the same at different scales. Fractal geometry has helped us categorize and quantify the shapes of objects that were previously too complex to evaluate. Of course, the subject of fractal geometry can be quite sophisticated and can involve very advanced mathematics. However, some mathematical manipulations that help students understand fractals are quite simple. Furthermore, simply making drawings or constructing models is perhaps the best way to explore the idea of self-similarity. Fractals provide a wonderful way to introduce students to a different way of thinking about math and geometry.

273

Materials

For each student:

- Student Sheets
- Pencils/pens
- Unlined paper
- Graph paper
- Ruler
- Construction paper
- Scissors

Engage

Show the students several visual examples of both natural and algorithmically (computer) generated fractals. You can use web resources to find the examples (there are links on p. 285 that may be helpful). Some examples of natural fractals are ferns, branching trees, snowflakes, river paths, coastlines, and so on. Have students brainstorm ideas about what is similar about these objects. What shapes do they have? Can we use our familiar shape categories (e.g., squares, triangles, cubes) to define them?

For more advanced students, introduce the idea of self-similarity, as explained above. For younger students, explain that sometimes patterns or shapes occur within an object at different scales. A fern is a typical example of a natural fractal. Its overall frond shape is repeated at smaller and smaller scales. Natural fractals have a limit to how many levels of self-similarity they can have (ferns have perhaps three or four levels). In contrast, mathematical fractals have infinite levels of self-similarity. Contrast fractal-like objects with nonfractal objects, such as simple geometrical shapes (an individual solid square or circle).

A Simple Fractal: The Letter L

The best way to gain understanding of fractals is to simply look at an example. Building fractals is a great way to introduce the concept of "algorithms." An algorithm is simply a recipe or a series of instructions. In the case of fractals, the algorithm is quite simple. You repeat a single instruction several times, and a fractal is generated. The instruction is simply to take an object of a certain shape, then make a new, bigger object of the same shape, using the original object as a building block. For example, here is an algorithm to make a fractal out of the letter *L*:

274

1. Draw (or create on a computer) a letter L.

2. Now make an L out of copies of your original letter L. We will use five copies of the original shape (but you could also use three).

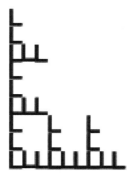

This is the crucial step in the algorithm for the students to fully understand. The new object is in the same general shape as the original object. The specific rule we used here was to apply a linear magnification of 3 to our original object (we used three Ls down and three across). In a linear magnification sense, our new L is 3 times bigger than our original. We will repeat this magnification in each step.

3. Now we perform another iteration and make a larger L out of the previous structure, again, three down and three across (five copies of the structure from step 2):

4. Repeat again. Take the whole structure you made in step 3 and make an L with five copies of it: three down and three across. Things begin to look interesting!!

275

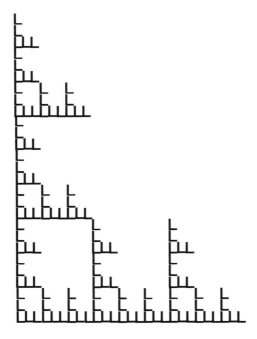

Use an example like the one above to introduce the idea of generating a fractal. Once students have the idea of an iterative algorithm (repeated instruction), they will be ready to move on to Student Data Sheet 1. It is good to emphasize both the math and the beauty of the fractal. It looks cool! But embedded in the structure is a mathematical design. By looking at the fractal carefully, you can determine the rules that generated it.

Explore

Dimensionality. Before going further, we will review some geometrical concepts. In particular, we need to review the concept of dimensionality. Objects are usually described as having one, two, or three dimensions. Although all objects are truly three dimensional, we can describe a flat piece of paper as being two dimensional, or a string or wire as being one dimensional. In the case of the paper and string, we ignore the finite thickness of the object and pay attention only to those dimensions that are most prominent (the length and width of the paper and the length of the wire). The dimensionality of the object describes how it fills space. More precisely, the dimension of the object describes how it fills space as it is scaled to larger or smaller sizes.

We will also introduce another term: *linear magnification*. By *linear magnification* we mean scaling an object in size such that any dimension of the object (length or width, in the case of the piece of paper) increases by the linear magnification. So if we have a piece of paper, and scale it by a linear magnification of 2, its length is increased by 2 and its width is increased by 2. We've simply increased the object size by 2. However, the new area of the object is 4 times the original area. So for a simple, two-dimensional object such as a piece of paper, a linear magnification of 2 increases the amount of two-dimensional space that it fills by a factor of 4.

The same space-filling idea can be applied to a three-dimensional object. If we increase the diameter of a solid sphere by a factor of 2, we increase the amount of three-dimensional space filled by that object by a factor of 8 (2 cubed). So conventional (nonfractal) one-, two-, and three-dimensional objects fill space in a particular and familiar way. As we shall see, fractals fill space in a very different way.

A Mathematical Fractal: The Sierpinski Triangle

The Sierpinski triangle was discovered by the Polish mathematician Waclaw Sierpinski (1882–1969) in the early 20th century and is what we would now call a fractal. Sierpinski was interested in self-similar sets of shapes. *Self-similarity* means that two objects share the same overall shape. As we go from iteration to iteration in the following exercise, each resulting shape has the same overall outline and is therefore self-similar to the iteration that preceded it (and all other iterations). A normal, solid triangle can be enlarged to make a self-similar large triangle, but the properties of the larger triangle are pretty much the same as the original. Both the small and the large solid triangle cover the same fraction of the area within their borders (all of it: 100%).

What is very curious about the Sierpinski triangle is that as we go through the iterations, making self-similar structures, it covers a smaller and smaller proportion of the area within its overall borders (3/4, then 9/16, then 27/64...). This property of the object means that it has a fractal dimension between 1 and 2. It is neither two dimensional nor one dimensional but somewhere in between.

Give all the students Student Sheet 1 and ask them to create the Sierpinski triangle. This activity can be done a number of ways. They can simply draw the triangles with pen on paper, or they can draw them on a computer (all of the fractals in this chapter were made by the authors with the drawing tools in Microsoft Word: copy, paste, repeat). The fractals can also be made using construction paper and scissors. Have the students generate dozens or hundreds

The Sierpinski Triangle.
In each step, a new triangle is made from three copies of the previous structure.

of small equilateral triangles and build the fractal up from there. How many levels can they achieve?

Student Sheet 1 provides the answers to the first few iterations of the Sierpinski triangle. The answers to interations 4–8 follow here. Iterations 7 and 8 may be beyond the students' capabilities, but they may make for a nice longer-term group project in which triangles are added over time to a big fractal on a chalkboard or poster board.

Iteration 1. Draw an equilateral triangle.

Iteration 2. Make two copies and touch vertices to make a larger triangle.

Iteration 3. Make two copies of this *whole structure* and arrange as you did in step 2.

Iteration 4. Repeat.

Iteration 5. Repeat.

Iteration 6. Repeat. (Not to scale.)

Iteration 7 and 8. Repeat. (Not to scale.)

Many resources on the web describe this fractal in detail, including *http://en.wikipedia.org/wiki/Sierpinski_carpet*

Explain

Explain that fractal geometry is a new way of describing the shapes of objects that occur in nature. Just as the line, square, and circle are mathematical tools that help us describe and evaluate the shapes of certain objects in our world, fractals help us with the more complex shapes around us, such as ferns, trees, and mountain ranges. They help us categorize and quantify shapes that seem to defy easy categorization.

Fractal Dimension

One of the fascinating properties of fractals is that they fill space in different ways than more familiar, nonfractal objects. We are used to categorizing geometrical objects as having one, two, or three dimensions. As mentioned above, fractals can have noninteger dimension. To determine the fractal dimension of an object, we perform the same sorts of iterations we did in the previous exercises, and determine the number of copies we need per iteration and the size (linear magnification) of the object scale relative to one another.

The fractal dimension (D) is related to the number of pieces (N) and the magnification (m) in the following way:

$$N = m^D$$

The fractal dimension D is then

$$\text{Log} (N) = \text{Log} (m^D)$$
$$\text{Log} (N) = D \text{ Log} (m)$$

$$D = \log (N)/\log (m)$$

> D = Fractal dimension
> N = Number of pieces
> m = Magnification

Example 1: Non-Fractal Objects. Let's do an example for which we know the answer and see how the equations work. A solid square is two dimensional.

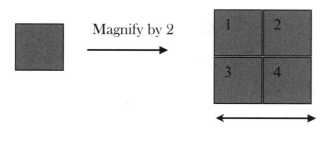

Magnify by 2

The new object must have the same shape, or must be self-similar to the original. It should still be square. So we need four copies of the original square to make the new, larger square. We've magnified by 2 (m = 2), and we need 4 squares to do it (N = 4).

$\mathcal{N} = m^D$

Where $m = 2$ and $\mathcal{N} = 4$. We need to solve for D, which is the dimension.

We take the log of both sides.

$\text{Log}\,(\mathcal{N}) = \log\,(m^D)$

The properties of logarithms allow us to pull the parameter D out in front.

$\text{Log}\,(\mathcal{N}) = D \log\,(m)$

Solving for D

$D = \log\,(\mathcal{N})/\log\,(m)$

$= \log\,(4)/\log\,(2)$
$= \log\,(2^2)/\log\,(2)$
$= 2 \times \log(2)/\log\,(2)$
$= 2$

The square is two dimensional.

Example 2: Fractal Objects. Now repeat the exercise with a fractal object and see how the equations determine fractal dimension. The first two Sierpinski triangle stages are shown below.

We are magnifying by 2. Magnifying by 2 means the width or height of the new object is twice as large.

$$m = 2 \quad \blacktriangle \longrightarrow \blacktriangle$$

Calculation:
$N = m^D \qquad m = 2; N = 3$
$\text{Log } (N) = \log (m^D)$
$\text{Log } (N) = D \log (m)$
$D = \log (N)/\log (m)$
$D = \log (3)/\log (2)$
$D = 1.585$

The new object must have the same overall shape, or must be self-similar to the original. So we need three copies of the original triangle to make the new, larger triangle. We've magnified by 2 ($m = 2$), and we need 3 triangles to do it ($N = 3$). The calculation shows that the dimension is 1.585.

Let's now look at going from iteration 2 to iteration 4 in the Sierpinski triangle. This should give the same answer if the object has a well-defined fractal dimension.

We are magnifying by 4. Magnifying by 4 means the width or height of the new object is 4 times as large.

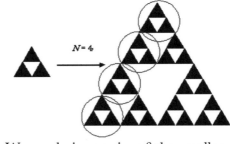

We need nine copies of the smaller triangle to make the new, larger triangle. We've magnified by 4 ($m = 4$), and we need nine copies to do it ($N = 9$). $D = \log (9)/\log (4) = 1.585$

We get the same answer.

Another very interesting potential topic of discussion is *why* certain natural objects have fractal geometry. Students may have some interesting insights or theories on this, which will certainly be informed by their experience with this investigation.

Extend

For a more challenging addition to this activity, have students explore the fractal dimensions found on Student Data Sheet 2. This investigation will introduce the idea of objects with dimension between 1, 2, and 3 integer dimensions.

Sections 1, 2, and 3 of Student Data Sheet 2 introduce students to a method of determining the dimension of a geometrical object based on the concept of self-similarity. They will gain confidence in this method by verifying that a line, square, and cube are one, two, and three dimensional, respectively. They will then move on to determining the fractal dimension of the Sierpinski triangle in section 4.

In Section 5, the students are challenged to determine the dimensionality of what is known as the Koch curve and in section 6 to make a fractal with dimension between 0 and 1.

Evaluate

Check for student understanding.

Ask the students to express in their own words the difference between something that is a fractal and something that is not. Have them define *self-similarity* in their own words. Invite the students to create their own fractal and determine how well it fits the definition of fractal geometry. For more advanced students, challenge them to evaluate the dimension of their own fractals or to set out to create a fractal that has dimension within a certain range (1–1.5 versus 1.5–2).

Most important, this exercise is intended to instill in students a sense that mathematics is interesting and imaginative. Fractals provide students the opportunity to go on their own personal adventures, exploring the intersection of mathematics and science through the production of their own unique creations.

References

www.math.umass.edu/~mconnors/fractal/fractal.html
http://math.rice.edu/~lanius/frac/
http://local.wasp.uwa.edu.au/~pbourke/fractals/

An extension of this concept is the Pythagorean Tree. The web has a number of excellent resources (search for "Pythagorean Tree"). One site has a generator program for various versions of this fractal:

www.cevis.uni-bremen.de/fractals/nsfpe/Pythagorean_Trees/PT.html

Building the Sierpinski Triangle

The Sierpinski triangle is a special mathematical set discovered by Waclaw Sierpinski in the early 1900s.

Iteration 1. Draw an equilateral triangle.

Iteration 2. Make two copies and touch vertices to make a larger triangle.

Iteration 3. Make two copies of this *whole structure* and arrange as you did in step 2.

286

Iteration 4. Repeat.

Iteration 5. Repeat.

Iteration 6. Repeat. (This will be challenging!!!)

Fractal Dimension

One of the strange properties of fractals is that they can have dimension different from 1, 2, or 3. In fact, they can have "noninteger" dimension, meaning that their dimension can be somewhere between 0 and 1, between 1 and 2, or between 2 and 3. This investigation challenges you to calculate the fractal dimension of different objects.

To determine the dimension of an object, we perform the same sort of steps we used in the previous exercises. For each step, we look at how many copies of the original piece we need to make the next bigger one. We also look at how much bigger the new piece is. By relating the number of copies of the original we need (N = number of pieces) and how much bigger the new piece is (m = magnification), we can determine the "fractal dimension," D, through the following equation:

$$N = m^D$$

D = Fractal dimension
N = Number of pieces
m = Magnification

The fractal dimension D is then

$$\text{Log}\,(N) = \text{Log}\,(m^D)$$
$$\text{Log}\,(N) = D\,\text{Log}\,(m)$$
$$D = \log\,(N)/\log\,(m)$$

Let's look at some familiar objects first to see how the equations work and to make sure they give us the answer we expect.

1. A line

Let's look first at a line, which we know is one dimensional. If we magnify the line by a factor of 2, we need to simply place two of the original pieces side by side. This object is "self-similar to the first," meaning that it has the same shape.

So the magnification is 2 (m = 2) and the number of pieces we need is two. Use the formula

$$D = \text{Log}\,(2)/\text{Log}\,(2) = 1$$

The line has a dimension of 1. It's one dimensional! Of course!

2. A square

Let's now look at a familiar two-dimensional object: a square. If we magnify by a factor of 2, we need four pieces. When we magnify by 2, we mean that we "blow up" the object so that the length of any side is twice as long. It's like changing the magnification on a microscope or a telescope by a factor of 2. The resulting object must have the same shape, or in other words, the new object is self-similar to the original: it is a square, just larger. So the magnification is 2 ($m = 2$) and the number of pieces required is 4 ($N = 4$).

$$D = \text{Log}\ (4)/\text{Log}\ (2) = 2\ \text{Log}\ (2)/\text{Log}\ (2) = 2$$

The square is two dimensional.

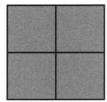

Note that we could also magnify by 3 and get the same answer. Magnifying by 3 means that the length of the side of the new square is 3 times wider. If the square is 3 times longer on each side, we need nine squares to make the new square. So $m = 3$ and $N = 9$. $D = \text{Log}\ (9)/\text{Log}\ (3) = 2\ \text{Log}\ (3)/\text{Log}\ (3) = 2$. It is still two dimensional.

3. A cube

Lets try a three-dimensional object like a cube. Magnify by a factor of 2. Again this means the new, bigger cube is twice as long along each side. To make a cube twice as long along each side, we need 8 cubes.
So $m = 2$ and $N = 8$ (we need eight cubes to make the bigger cube).

$$D = \text{Log}\ (8)/\text{Log}\ (2) = \text{Log}\ (2^3)/\text{Log}\ (2) = 3\ \text{Log}\ (2)/\text{Log}\ (2) = 3$$

It is three dimensional!!

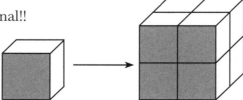

288

4. NonInteger Dimension: The Sierpinski Triangle

Check: Let's go from the iteration 2 triangle to the iteration 4 triangle. We've magnified by a factor of 4 and we need nine copies of the iteration 2 triangle to make the iteration 4 triangle. So $m = 4$ and $N = 9$

$D = \text{Log}(9)/\text{Log}(4)$

$D = \text{Log}(3^2)/\text{Log}(2^2) = 2\,\text{Log}(3)/\,2\,\text{Log}(2) = \text{Log}(3)/\text{Log}(2)$

$D = 1.585$

Again it works out to $D = 1.585$.

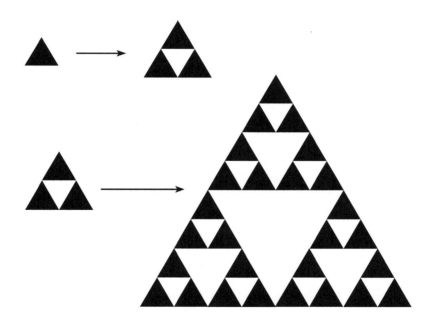

In going from iteration 1 to iteration 2 we are magnifying by a factor of 2 (each side of the triangle is twice as long). So $m = 2$. We need three triangles to do so. So $N = 3$.

$D = \text{Log}(3)/\text{Log}(2)$

$D = 1.585$

The Sierpinski triangle has dimension 1.58. It is between 1 and 2.

5. Challenge

What is the fractal dimension of the following fractal?

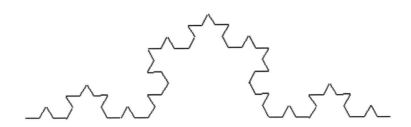

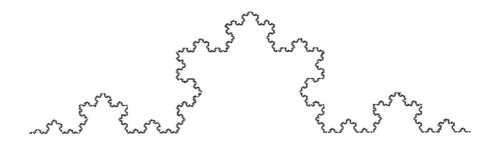

Answer:
As we go from iteration 1 to iteration 2, we need four pieces ($N = 4$), and we've magnified by a factor of 3 ($m = 3$). This is readily apparent by observing that the object is 3 times longer and taller in the next iteration.

$$D = \text{Log}(4)/\text{Log}(3) = 1.262$$

6. Challenge

Can you make a fractal that has fractal dimension between 0 and 1?

Example: Here is one possible answer, although there are many. The following fractal is called *Cantor's Dust*.

Iteration 1: _____

Iteration 2: _____   _____

Iteration 3: _____   _____   _____   _____

Iteration 4 (scaled):

     ___ ___   ___ ___   ___ ___   ___ ___

Iteration 5 (scaled):

     __ __   __ __   __ __   __ __

The dimension of this fractal:

Each iteration magnifies by 3 and requires two copies.

$D = \mathrm{Log}\,(2)/\mathrm{Log}\,(3) = 0.631$

291

Chapter 23
Screening My Calls:
Scale & the Electromagnetic Spectrum

Overview

Colors are all around us. The light from the sun is yellow at midday and red toward sunset. The sky is blue and the leaves are green. How are red light, blue light, and green light different, anyway? It's simply a matter of scale! Light is an electromagnetic wave. Just like water waves or a plucked guitar string, a light wave has a wavelength, or a characteristic distance between peaks. The wavelength of the light determines its color. Longer wavelengths tend toward the red, and shorter wavelengths tend toward the blue. Light is just one type of electromagnetic radiation; it belongs to the visible portion of the electromagnetic (EM) spectrum. The other regions of the EM spectrum include everything from gamma rays to radio waves. They are all the same thing: electromagnetic waves. But their properties vary dramatically as the scale of the wavelength changes. In this investigation students create, test, and explore a Faraday cage, which familiarizes them with the scale of cell phone signal wavelengths.

Objectives

- To develop an understanding of electromagnetic (EM) radiation.
- To be able to identify different types of EM.

Process Skills

- Observing
- Predicting
- Measuring
- Analyzing data

Activity Duration

45 minutes

293

Background

It may surprise you to know that every cubic inch between your eyeball and this page is full of electromagnetic radiation: visible light, radiowaves, microwaves, infrared radiation, and much more. Then again, maybe it's not so surprising. You already know that if your cell phone is placed within that space, you'll receive a call; if your radio antenna were sitting on your lap, you'd receive your favorite radio program. You are also seeing the page, which means that there are light waves passing all around. The space you live in is full of electromagnetic (EM) radiation of all wavelengths. Some of this radiation carries information (radio); some gives us a sunburn

FIGURE 1.
The electromagnetic spectrum.

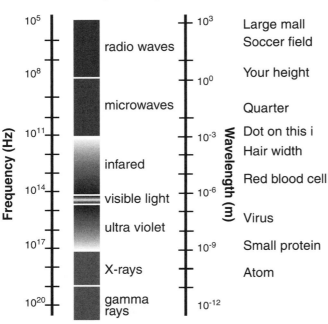

move through water; sound waves move through air (or solids or water). In a vacuum, by definition, there is no "stuff," so these other types of waves cannot move through it. EM radiation, on the other hand, moves through the vacuum with ease. It is precisely for this reason that we can see the light from the Sun and stars. The light emitted from these celestial bodies travels through vast distances of the vacuum of space to reach our eyes. Sound cannot travel one millimeter in a vacuum, no matter how loud the source!! All EM radiation also travels at roughly the same speed. In a vacuum, EM radiation travels at the "speed of light" or 3.0×10^8 m/s (186,000 miles/sec). This speed can vary slightly as light passes through glass or water, but it is reasonably accurate to use that number as the speed of light through air.

Energy. The different wavelengths of EM radiation have different frequencies and energies. These three parameters—wavelength, frequency, and energy—are not independent. If you know one, you know the other two. EM radiation of very small wavelength has very high frequency and energy. EM radiation of very large

(ultraviolet); and some comes directly from our warm bodies (yes, even we radiate in the infrared!).

What is it? EM radiation is both familiar and mysterious. The light from our desk lamp is as ordinary a sight as any in our day. But what is light? What is EM radiation? Light is a wave of oscillating electric and magnetic fields. It shares some characteristics with other types of waves: It has a wavelength, a frequency, and a velocity. But EM radiation is very different from other types of waves in one very special way: It does not require a medium in which to propagate. Water waves

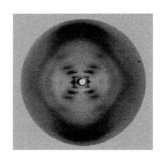

FIGURE 2.
Rosalind Franklin's X-ray diffraction image of DNA, which led to the discovery of the double helix.

294

FIGURE 3.
Infrared image of a tiger. Note that the face and eyes are radiating more, indicating that they are warmer.

From *http://coolcosmos.ipac. caltech.edu/image_galleries/ ir_zoo/index.html.*

wavelength has very low frequency and very low energy. Starting with EM radiation of the smallest wavelength, the different ranges of the EM spectrum are gamma rays, X-rays, ultraviolet radiation, visible light, infrared radiation, microwave radiation, and radio waves (see Figure 1).

Gamma Rays. These are the most energetic and perhaps the most mysterious. They have wavelengths that are smaller than the atomic scale. Because they are so energetic, they can cause the most damage to living systems. This can be both a good and a bad thing. Some cancer therapies use gamma radiation as a way of killing unwanted cells.

X-rays. X-rays are familiar to most people as the type of radiation we use to observe broken bones. X-rays pass mostly unperturbed through tissue but are reflected and absorbed by the harder mineral material (bone) within our bodies. Another very important property of X-rays is their wavelengths' correspondence to atomic-length scales. This is what allows us to use X-ray diffraction techniques to determine the structure of molecules and proteins (see Figure 2). It is this type of radiation that allows us to "see" the atomic scale, precisely because its wavelength corresponds to atomic sizes.

Ultraviolet. Ultraviolet light lies between the violet end of the visible range and X-rays. These are the rays of EM radiation that give us sunburns and cause hair to bleach.

Visible. Taking up a very small range of the EM spectrum, the visible range is the range of radiation that we see. Violet light is on the high-frequency end and red light is on the low-frequency end. All colors we experience lie in this range.

Infrared. Located just up from the visible range in wavelength, infrared radiation is slightly less energetic. Some animals, such as snakes, can actually see in the infrared, so that they can see other animals in what we would perceive as complete darkness. It turns out that all objects radiate EM radiation. Even you!! Because we live at a certain temperature, our atoms and molecules jiggle and wiggle and occasionally emit radiation. This radiation is in

FIGURE 4.
Cosmic microwave background.
(Source: NASA / WMAP Science Team.) The universe is full of radiation. This is a map of the whole sky showing the different intensities of microwave radiation coming from different directions. It gives us clues to the structure and origins of the universe.

295

the infrared region. Some cameras now have the ability to see this type of radiation (see Figure 3). Infrared cameras can see objects, especially living ones, which tend to be warmer than surrounding, nonliving objects. For more information go to: *http://coolcosmos.ipac.caltech.edu/image_galleries/ir_zoo/index.html*

Microwave. The microwave oven in your kitchen makes EM radiation. This radiation happens to be at the correct frequency to jiggle water molecules (~2.45 GHz). As the water molecules in your food jiggle, they warm up everything around them and heat your food! Take a look at your microwave. In the window there is a wire mesh. Because the wavelength of the microwaves is about 12 cm, they cannot penetrate the mesh. This is called a Faraday cage and is the subject of this exercise.

Radio. Aside from visible light, radio waves may be the most familiar EM radiation. Though we cannot see it, it carries all of the information that we rely on in our modern lives, including TV and radio broadcasts, our cell phone calls, and wireless internet networks. The wavelength of this type of radiation is quite long, from centimeters to kilometers!

EM Region	Wavelength	Frequency [Hz]
Gamma rays	< 0.01 nm	$> 3 \times 10^{19}$
X-rays	0.01 nm–10 nm	$3 \times 10^{16} - 3 \times 10^{19}$
Ultraviolet	10 nm–400 nm	$7.5 \times 10^{14} - 3 \times 10^{16}$
Visible light "light"	400 nm–700 nm	$4.3 \times 10^{14} - 7.5 \times 10^{14}$
Infrared	700 nm–1 mm	$3 \times 10^{11} - 4.3 \times 10^{14}$
Microwave	1 mm–10 cm	$3 \times 10^{9} - 3 \times 10^{11}$
Radio	> 10 cm	$< 3 \times 10^{9}$

Materials

Each group will need:

- Cell phone or a small, battery-powered radio
- Small cardboard boxes with lids, large enough to hold a cell phone or small radio
- Aluminum foil
- Scissors
- Stapler
- Transparent tape
- Ruler

Note:

- Optional: 2–3 square feet of aluminum screening (available at any hardware store)
- Optional: Instead of aluminum foil, use two aluminum foil pans to enclose the cell phone or radio.

Engage

Discuss light with your class, since this is the EM radiation they are most familiar with. Describe and discuss how light moves, concentrating on things they know: Light can bounce off things (mirrors), travel through things (windows), and can be absorbed (black cloth). During most of our day, light surrounds us everywhere. Only when we are shut in a room, or at night in a dark neighborhood, do we experience the absence of light. Mention other types of EM radiation that they are familiar with—radio waves (for radios, TV, and cell phones), microwaves in their kitchens, and ultraviolet waves that give them sunburns. Point out that these are all types of EM radiation and have some of the same properties as visible light (they travel through some things and not through others). One important concept to get across is that these waves are all around us, even when we cannot see them. The fact that we can receive a cell phone call or tune in a radio show almost anywhere we go tells us that these waves (in this case, radio waves) are all around us all the time.

Use the EM spectrum chart, or find one on the web, to aid discussion of the different parts of the EM spectrum. A discussion of the length scales will help. Look up the typical frequencies for cell phones (if you are using a radio, look up the typical ranges of FM and AM radio broadcasts).

Explore

Have students look up the typical frequencies for cell phone signals if you have access to the internet in the classroom, or bring in this information. One source of information is *http://en.wikipedia.org/wiki/Cellular_frequencies*. Typically cell phones will be in the 800 MHz range, though in some cases they may be as high in the 1,900 MHz (1.9 GHz) range. These frequencies of electromagnetic radiation correspond to wavelengths that are a few tens of centimeters long.

Exercises 1 and 2

In these exercises you can use either a cell phone or a radio to act as a receiver for radio wavelength EM radiation. Students construct what is called a *Faraday cage*, which is simply a metal cage or box that shields out the EM radiation and prevents reception (no cell phone reception; static on the radio). The first stage of this exercise is to show that you can completely screen out radio signals by

297

building a box covered in aluminum foil. (Actually any sealable metal enclosure will do. A metal tea tin or metal index card file will work, for example.) Simply wrapping a cell phone or small battery-powered radio will work. Make sure to emphasize the "control" experiment: Check for reception on the cell phone before and after placing it in the Faraday cage, to verify the effect. Steps are listed in the Student Data Sheet.

Exercises 3 and 4

What becomes more fun and illuminating is to show that a cage of metal with holes in it (which visible light can easily penetrate) stops radiation of larger wavelengths. If the holes in the cage or screen are small relative to the wavelength of the radio waves, then it is essentially like a solid barrier to that radiation. Within the cage it is completely "dark" with respect to radio radiation.

A simple rule of thumb for screening EM radiation is that the mesh size, or the size of the holes in your screen, must be 1/10 of the wavelength of the radiation you are trying to screen. Most cell phones operate in the 800–900 MHz range, which means that the wavelength is approximately 30–40 cm. With a mesh size smaller than 3 cm, you should be able to block out phone reception! Moreover, you can see right through a mesh of this size. It clearly illustrates the difference between visible light and EM radiation of much larger wavelength. If the exercise is done properly, your Faraday cage will allow you to see into the box (visible EM radiation gets through) that is "dark" to the cell phone signal. If you have access to aluminum screening, have your students make a cage. Make sure that all sides are stapled shut. In this case the mesh size is quite small, so you should screen very effectively.

Next, in Exercise 4, have the students make their own mesh with aluminum foil (Figure 5). You can achieve this by simply taking aluminum foil and poking holes in it, or by using strips of foil to make a grid as a lid for your foil-covered box. If you use strips, make sure that a grid is made (strips going perpendicular to each other) with openings no larger than a centimeter or two. Have the students experiment with the spacing of the strips. Perhaps have one group make a mesh of 1 cm holes, another 2 cm, and so on, up to 10 cm. Keep in mind that if you are using a radio, all of these sizes should screen effectively, since the wavelength for the FM radio range is so long (a 90 MHz radio broadcast has a wavelength of 3.3 m).

FIGURE 5.
Cell phone in Faraday cage.

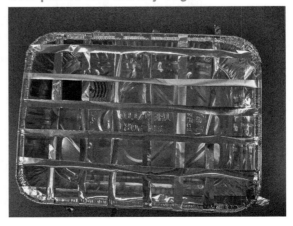

Exercise 5

Have the students construct a mesh with holes that are long along one direction and short along another. For cell phone signals (whose wavelength is about 30 or 40 cm), making a Faraday cage with long holes (say 10–15 cm) along one direction and 1 cm holes along another will likely let the signal through. As the students add strips along the perpendicular direction, the signal will be screened out. Have the students brainstorm their ideas about this effect. What does this indicate about EM radiation?

Helpful hint: Most phones have an indicator on their display showing how strong the reception is at a given moment. If the students can monitor this display while the phone is enclosed within the various Faraday cages (other than when they are totally enclosing the phone in foil), they will be able to see how the signal is changing from moment to moment. This will be especially engaging for Exercise 5, in which the signal should start to disappear as the perpendicular strips are added.

Explain

Electromagnetic radiation has a property known as *polarization,* which can be thought of as the orientation of the EM wave. It is like a ribbon: thin in thickness but wide along the other direction. When the first set of strips are set down, radiation can still get through—in particular, the radiation that is oriented (polarized) along the direction of the strips. Again you can think of it as ribbons slipping through the long, thin holes. When the perpendicular strips are laid down, no radiation can get through. This is essentially how polarizing sunglasses work. They let light through with one orientation but not the other. If you cross two polarizers, then no light gets through. This is essentially what the students do as they add the strips in the perpendicular direction.

Extend

Have students calculate the wavelength of EM radiation if they know the frequency and vise versa.

If I know frequency, how do I determine wavelength? An equation that describes the speed of a wave as it relates to the wavelength and frequency is called a *dispersion relation*. In the simplest case (light traveling through a vacuum) the dispersion relation for light looks like this:

$$\text{Speed} = \text{frequency} \times \text{wavelength, or}$$

$$c = f \times \lambda$$

It is reasonably accurate to use this equation even when air is the medium. What is useful about this equation is that you can figure out the wavelength

299

if you know the frequency. Often for radio waves (our GHz cell phones or AM and FM radio bands) we know the frequency. We simply use the equation on page 299 to determine the wavelength using $c = 3 \times 10^8$ m/s as our speed of light.

$$\lambda = c / f$$

So if you have a cell phone that uses 800 MHz frequency, its wavelength is:

$$\lambda = c / f = (3.0 \times 10^8 \text{ m/s})/(800 \times 10^6 \text{ Hz})$$
$$= (300{,}000{,}000 \text{ m/s})/(800{,}000{,}000 \text{ Hz})$$
$$= 0.375 \text{ m}$$
$$\sim 38 \text{ cm}$$

AM radio broadcasts happen in the high hundreds of kHz. So an AM radio broadcast at 800 kHz frequency has a wavelength of:

$$\lambda = c / f = (3.0 \times 10^8 \text{ m/s})/(800 \times 10^3 \text{ Hz})$$
$$= (300{,}000{,}000 \text{ m/s})/(800{,}000 \text{ Hz})$$
$$= 375 \text{ m}$$

Almost a quarter-mile long!!!

Conversely, if we know the wavelength and want to know the frequency:

$$f = c / \lambda$$

Evaluate

Check for student understanding:

1. What is radiation?
2. Name three types of radiation.
3. What is the frequency of a typical cell phone signal?
4. What is the wavelength of a typical cell phone signal?
5. How does a Faraday cage work to block radio signals?

For more information:

- *http://science.hq.nasa.gov/kids/imagers/ems*
- *http://hyperphysics.phy-astr.gsu.edu/hbase/ems1.html#c1*

300

Prelab

Look up the typical frequencies of cell phone signals, or have your teacher provide this information.

Exercise 1: Control experiment.

Make sure your cell phone is working properly by calling it. Make sure the ringer is loud enough that you can hear it inside your Faraday cage. You should repeat your control experiment before each trial below to make sure the phone is working properly.

Exercise 2: Construct a Faraday cage from solid foil sheets.

1. Take a small cardboard box (large enough to hold a cell phone); a small shoe box will work.
2. Place the phone within the cardboard box and close the lid. Does your phone ring? Why or why not?
3. Cover the box and the lid with aluminum foil. Use tape or stapler to affix foil to the box and lid. Make sure the lid fits snugly onto the box.
4. Place the cell phone into the box and replace the lid. Again, make sure the lid is on snugly.
5. Call the cell phone. Does it ring? Why or why not?
6. Open the lid slightly. Does the phone ring now?
7. Try to adjust the lid so that there is a small opening, but the phone doesn't ring. How big can you make the hole?

Exercise 3: Construct a Faraday cage from aluminum screening.

1. Take a piece of aluminum screening. The screen should be long enough to make a cage for your phone. Make a cylinder with your screen, and close off one end by folding it over and stapling it. Make sure the cylinder is wide enough to accommodate your cell phone.
2. Do another control ring on your phone. Make sure it rings loudly when you call it.
3. Place your phone within the screen cylinder, fold over the opening, and staple.

301

4. You should have a completely closed screen enclosure. You should be able to see your phone.
5. Call your phone. Does it ring? Why or why not?

Exercise 4: Construct a Faraday cage of foil with holes.

How small do the holes have to be to screen out the radiation? We will test this by modifying the box you made in Exercise 2 above.

1. Remove the foil from the lid of your box.
2. Do a control experiment. See whether your phone rings without the foil on the lid. It should. If it does not, make sure it rings outside of the box. If it does ring outside the box, but continues not to ring in your box, it may be too deep within the box. Raise the phone up near the opening by putting something under it. Make sure that it rings when it is in the box with the lid off.
3. Make foil strips ½ inch wide.
4. Make a grid of strips on your lid. Conduct different tests, as you vary the spacing of the strips to make holes of different sizes. See how large the holes must be to allow the radio waves to penetrate your box. How does this size compare to the wavelength? A rule of thumb for screening EM radiation is that the mesh size (size of holes) should be 1/10 the wavelength of the radiation for effective screening.

Exercise 5: Construct a Faraday Cage with a foil "polarizer."

What if your holes are long in one direction and short in another? Will the radiation get in?

1. Repeat Exercise 4, but only place strips along one direction. Make sure to tape the ends of the strips onto the foil affixed to the bottom of the box. If your lid is a rectangle, add the strips along the long direction. Do you still get reception? Why or why not?
2. Now make some more foil strips long enough to stretch across your lid. Place these strips perpendicular to the strips that are already affixed to your lid. Make sure to make good contact between the ends of these new strips and the aluminum on the box bottom. Do you still get reception? Why or why not?

Student Data Sheet
Screening My Calls:
Scale & the Electromagnetic Spectrum

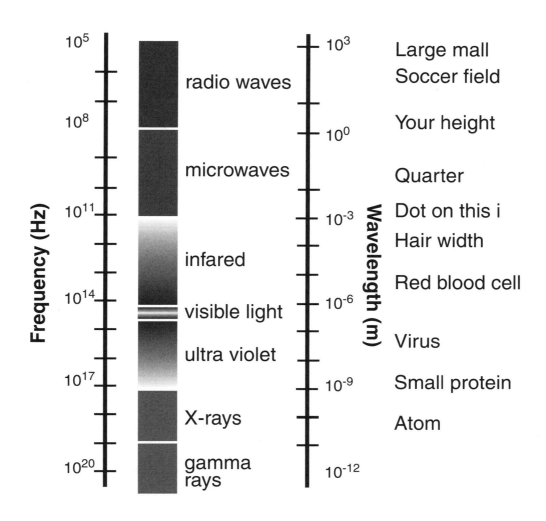

EM Region	Wavelength	Frequency [Hz]
Gamma rays	< 0.01 nm	$> 3 \times 10^{19}$
X-rays	0.01 nm–10 nm	$3 \times 10^{16} - 3 \times 10^{19}$
Ultraviolet	10 nm–400 nm	$7.5 \times 10^{14} - 3 \times 10^{16}$
Visible light "light"	400 nm–700 nm	$4.3 \times 10^{14} - 7.5 \times 10^{14}$
Infrared	700 nm–1 mm	$3 \times 10^{11} - 4.3 \times 10^{14}$
Microwave	1 mm–10 cm	$3 \times 10^{9} - 3 \times 10^{11}$
Radio	> 10 cm	$< 3 \times 10^{9}$

Chapter 24
Stringy Chemistry & States of Matter

Overview

Matter is made up of atoms and molecules. The objects we see and touch every day have billions of billions of molecules clumped together in various ways. The properties of matter depend largely on how those molecules interact with each other. Solids, liquids, and gases are familiar to students as the different states of matter. Why are some substances gases and some solid at room temperature? This exercise helps students explore the basic concepts behind intermolecular bonding and how it affects states of matter and the properties of materials. One important concept that this exercise emphasizes is that molecules come in many different sizes. The size of the molecules is one of the most important determinants of the properties of a substance.

Objectives
- To be able to describe how the length of a molecule is related to the strength of bonding.
- To be able to describe how the size of a molecule is related to its behavior.

Process Skills
- Observing
- Modeling
- Analyzing data

Activity Duration
60 minutes

Background

When it comes to the properties of materials and substances, the size of the molecules involved is extremely important. Size matters in chemistry! As we scale molecules up from small to large, new properties emerge. All else being equal, larger molecules cohere to their molecular neighbors more strongly than smaller ones. That is why small molecules, such as diatomic oxygen (O_2) and nitrogen (N_2), tend to be gases at room temperature. Larger molecules tend to form liquids and solids. This exercise focuses on one of the simplest examples of this trend: saturated hydrocarbons. These chain molecules are what make up gases such as methane and propane, liquids such as gasoline (octane) and mineral oil, soft solids such as Vaseline (petroleum jelly), and hard solids such as the polyethylene in your water bottle. All of these substances are made of carbon and hydrogen only. In fact, the molecules that make them have the same basic structure: a line or chain of carbon atoms decorated with hydrogen atoms. The differences in their properties, including the dramatic change from gas to liquid to solid, are due to the increasing length of the individual molecular strings or chains.

305

Hydrocarbons

Saturated hydrocarbon is the name for a whole class of carbon chain molecules that include the familiar gases methane, propane, and butane, as well as the liquid octane (in gasoline) and the polymer polyethylene. These molecules all have the same basic structure: a backbone of carbon atoms with hydrogens attached. This class of molecules is also referred to as the *alkanes* or the *paraffins*. Figure 1 shows an example of an alkane or saturated hydrocarbon molecule. It is the structural formula for propane. It has three carbon atoms along its backbone, with eight hydrogen atoms attached. In alkane molecules, each carbon atom bonds with four neighboring atoms. The carbon atoms on the ends of the molecule bond with one neighboring carbon atom and three hydrogen atoms. The internal carbon atoms bond with their two neighboring carbon atoms and two hydrogen atoms off

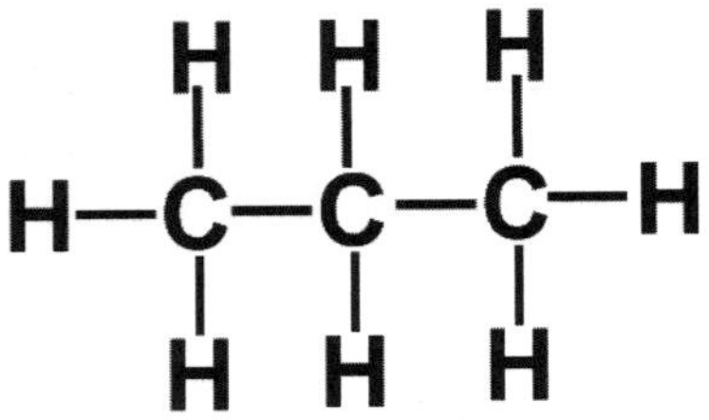

FIGURE 1.
The structural formula of propane.
The molecule can also be represented by its basic molecular formula, C_3H_8. Alkanes always have two hydrogen atoms for every carbon atom, plus two more hydrogen atoms to cap the ends. So if an alkane has N carbon atoms, it will have 2N + 2 hydrogen atoms. Sometimes alkanes are represented by the following generic formula: C_NH_{2N+2}.

to the side of the main chain. The different alkanes only differ in the number of carbons along the backbone. There can be as few as one (as in the case of methane), many hundreds, or even many thousands in the case of the polymer known as *polyethylene*.

Properties of Alkanes

One of the interesting problems that chemists and materials scientists wrestle with is how to predict or connect the properties of the substances that molecules compose to the structure and properties of the individual molecules themselves. Put more simply, can you look at the structural formula of the molecule and make successful predictions about the properties of the substance? (Your students will make a prediction at the end of this exercise.)

Alkanes provide an interesting and simple lesson in this context. Every alkane is made up of only two types of atoms and has a similar structure differing only in length. However, the properties of the molecules differ dramatically depending on their length. Methane, with one carbon atom, is a gas; octane, with eight, is a liquid. Mineral oil, petroleum jelly, and candle wax (petroleum based) are made of alkanes with chain lengths in the 20 to 40 carbon range. As we get to much higher numbers of carbon atoms (hundreds and thousands) the molecules make up harder plastic, which is known as polyethylene. Why is this?

It turns out that it is simply a matter of stickiness. Alkanes interact or stick to each other through intermolecular forces known as *van der Waals forces*. Compared to many other types of forces between molecules, these are relatively weak (hydrogen bonds between water molecules are much stronger, for example; that is why water is a liquid at room temperature, though it is roughly the same size as methane). Molecules that are bonded more strongly to each other are harder to slide, push, and pull relative to each other. The stronger the bonds, the harder they are to bend and break. Methane molecules are very small and interact very weakly through van der Waals forces. Because the interactions between methane molecules are so weak, they tend to fly off from each other at room temperature. Thus methane is a gas. Octane molecules are larger and tend to stick more. They don't fly off from one another, but they can easily slide and slip around each other. Thus octane is a liquid. As the chains get even longer, the slipping and sliding gets harder, and the substances get more viscous (mineral oil), eventually becoming a waxy, gel-like solid at carbon lengths near 18. At very long chain lengths, as in polyethylene, the chains are so entangled and mixed together that they simply vibrate under thermal motion and cannot really move relative to each other (like the stands of twine in a rope). That is why polyethylene is a hard plastic.

To summarize, the properties of a substance are determined by how easily the carbon chains can slip, slide, or even break away from each other. It should also be emphasized at this point that at the molecular scale, temperature affects the thermal motion of the molecules. All of these molecules are wiggling, shaking, and moving about. The stickiness to their neighboring molecules is what is keeping them in place. If the stickiness is not great enough, the molecules will fly apart (gas) or easily slip and slide around (liquid). Take a look at the Alkanes Reference Sheet on page 311. It shows the structural formula for some representative alkanes and the boiling and melting points of the first 10 alkanes as well as eicosane (20 carbons). Note the trends. Boiling and melting points rise continuously with the length of the chains.

In the exercise, students will make simple models of alkane molecules out of yarn of different lengths and mix them together to form model substances. This exercise is a direct analogy to the real situation. The longer the molecule (length of yarn), the more entangled and stuck together a group of strands will become. Your students will study how the length of the string affects how well a clump or ball of yarn molecules stay together. This exercise will help them visualize in a tangible way how the size of molecules and the strength of their interactions affect the properties of the substance they compose.

307

Materials

Each group will need:

- Mineral oil
- Petroleum jelly
- Paraffin candles (typical inexpensive candles)
- HDPE plastic bottle (any plastic bottle with the recycling symbol and the number 2; most plastic beverage bottles are made of HDPE; HDPE stands for high-density polyethylene)
- Light to medium yarn (15 to 20 meters per group) or a coarse garden string
- Scissors
- Cardboard or plastic box (shoe box size is ideal)

Engage

For Part I, form the students into groups of four or five and hand out the various substances: a small vial of mineral oil, petroleum jelly, small candles, and an HDPE water bottle (or any other HDPE plastic you have available). Have them explore the feel and mechanics of the various materials. This may be a little messy, so have paper towels on hand to clean up hands and surfaces. Encourage the students to explore the viscosity of the fluidlike materials and the hardness of the solid materials. Which substances are the hardest or the softest? Do the substances fall easily into the classic categories of solid and liquid (the petroleum jelly might be the odd substance; it is a gel, which is a very soft form of solid)? Ask the students to brainstorm about what makes a substance a liquid or a solid or a gas. Also, remind them that the temperature is important when discussing the states of matter. A substance that is solid at room temperature will become a liquid a higher temperature.

After the students have explored for a few minutes, point out that each of these substances is made of chain molecules. Explain that the chains are the same in every respect except their lengths. Explain the structure of alkanes on the board. Have the students brainstorm how the length of the chains affects the properties of the material. Which substance is made of long molecules and which of short? Why do you think so?

Explore

Hand out the Student Data Sheet and have the students work in their groups on the brainstorming questions, based on their exploration of the various substances you have handed out.

Begin Part II of the exercise. Have each group prepare piles of yarn or string of different lengths. Make sure to remind students that the different lengths should remain separated throughout the exercise. The different string lengths are analogous to the lengths of the alkane molecules. The students are essentially making model molecules and will combine them to form model substances or pieces of matter with groups of these molecules. Once the different groups of molecules are prepared, have the students combine them (each type separately) by balling them up tightly in their hands. Once they are balled up, have them work the strands together with their hands as well as they can. Emphasize that explicitly tying strands is not allowed, but entangling strands through working the bundle is definitely encouraged. The bundles made of longer strands (1 m and 20 cm) should form a fairly tight bundle if worked well. The bundles made of smaller strands should stay together but may fall apart more easily (this is the point!). The students should entangle each group as thoroughly as they can (with equal effort for each).

Once the bundles are made, they should place them one at a time (a separate trial for each) into their boxes and shake vigorously. This action is simulating temperature. Actual molecules are undergoing very vigorous shaking and bumping all of the time. The shaking the students are doing simulates what a group of molecules actually experiences. Have the students shake each bundle separately and thoroughly and carefully observe the results. Have them answer the questions at the end of the Student Data Sheet. Most important, have them identify trends. What changes as the molecules get longer? How is this related to the properties of the substance?

Explain

Ideally what the students will find is that the bundles made of the shortest lengths of yarn fly apart, come back together, and fly apart again. This case is analogous to the gas phase, in which molecules are flying about disconnected from other molecules aside from brief collisions. The bundles made of intermediate-length fibers may partially fall apart but remain in one overall, unraveled clump. This is analogous to liquid, in which molecules can slide and reorient but do not fly apart from each other. The bundles made of long chains should keep their shape fairly well if they have been properly entangled. This is analogous to a solid.

Point out to students that the cases where the object falls apart are analogous to melting or boiling. Thermal energy shakes the substances apart (especially those substances with weaker intermolecular bonding). Emphasize question 3 at the end of the Student Data Sheet. Have the students predict which stringlike molecule would be solid, which would be a liquid, and which would be a gas. The long chain would be a solid, the intermediate length would be a liquid, and the small chain would be a gas. Students should be able to give a logical reason why they chose these answers: Longer chains mean more interaction and entanglement and less chance for the molecules to come apart.

Extend

This exercise can lead directly into discussions in more depth about states of matter and transitions between them (melting, boiling). The crucial concept the exercise provides is how the inherent moving and shaking of molecules due to ambient thermal energy competes with the strength of the sticky interactions among molecules.

Evaluate

Check for student understanding:

1. What is an alkane?
2. What atoms make up an alkane?
3. What happens when a carbon chain gets longer?
4. How is molecular size related to states of matter?
5. Would you expect a material that is solid at room temperature to have a higher or lower melting point than another material that is a gas at room temperature?

310

Alkanes Reference Sheet

The molecules depicted on this page are called *alkanes* or *saturated hydrocarbons*. They all consist only of carbon and nitrogen and share a structure of a carbon backbone with hydrogens attached. The molecules differ only in their length, but the properties of substances made of each of them differ dramatically. The table on the next page shows how melting and boiling points change as the length of the chain increases. Methane, ethane, propane, and butane are gases at room temperature (note their boiling points are below room temperature or ~20°C). Pentane through decane are liquids at room temperature. Eicosane, with 20 carbons, is a waxy solid. This trend is due to the increased strength of interactions between molecules as they get longer. In a simple sense, there is simply more surface area with which longer molecules touch and interact. This increases the amount of energy required to pull them apart.

Eicosane ($C_{20}H_{42}$)

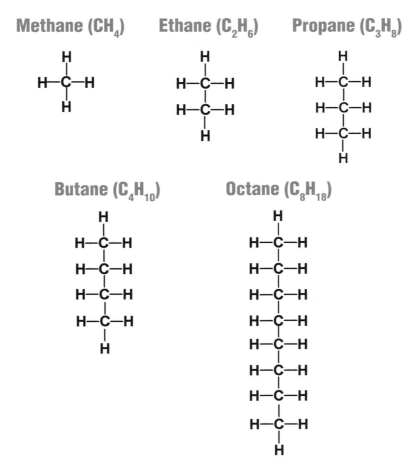

Methane (CH_4)

Ethane (C_2H_6)

Propane (C_3H_8)

Butane (C_4H_{10})

Octane (C_8H_{18})

311

Student Data Sheet
Stringy Chemisty & States of Matter

Alkane Melting and Boiling Points

Alkane	Formula	Melting Point (°C)	Boiling Point (°C)	State
Methane	CH_4	-183.0	-164.0	Gas
Ethane	C_2H_6	-183.0	-89.0	Gas
Propane	C_3H_8	-190.0	-42.0	Gas
Butane	C_4H_{10}	-138.0	-0.5	Gas
Pentane	C_5H_{12}	-130.0	36.0	Liquid
Hexane	C_6H_{14}	-95.0	69.0	Liquid
Heptane	C_7H_{16}	-91.0	98.0	Liquid
Octane	C_8H_{18}	-57.0	125.0	Liquid
Nonane	C_9H_{20}	-51.0	151.0	Liquid
Decane	$C_{10}H_{22}$	-30.0	174.0	Liquid
Eicosane	$C_{20}H_{42}$	37.0	343.0	Solid

312

Student Data Sheet
Stringy Chemisty & States of Matter

Name _____

Procedure

Part I

Your teacher will pass out samples of several different substances. Explore the feel of the different materials.

Brainstorm with your group:

1. Why are some substances gases at room temperature, while others are liquids and solids?
2. How do you think a substance made of larger molecules would differ from a substance made of smaller molecules?
3. What makes some substances harder and some softer?

Part II

Model the solid, liquid, and gas behavior of hydrocarbon chains.

1. Your group will need about 15–20 m of yarn or string. Cut pieces into the lengths listed below. Keep each group separate.

   - 5 pieces of 1 m length
   - 20 pieces of 20 cm length
   - 25 pieces of 10 cm length
   - 50 pieces of 3 cm length
   - 150 pieces of 1 cm length (or less)

2. Take each group of strands of the same length and clump them into a ball. Really work them together, BUT NO TYING. Work the outside strands into the middle of your bundle to really get them entangled. But again, no tying ends of strands with other strands. Just mix them together as well as you can.

3. You will now use a small box as your "reaction chamber." Place your bundles inside and shake your box vigorously, so that the bundle bounces and is knocked around. Shake hard for at least 10 seconds, and make sure to shake in various directions (not just up and down with the same motion the entire time). Before starting your observations, hypothesize what you think will happen. What trends do you predict?

313

Student Data Sheet

Stringy Chemisty & States of Matter

Hypothesis:

_____

_____

_____

_____

4. For each bundle record your observations. How does the strand hold up under shaking? Count the pieces after shaking. Did some bundles stay together better? If you have other ways of measuring the outcome, create a new measure in the column provided.

Data Table

Strand Length	Number of Separate Pieces	Appearance	Comments
1 m strand bundle			
20 cm strand bundle			
10 cm strand bundle			
3 cm strand bundle			
1 cm strand bundle			

Questions

314

1. **What trends did you observe? Did the bundles of longer pieces behave differently than the bundles of shorter pieces?**

2. What do you think explains these trends? If you observed a difference, what is your explanation for it?

3. Three long chain molecules are shown below. One molecule, when mixed with thousands of copies of itself, is a gas at room temperature; another is a liquid; and the third is a solid. By each molecule, write either solid, gas or liquid.

Molecule A	Molecule B	Molecule C
_____	_____	_____

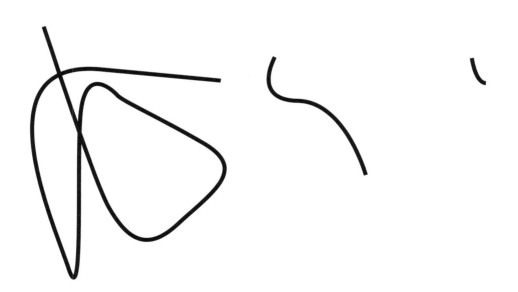

315

Chapter 25
Our Amazing Senses

Overview

We interact with the world through our senses. We see, hear, smell, and touch the universe around us. What exactly are these sensations? In a way, our sensations are measurements. Our sensory organs are finely tuned instruments that not only detect but also measure different environmental inputs. In particular, our eyes, ears, and nose are extraordinary sensors. The tasks these organs face are incredibly challenging. Typical light and sound intensities can vary by a factor of one billion. We detect chemicals in the air with parts per billion sensitivity. Our sensory organs are finely adapted to accommodate this huge range of input intensities. In this investigation students examine the magnitude of different signals that our senses detect.

Objective

- To develop an understanding of the range of stimuli that our senses detect.

Process Skills

- Observing
- Estimating
- Measuring

Activity Duration

60 minutes

Background

In our daily lives we receive huge amounts of information through our senses. This information comes in many different forms: light, sound, smell, taste, and tactile input. Each type of information that we receive is complex. Our senses are finely adapted to accommodate the complexity of the information. For example, our ears are capable of detecting very faint sounds as well as very loud ones; they are capable of hearing sounds over a large range of frequencies (20 Hz–20,000 Hz), low pitches and high pitches. Our eyes detect not only the level of brightness, but also color (the frequency of the light rays). Our noses can detect as many as 10,000 distinct scents and measure the intensity of each. In other words, our senses have multidimensional detection capabilities. An amazing thing! The investigations focus on the sensitivity of the senses to the magnitudes of different inputs: the loudness range of sound, the brightness range of light, and the range of scent strengths.

Engage

Explain to your students that in this series of investigations they will explore the magnitudes of sensory input intensity (brightness, loudness, smelliness). In Part I they will investigate the magnitudes of sounds. In Part II they build a model depict-

317

ing "one part per million" and "one part per billion." In Part III they make a series of dilutions that will allow them to investigate how sight and smell perception differ for very small amounts of materials.

Part I. Sound

Materials

- Student Data Sheets

Ask your students, *How many times louder is your voice when you scream than when you whisper?*

Explore

Pass out Student Data Sheet 1. Students should discuss how many times louder a normal speaking voice and a class of yelling students would be, compared with a whisper. After students predict, share the actual measurements.

Part II. Modeling Parts per Billion

Materials

- Materials for constructing a 1-meter cube, such as boxes and cardboard
- Clay
- Student Data Sheet 2

This investigation provides students with an intuitive visual experience of the concepts of parts per million and parts per billion. They build a model that represents a volume of air with a single scent molecule within. They will first construct a model volume or chamber that is 1 cubic meter in volume. They will then calculate the size of their model molecule. The calculation will determine the equivalent volume of one-millionth and one-billionth of a cubic meter.

Have students build a 1-meter cube. This can be done by finding a very large box and modifying it, or simply using scrap cardboard to construct a cube. Be sure to keep one face open to enable them to see into the interior. If materials are available, try building a frame of a 1 m cube out of tinker toys or other building materials (e.g., meter sticks or bamboo sticks). This will

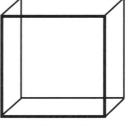

Model of 1 m Cube

require some engineering but will be a fun and challenging project on its own. A very simple method would be to take twelve 1 m lengths of string and have the students hold them in the shape of a cube.

One Part per Million Volume Calculation

The students begin by calculating the volume of the object they will place within the cube. The cube is 1 meter on a side. This is our air volume or Vair. Its volume is:

$$V_{air} = (1 \text{ m})^3 = 1 \text{ m}^3$$

To determine how to construct a model that represents 1 one-millionth of this volume we first determine the volume of the model particle, $V_{particle}$. We then take the cube root to determine the size of the edge of the particle.

$$V_{particle} = (V_{air}) / 1,000,000 = (1 \text{ m}^3) / 1,000,000 = 0.000001 \text{ m}^3 = 10^{-6} \text{ m}^3$$

$$V_{particle} = 10^{-6} \text{ m}^3$$

We now take the cube root to determine the edge length of a cube of this volume or the edge length of our particle, L_{edge}:

$$L_{edge} = (V_{particle})^{1/3} = (10^{-6} \text{ m}^3)^{1/3} = 10^{-2} \text{ m, or 1 cm}$$

$$L_{edge} = 1 \text{ cm}$$

The model molecule, if it is to take up 1 one-millionth of the volume of the 1 m cube, must be 1 cm on a side. Have students construct a 1 cm cube with clay, Legos, or other materials.

One Part per Million Volume Calculation

To determine how to construct a model that represents 1 one-billionth of this volume, we first determine the volume of the model particle, $V_{particle}$. We then take the cube root to determine the size of the edge of the particle.

$$V_{particle} = (V_{air})/1,000,000,000 = (1\ m^3)/1,000,000,000 = 0.000000001\ m^3 = 10^{-9}\ m^3$$

$$V_{particle} = 10^{-9}\ m^3$$

We now take the cube root to determine the edge length of a cube of this volume or the edge length of our particle, L_{edge}:

$$L_{edge} = (V_{particle})^{1/3} = (10^{-9}\ m^3)^{1/3} = 10^{-3}\ m,\ or\ 1\ mm$$

$$L_{edge} = 1\ mm$$

The model molecule, if it is to take up 1 one-billionth of the volume of the 1 m cube, must be 1 mm on a side. A large sand grain or large salt grain is roughly 1 mm. Students could also try to ball up small particles of clay to represent their 1 mm cube molecule.

NATIONAL SCIENCE TEACHERS ASSOCIATION

Part III. One Part per Billion

Note: Part III is adapted from Jones, M., A. Taylor, B. Broadwell, and M. Falvo. 2007. *Nanoscale Science*. Arlington, VA: NSTA Press.

Just how big is 1 part per billion? Can you see a part per billion? Students use dilutions in this investigation.

Materials

Each group will need:

- White paper
- 1 ml dropper
- Food coloring
- 200 ml of water
- Rinse cup of water
- 9 small cups (clear or white) or beakers
- 1 ml mouthwash (not to be distributed until the EXTEND section)
- 2 graduated cylinders (10 ml)
- Student Data Sheet 3

Procedures

Begin the investigation by asking the students, *Would you rather have air pollution levels that were 10 parts per million or 10 parts per billion? Why?*

Note: Explaining Dilution

Students will need to have an understanding of solutions and how their concentrations are calculated to complete the activity.

Hold up a beaker with 95 grams of water (95 milliliters). Ask the class, *If I wanted to make this a 5% sugar solution, how much sugar do I need to add to it?* Write "95 grams of water" on the board. Once you have received the answer 5 grams, write "5 grams of sugar + 95 grams of water = 100 grams of solution." Write the fraction "5 grams of sugar/100 grams of solution." If the students seem to have difficulty understanding percentage, then you may want to be prepared to add other examples.

Hold up a beaker of water and red food coloring (a 10% solution). Tell the students that this is a 10% solution. Ask, *Tell me how I would make this solution out of water and food coloring.*

Further explain that 10 parts of food coloring were added to 90 parts of water. You can demonstrate this by putting 9 drops of water in a clear cup or beaker, and then adding 1 drop of food coloring.

321

Explore

It is suggested that students work in pairs. Each pair should have nine small cups or beakers, placed on a blank, white piece of paper to help them see the color change. Explain that they will perform a series of dilutions, each larger by a power of 10. This is referred to as *a serial dilution*. Distribute Student Data Sheet 3.

You may need to get them started by doing cups 1 and 2 as a class. You may also need to help them calculate the concentrations for these cups. Explain and write on the board that cup 1 has a 10% solution, or 1/10 solution. If they add 1 ml of a 1/10 solution to 9 ml of water, the solution will now be 1/10 of 1/10, which equals 1/100, or 1%, or 1 part per hundred. Have them calculate the concentration of cup.

Ask students to discuss the results of their investigation.

Discuss with the students that *parts per billion* typically is used when working

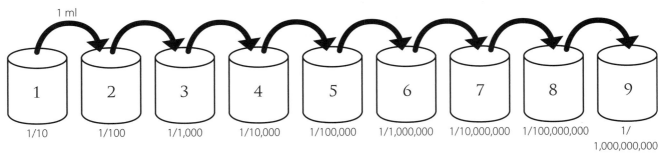

1 ml

| 1 | 2 | 3 | 4 | 5 | 6 | 7 | 8 | 9 |

| 1/10 | 1/100 | 1/1,000 | 1/10,000 | 1/100,000 | 1/1,000,000 | 1/10,000,000 | 1/100,000,000 | 1/1,000,000,000 |

with extremely small amounts. At a certain dilution level, the color is no longer apparent, but the dye is still present. We cannot see objects that are at scales of 1 part per billion, but they do exist. It is important for students to understand that even when things are too small to be seen, that does not mean that they don't exist or that they are too small to have an effect.

Next, students further develop their understanding of the size of one-billionth by repeating the dilution activity using their sense of smell.

Note: Students' results in the data table may vary.

322

Our Amazing Senses

Answer Sheet

Teacher Key: Dilution Activity

Cup	Color	Concentration
1	Black-green	0.1
2	Dark green	0.01
3	Medium green	0.001
4	Very light green	0.0001
5	Slightly green	0.00001
6	Clear	0.000001
7	Clear	0.0000001
8	Clear	0.00000001
9	Clear	0.000000001

1. **In which cup did the solution first appear colorless?**

   Answer: This may vary, but it should become colorless at cup 5 or 6.

2. **What is the concentration of food coloring in this cup?**

   Answer: Cup 5 = 1/100,000 or 10 ppm
   Cup 6 = 1/1,000,000 or 1 ppm

3. **Do you think there is any food coloring present in this cup of diluted solution, even though you cannot see it? Explain.**

   Answer: Yes, the solution is still present with each dilution because a tiny amount was transferred from one cup to another.

4. **What is the concentration of cup 9? Explain your answer in your own words.**

323

Our Amazing Senses

Answer: 1/1,000 ppm or 1 part per billion. There is one part of the dye for every billion parts of water.

Extend
Investigating Smell

Distribute to each group 1 ml of mouthwash, nine clean cups (or beakers), and Student Data Sheet 3. Students will use smell in this investigation, as well as color, as they make serial dilutions. Students are able to detect the presence of mouthwash by smell, even after they can no longer see it. This provides an opportunity to discuss how things at the nanoscale are present even though they cannot be seen.

Evaluate

Cup	Color	Smell	Concentration
1	Slightly green	Strong	0.1
2	Clear	Medium	0.01
3	Clear	Medium	0.001
4	Clear	Slightly	0.0001
5	Clear	Slightly	0.00001
6	Clear	Barely	0.000001
7	Clear	Barely	0.0000001
8	Clear	None	0.00000001
9	Clear	None	0.000000001

As a whole class, talk about the answers to the Discussion questions on Student Data Sheet 4.

324

Our Amazing Senses

Teacher Key—Going Further

1. **In which cup did the solution first appear colorless?**

   Answer: This will vary depending on initial darkness of solution.

2. **In which cup did the solution first appear odorless?**

   Answer: Around cups 6 or 7.

3. **At what point do you think you will no longer be able to smell the solution?**

   Answer: This will vary.

4. **Which cup holds the "nano" percent solution?**

   Answer: This can vary as well. If they followed the same procedure as in the previous dilution activity, then the answer is cup 9.

5. **What is the actual percentage solution of this "nano" mixture, written in numerical format?**

   Answer: 1 ppb or 1/1,000,000,000

6. **Explain how you made a "nano" percent solution.**

   Answer: This may vary; however you should take a close look at students' procedures to assess their understanding of 1 ppb.

Explain

The huge range of intensities in light, sound, and smells that our sensory organs must manage presents a very fundamental problem: How can we be sensitive to small variations of light in a darkly lit room, but then the next moment be able to walk out into sunlit day and navigate in the brighter world? When we do this, we are measuring light intensities but on extremely different scales. To put this in perspective, the same changes when measuring distances would be equivalent to making fine millimeter measurements one moment and measuring distances of millions of kilometers the next! Our sensory instruments provide us with the remarkable ability to switch from one extreme in intensity scale to another.

325

Sight

Our eyes provide us reliable visual information both in a room lit by a single candle and on a sunny summer day at the beach. Light intensity, or luminance, in these two cases can vary by a factor of over 1 billion. Our eyes are uniquely adapted to detect these ranges of light. Light is a wave of oscillating electric and magnetic fields. It shares some characteristics with other types of waves: It has a wavelength, a frequency, and a velocity.

Although humans can see a wide range of the spectrum (typically in the 400 to 700 nanometer range), some animals cannot see as well as humans, and others can see parts of the spectrum that we cannot see. Animals such as prairie dogs and squirrels are red/green color-blind. Bees can see ultraviolet light that allows them to locate nectar on flowers that reflect ultraviolet frequencies.

For further information:
- *www.pigeon.psy.tufts.edu/ecp.htm*
- *www.engmu.edu/rehab/rehab167/mod2/seeing*

Hearing

Our sense of hearing is quite remarkable. Our ears are capable of detecting the sound of a friend whispering in a quiet room but can also accommodate the sounds of jet engines and nearby thunderclaps. The range of sound intensity these examples bracket is astonishingly large. Sound is simply a pressure wave that travels through air (sound actually travels through all matter: solid, liquid, gas). Sound intensity is defined as the power transported per unit area by this pressure wave through the air (or whatever medium it is traveling through).

Our ears are remarkable for a variety of reasons. First, they are incredibly sensitive. We can hear the rustle of leaves in a gentle breeze or the drop of a pin in a quiet room. These events produce sound pressure waves in the air that reach our ears. These sound pressure waves are simply variations in the pressure around the average atmospheric pressure. These very quiet sounds at the threshold of our hearing capability are produced by variations in pressure that are less than one-billionth of atmospheric pressure. Second, our ears have an enormous range over which they can detect sound intensities. Our ears are capable of detecting sound intensities over a range of 13 or 14 orders of magnitude or powers of ten. This means that the loudest sound your ears can handle is 10^{14} or 100 trillion times the intensity of the quietest detectable sound! What is interesting is that our perception of sound is such that we don't really perceive this 100-trillion-fold range. A powerful jet engine might seem 100 times louder to us than a normal conversation, or perhaps 1,000 times louder, but not a billion or a trillion times louder (which in fact it is, in sound intensity terms). Our *perception* of sound intensities seems to follow a logarithmic relationship to the actual sound intensity. Simply put, a sound that is 10 times the intensity of another is perceived by our brain as being only twice as loud.

For further information:
- *www.sengpielaudio.com/TableOfSoundPressureLevels.htm*
- *http://hyperphysics.phy-astr.gsu.edu/Hbase/sound/intens.html#c3*
- *http://hyperphysics.phy-astr.gsu.edu/Hbase/Sound/db.html*

Smell

We smell when our noses detect molecules of volatile materials. Our noses have different olfactory receptors that allow us to detect different odors. It has been estimated that we can detect over 10,000 different smells. Each receptor is the result of a different gene that codes for that specific odor.

Smell and taste are both chemical senses that detect different molecules in the environment. The sense of smell is more acute and can detect molecules at a greater distance than the sense of taste. Both smell and taste play critical roles in helping us to detect dangerous situations such as a gas leak or food that has spoiled. Animals use smell to communicate a variety of types of information, including territory boundaries, predator presence, reproductive readiness, or the location of other members of their species. It has been reported that our noses can detect a few parts per trillion for some odors. In one case, people in Kansas reported that their water tasted bad. Biologists traced the bad taste to a chemical known as *geosmin* that is given off when bacteria die in the water. The level of geosmin was only 30 parts per trillion (*http://www.news. ku.edu/2007/february/12/watertaste.shtml*).

For further information:
- *http://health.howstuffworks.com/question139.htm*
- *www.cardiff.ac.uk/biosi/staffinfo/jacob/teaching/sensory/olfact1.html*
- *www.rense.com/general7/whyy.htm*

327

Extend

There are many interesting areas for further investigation related to the sensitivity of the senses. Your students can investigate different animal senses to find the species with the best sense of smell. Challenge them to find out how the sense of smell helps animals survive. Pheromones are another area that is interesting to explore. Invite your students to learn more about how scientists design experiments to see if pheromones exist and to design an experiment to see if humans have pheromones.

Evaluate

Check for student understanding:

1. How many times louder was the sound when the class shouted than when you whispered?
2. Is our perception of sound linear or logarithmic?
3. If a sound is 10 times the intensity of another sound, how much louder does it sound?
4. What is the largest difference at which a human can perceive a smell? Would it be parts per thousand, parts per million, parts per billion, or parts per trillion?

TABLE 1.
Sound Intensities

Sound	Intensity in decibels (dB)	Intensity in watts per meter squared (W/m²)
Eardrum rupture	>160 dB	10,000
Jet engine (at 30–50 m)	140 dB	100
Threshold of pain	120 dB	1
Chain saw at 1 m	110 dB	0.1
A room full of shouting students	80 dB	0.0001
Normal conversation	60 dB	0.000001
Whisper	20 dB	0.0000000001
A paper clip dropping form 10 ft.	10 dB	0.00000000001
Threshold of hearing	4 dB	0.0000000000025

Adapted from data within the following sources:

Ohanian, H. 1985. *Physics.* New York: Norton.

www.sengpielaudio.com/TableOfSoundPressureLevels.htm

http://hyperphysics.phy-astr.gsu.edu/Hbase/sound/intens.html#c3

http://hyperphysics.phy-astr.gsu.edu/Hbase/Sound/db.html

http://people.seas.harvard.edu/~jones/cscie129/nu_lectures/lecture8/images/soundspl.gif

www.osha.gov/dts/osta/otm/noise/health_effects/soundpressure_aweighted.html

TABLE 2.
Light Intensities

Light Source	Luminance candelas per meter squared (cd/m²)	Luminance (log scale)
Photo flash	100,000,000	8
Sunny day	100,000	5
Indoor lighting	100	2
Candle	1	0
Moonlight	0.01	-2
Starlight	0.001	-3
Threshold	0.000001	-6

Adapted from data within the following sources:

http://webvision.med.utah.edu/

http://webvision.med.utah.edu/imageswv/table3.jpeg

www.telescope-optics.net/eye_spectral_response.htm

Name _____

Part I : How Much Louder?

Sound intensity is a measure of how loud a sound is. How much louder are some sounds than others?

Sound level 1. Wait until your teacher has quieted the class. Have one member of your group whisper so quietly that you can barely hear her. Make sure to coordinate with other groups so that only one person is whispering in the room at a time. It should be silent in the room except for one person whispering. Call this a sound level of 1.

Sound level 2. Have one person speak in a normal voice that all students in the room can hear.
- How much louder is this sound than the whispered sound?
- Make an estimate of this sound level. Assign a number to it that provides a magnitude relative to the whisper sound level.

Sound level 3. When your teacher gives you the signal, you and all of your classmates should yell as loudly as you can for 3 seconds.
- How much louder is this sound than level 1?
- How much louder is this sound than level 2?
- Assign a number to the sound intensity.

Sound	Sound Description	Your Estimate of Sound Intensity	Actual Relative Intensity (Estimate Provided by Teacher)
Sound level 1	Whisper	1.0	1.0
Sound level 2	Normal speaking voice		
Sound level 3	All students yelling		

1. How far off was your estimate from the actual relative intensity for each level?

2. Why do you think your body does not interpret sound as a strict linear increase from one level to the next?

Name _____

Part II: Modeling Parts per Billion!

Though not as sensitive as those of bloodhounds or bears, our noses are still quite remarkable. Noses are sensors that detect molecules in the air. We can routinely detect concentrations of molecules in the air at 1 part per million (1 scent molecule for every million air molecules). In some cases, we can smell molecules at concentrations of 1 part per billion! What does 1 part per million or 1 part per billion look like?

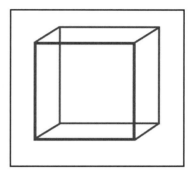

Your teacher will provide materials to build a 1 m cube. This cube will represent a volume of air in which you will place a model scent molecule. You will place your molecule within the chamber when you are finished.

1. Construct your cubic meter out of materials provided by your teacher. This cubic volume represents a volume of air you might breathe through your nose.

2. Determine the size of a particle that would take up 1 one-millionth of the volume within your cubic meter. Place the model molecule within the cube. If the volume of air represented by your cube passed into your nose, you would be able to detect the presence of the particle. This concentration of particles, 1 part per million or 1 ppm, is a very easy target for your nose if the scent particle in question is one for which our noses are sensitive.

3. Determine the size of a particle that would take up 1 one-billionth of the volume within your cubic meter. Place the model molecule within the cube. If the volume of air represented by your cube passed into your nose, you would be able to detect the presence of the particle. This concentration of particles, 1 part per billion or 1 ppb, is a harder target for your nose, but in some cases we can detect this extremely low concentration.

331

Name _____

Part III: Parts per Billion!

Problem

At what concentration (which cup) will the solution appear colorless?

Prediction (Write your hypothesis in the space below.)

_____

_____

Materials

Each group will need:

- White paper
- 1 ml dropper
- Food coloring
- 200 ml of water
- Rinse cup of water
- 9 small cups (clear or white) or beakers
- 2 graduated cylinders (10 ml)

Procedure

1. Number the cups or beakers 1 through 9.
2. Place white paper under the nine cups or beakers.
3. Using a graduated cylinder, put 1 ml of food coloring and 9 ml of water in cup 1. Be sure to rinse the graduated cylinder with water each time. Swirl the cup or beaker gently to mix solution.
4. In the chart on the next page, describe the color of the solution in cup 1, and write "0.1" under "Concentration" to represent a 10% solution.
5. In cup 2, add 1 ml of solution from cup 1 and 9 ml of water. Again, describe the color and calculate the concentration of the solution. Record results in chart.
6. In cup 3, add 1 ml of solution from cup 2 and 9 ml of water. Record results in chart.
7. Continue the dilution process as done above for cups 4 through 9. Record all results in the chart.

332

Results

Cup	Color	Concentration
1		
2		
3		
4		
5		
6		
7		
8		
9		

Conclusion

1. In which cup did the solution first appear colorless?

2. What is the concentration of food coloring in that cup?

3. Do you think there is any food coloring present in the cup of diluted solution even though you cannot see it? Explain.

4. What is the concentration of cup 9? Explain your answer in your own words.

333

Name _____

Part IV: Going Further

Your challenge is to dilute mouthwash to the point that it is a billionth percent solution. You will use the same process as you did for the first dilution investigation. In cup 1, add 1 ml of mouthwash and 9 ml of water. As you continue the dilution process for cups 2 through 9, record your observations of color and smell. Calculate and record the concentrations.

Cup	Color	Smell	Concentration
1			
2			
3			
4			
5			
6			
7			
8			
9			

Discussion

1. **In which cup did the solution first appear colorless?**

2. **In which cup did the solution first appear odorless?**

3. **At what point do you think you will no longer be able to smell the solution?**

4. **Which cup holds the "parts per billion" solution?**

5. **What is the actual percentage solution of this mixture, written in numerical format?**

334

Chapter 26
Beetlemice Multitudes!!!
Power Law & Exponential Scaling

Overview

Scaling describes how a quantity changes over time or with the size of a system. It can also be defined as how a quantity changes in relation to any another parameter. When you stop and think about it, all of the equations in math and science are scaling relationships: how the volume of a sphere scales with radius, how the force of gravity scales with the mass of the object, how a population of birds grows over time. The equations that describe these scalings between one parameter and another have particular mathematical forms. In this investigation students explore two types of mathematical scaling: power laws that describe geometrical relationships and exponential growth.

Objectives

- To develop skills in analyzing data.
- To become familiar with scaling data.
- To develop an understanding of power law and exponential scaling.
- To be able to apply power law to a novel data set.

Process Skills

- Analyzing data

Activity Duration

50 minutes

Background

One of the goals of scientific inquiry is to provide a quantitative description of natural phenomena. Physics, biology, chemistry, and geology all aim at determining quantitative relationships that help us refine theories and provide a better scientific understanding. These quantitative relationships are the mathematical and scientific equations that are the foundation of science. Ultimately these equations are nothing more than scaling relationships that describe how one measurable property changes as a function of another (e.g., population over time, electrostatic force with distance). The simplest mathematical relation between two parameters is called a *linear* relationship: One parameter is *linearly proportional* to another. For example, for objects of uniform density, mass is proportional to volume (this is a linear relationship between mass and volume).

Establishing scaling relationships helps us in many ways. First, these scaling equations help us make successful predictions. If we know that the intensity of light from a point source (such as a lightbulb) decreases as the square of the distance from the light bulb, then when we double our distance, we know the intensity of the light will be reduced by a factor of 4. Another very important way scientists use scaling is to determine underlying reasons for why things are the way they are. For example, if a set of data shows an exponential dependence of some parameter on time, this indicates geometric growth, or a growth rate that depends on the current size of that parameter.

335

Power Law Scaling

Perhaps the most familiar type of scaling is *power law* scaling. The name *power law* refers to the fact that one parameter is dependent on another parameter raised to some power. The following familiar relations are power laws relating geometrical measures of a circle or sphere to some power of the radius:

Linear Relationships
Diameter of a circle = 2 × Radius
Circumference of a circle = 2 × π × Radius (this is a linear relationship between circumference and radius)

Quadratic (Square) Relationships
Area of circle = π × (Radius)^2
Area of a sphere = 4 × π × (Radius)^2

Cubic Relationships
Volume of a sphere = 4/3 × π × (Radius)^3

These are simple geometrical relationships, but they are important examples; many of the power laws that exist in science are rooted in some geometrical aspect of the system.

Exponential Scaling

Exponential scaling is probably most commonly encountered in growth rate applications and is referred to as *exponential growth*. This phrase is commonly used to describe very high rates of growth and is very often used in a nonprecise mathematical way. Not all very rapid growth is exponential growth, and not all exponential growth is particularly rapid.

It is actually simple to provide a technically correct description of exponential growth in common language: If the rate of growth of a system depends on the current size of the system, that system is growing exponentially. The bigger it is, the faster it grows. Money in your bank account and populations are systems where this sort of growth can commonly occur.

Materials

- Student Data Sheets
- Scratch paper for calculations
- Calculator

336

Engage

Explain that there are different ways in which quantities can scale. Two types that are quite common are *power law scaling* and *exponential scaling*. Explain that geometrical relations that they are familiar with, such as the area of a circle or the volume of a cube, are power law relationships. One parameter depends on another taken to some power (or exponent). Explain that exponential scaling is another common type of scaling that often is related to growth, such as growth of populations or growth of money in your bank account. Explain that exponential growth is characterized by the rate of growth being proportional to the current population. The more there is, the faster it grows.

Explore

Use the board to explain some of these concepts mathematically. Use a simple population example to illustrate how exponential growth works. Use a paper-tearing example. Have students tear a piece of paper in two (step 1). Explain that you will then take each piece and split it in two, then repeat, splitting each existing piece in two at each step. Ask them to predict how many pieces they will have after 5, 6, or 7 steps, or even 20 steps. Ask how many steps can be performed before the pieces are too small to continue. Then have them proceed to tear each piece in two and repeat. Have them write down how many pieces are left after each step. Create a table on the board and record the number of pieces for each step. Challenge the students to determine an equation that would describe the number of pieces at each step.

Number of pieces = 2 × 2 × . . . × 2 (where the number of 2s is the number of tearing steps).

Number of pieces = 2^N , where N is the number of tearing steps.

If your class is patient, they may get to step 6 ($2^6 = 64$ pieces), step 7 ($2^7 = 128$ pieces), or even step 8 ($2^8 = 256$ pieces!).

Student Data Sheets

Beetlemice Multitudes

In this investigation students examine the growth rate of an imaginary animal—the beetlemouse. Describe the imaginary context: Read the introductory paragraph on Student Data Sheet 1. The activity allows students to look at exponential growth rates. Distribute Student Data Sheet 1.

Introduce the investigation by explaining that beetlemice split in two every hour. At noon on day 1, you place one beetlemouse into the warehouse. One hour later it splits into two. For question 2, they will need a calculator, though some very adventurous students may want to try to do the calculation by hand.

Investigating Mystery Spheres and Cubes

Hand out Student Data Sheet 2, Mystery Spheres and Cubes. This second investigation involves students in determining whether a set of cubes and spheres is solid or hollow. Describe the imaginary context: Read the introductory paragraph on Student Data Sheet 2.

Encourage the students to analyze the spheres separately from the cubes. The spheres are solid, and the cubes are hollow. Simply evaluating the mass and the size of a sphere or cube will not allow them to determine whether it is hollow or solid. However, if students analyze how the *mass changes with size*, in particular by looking at ratios of masses and sizes, they can answer the question. In fact, only two (any two) of each set are needed to determine the scaling, which will determine whether they are solid or hollow.

Remind the students that the surface area of a sphere is $4 \times Pi \times (radius)^2$ and the volume of a sphere is $4/3 \times Pi \times (radius)^3$. The volume of a cube is simply the cube of the length of one of its sides. The surface area of a cube is 6 times the area of one of its faces, since there are 6 faces on a cube.

Explain

Beetlemice Multitudes Solution

The beetlemice split in two every hour. At noon on day 1, you place one beetlemouse into the warehouse. One hour later it splits into two. At two hours you have 2×2. At three hours they have split three times ($2 \times 2 \times 2$), or 2^3 (there will be eight beetlemice). Every hour, we multiply the existing number of beetlemice by 2. Let's use the symbol $P(t)$ to represent the population of beetlemice at time t, where t is the number of hours.

$P(t) = 2 \times 2 \times 2 \ldots 2$ (where the number of 2s is equal to the number of hours)

For example: $P(2 \text{ hrs.}) = 2 \times 2 = 2^2 = 4$

And $P(5 \text{ hrs.}) = 2 \times 2 \times 2 \times 2 \times 2 = 2^5 = 32$

338

Beetlemice Multitudes!!!

Answer Sheet

We can write down a general equation for the population at time t:

$P(t) = 2^t$ where t is the time in hours since introduction of the beetlemice.

Ask your students:

1. When you leave work just after 5 o'clock on that first day, how many beetlemice are there? Would they be crowded in the warehouse?

At 5 o'clock, the beetlemice undergo their fifth splitting. So

$P(5 \text{ hrs.}) = 2^5 = 32$

Next, challenge your students to think about the next day:

2. When you arrive the next morning just after 8 a.m., how many beetlemice are there?

At 8 a.m. the next morning, the beetlemice undergo their 20th splitting, since it has been 20 hours since their introduction into the warehouse.

$P(20 \text{ hrs.}) = 2^{20} = 1,048,600$

3. How much room do these beetlemice take up at this point?

Each beetlemouse is 10 cm wide and 10 cm long; in units of meters, they are 0.1 m wide and 0.1 m long.

So the area each beetlemouse takes up is roughly equal to
$(0.1 \text{ m}) \times (0.1 \text{ m}) = 0.01 \text{ m}^2$

The total number of beetlemice is roughly 1 million (1,000,000). The total area the beetlemice take up if they are packed closely together would be

Total area of beetlemice = area of each beetlemouse x number of beetlemice

= 1,000,000 beetlemice × 0.01 m²/beetlemouse = 10,000 m²

339

4. Can they remain in the warehouse?

The total floor area of the warehouse is 25 m × 10 m = 250 m².

The 1 million beetlemice are taking up 40 times the area of the warehouse floor. No they can't!! They are 40 beetlemice deep!!

Related Websites

- Exponential Growth: This website has a series of applets that allow students to see animations of population growth for fish. *www.otherwise.com/population/index.html*
- World Wide Web Exponential Growth: Students can see data showing how use of the internet has grown exponentially since 1993. *www.usna.edu/MathDept/website/courses/calc_labs/Expon/Application.html*
- Are you smarter than yeast? This video clip shows yeast dividing with exponential growth. Students can learn how to determine the doubling time and the rule of 70. The video ends with the challenge to students to consider consumption and waste for human activity. *www.youtube.com/watch?v=hM1x4RljmnE*

Spheres Solution

If the spheres are solid, then their mass is proportional to their total volume. If we pick any two of the spheres, we can look at what the ratio of their masses should be if they are solid and made of the same material (same density):

$$\frac{M_1}{M_2} = \frac{Volume_1}{Volume_2} = \frac{\frac{4}{3} \times \pi \times r_1^3}{\frac{4}{3} \times \pi \times r_2^3} = \frac{r_1^3}{r_2^3} = \left(\frac{r_1}{r_2}\right)^3$$

where M_1, M_2 are the masses of sphere 1 and sphere 2, and r_1 and r_2 are the radii of the two objects respectively. This equation shows that if the spheres are solid, the ratio of the masses would be equal to the cube of the ratio of their radii.

If the spheres are hollow, their masses would be proportional to their surface area (approximately; if the spheres were very, very thin shells this would be the case). The ratio of the masses of any two spheres would then be:

$$\frac{M_1}{M_2} = \frac{SurfaceArea_1}{SurfaceArea_2} = \frac{4 \times \pi \times r_1^2}{4 \times \pi \times r_2^2} = \frac{r_1^2}{r_2^2} = \left(\frac{r_1}{r_2}\right)^2$$

340

If the spheres are hollow, the ratio of their masses would be equal to the square of the ratio of their radii.

If we pick any two spheres, we will be able to see how the spheres' masses scale with radius. For example, let's pick the 7 cm sphere and the 3 cm sphere. The ratio of their masses is

$$\frac{M_{7cm}}{M_{3cm}} = 359g \: / \: 28.2 \: g = 12.7$$

The ratio of their radii is $\left(\dfrac{r_1}{r_2}\right) = 7cm/3cm = 2.33$

The cube of radii ratio is $\left(\dfrac{r_1}{r_2}\right)^3 = (2.33)^3 = 12.6$

The square of the radii ratio is $\left(\dfrac{r_1}{r_2}\right)^2 = (2.33)^2 = 5.42$

The cube of the ratio of the radii matches almost exactly with the ratio of the masses. This indicates the spheres are solid.

Extend
Advanced Solution to the Spheres Problem

For more mathematically advanced students, a more rigorous solution can be explored. This solution for the sphere case is outlined here.

In this solution, we assume that the mass of the object is equal to some geometrical factor, A, multiplied by some power of the radius. This is consistent with both the equation for the surface area of a sphere and the volume. In the case of the surface area, the geometrical factor is $4 \times Pi$, and the power of the radius is raised to the power of 2 ($4 \times Pi \times r^2$). In the case of the equation for the volume of a sphere, the geometrical factor is $4/3 \times Pi$, and radius is raised to the power of 3. So we make a generic equation for the volume of the sphere that does not assume either case:

$$M = A \times r^N$$

where M is the mass of the object, A is the geometrical factor, and N is the power or exponent of the radius. We want to solve for N, which will determine whether our mass depends on the square or the cube of the radius, which will in turn tell us if the spheres are hollow or solid. We accomplish this by taking the ratio of the masses of two different spheres, 1 and 2.

$$\frac{M_1}{M_2} = \frac{A \times r_1^N}{A \times r_2^N} = \frac{r_1^N}{r_2^N} = \left(\frac{r_1}{r_2}\right)^N$$

The equation simplifies to $\dfrac{M_1}{M_2} = \left(\dfrac{r_1}{r_2}\right)^N$

To solve for N, we need to take the logarithm of both sides. $\log\left(\dfrac{M_1}{M_2}\right) = \log\left(\dfrac{r_1}{r_2}\right)^N$

Using the properties of logarithms, we can take the exponent N and place as a prefactor multiplied by the log of the radii ratios.

$$\log\left(\frac{M_1}{M_2}\right) = N \times \log\left(\frac{r_1}{r_2}\right)$$

Solve for N. $\quad N = \dfrac{\log\left(\dfrac{M_1}{M_2}\right)}{\log\left(\dfrac{r_1}{r_2}\right)}$

The equation above allows us to take our mass and radii data and solve for the exponent N. If we take the case of the 4 cm and 3 cm spheres:

$$N = \frac{\log\left(\dfrac{M_{4cm}}{M_{3cm}}\right)}{\log\left(\dfrac{r_{4cm}}{r_{3cm}}\right)} = \frac{\log\left(\dfrac{67.0g}{28.2g}\right)}{\log\left(\dfrac{4\,cm}{3\,cm}\right)} = \frac{\log(2.376)}{\log(1.333)} = 3.01$$

N equals very nearly 3 (the error is due to rounding). This means the masses are proportional to the cube of the radius, indicating that they are solid.

Evaluate

Check for student understanding:

1. If human populations grew like beetlemice, what would be the implications for our ecology?
2. Do humans have exponential growth rates?
3. What keeps populations in the wild from growing exponentially?
4. Can you suggest a real situation in which scientists would have to determine whether something is solid or hollow, as in the case of the mystery spheres and cubes?
5. Would you want your bank account to grow exponentially or by simple linear growth?

Name _____

Beetlemice Multitudes

You are a famous zookeeper assigned to a challenging species containment project. A new species has been discovered in the deep jungles of the Brazilian Amazon. It is a mysterious animal that is as yet unclassified. It has been dubbed the *Brazilian beetlemouse* because it has six legs and an iridescent shell like a beetle's but a head and face like those of a mouse. The very strange thing about this animal is that each individual reproduces by splitting in two every hour, resulting in two fully grown beetlemice.

You are challenged with housing this animal in a warehouse on the edge of the zoo grounds. The warehouse is roughly the size of a tennis court (10 m × 25 m). The beetlemouse is about 10 cm wide by 10 cm long by 5 cm high—quite small, so you should have no problem with room. The truck arrives at noon with the first beetlemouse. It has been kept in a dark, cold chamber, which has kept it from splitting. When released into the warehouse, however, it begins to split into two every hour, making more and more beetlemice, which in turn split in two after one hour. You watch for the rest of the day and see that the numbers are reasonably small after a few hours.

Use a separate paper to work out the following questions and place your answers here. Save your work!!

1. **When you leave work at 5 o'clock on that first day, how many beetlemice are there? Would they be crowded in the warehouse?**

2. **When you arrive the next morning at 8 a.m., how many beetlemice are there?**

3. **How much room do the beetlemice take up at this point?**

4. **Can they remain in the warehouse?**

Name _____

Mystery Spheres and Cubes

You are a science detective who has been called to solve an important mystery. The local science museum has received some mysterious objects recently discovered in a remote region of the Gobi Desert. There are two sets of objects. One set consists of four red spheres. The other is a set of four gray cubes. The two sets of objects appear to be made of different, unknown materials. Among the many important questions the scientists who are studying these objects want to know is the following: *Are the objects solid or hollow?* All nondestructive methods of answering this question have failed (X-ray imaging for example). The scientists do not want to damage the objects but need to know whether they are solid or hollow. Can you help them?

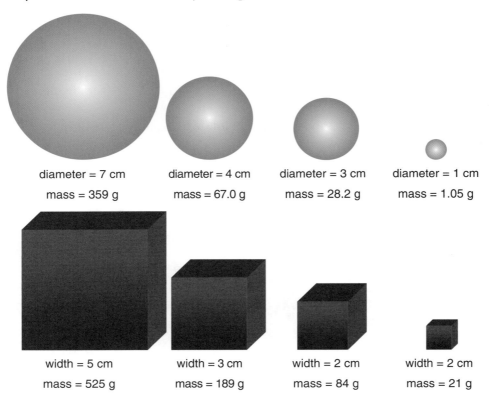

| diameter = 7 cm | diameter = 4 cm | diameter = 3 cm | diameter = 1 cm |
| mass = 359 g | mass = 67.0 g | mass = 28.2 g | mass = 1.05 g |

| width = 5 cm | width = 3 cm | width = 2 cm | width = 2 cm |
| mass = 525 g | mass = 189 g | mass = 84 g | mass = 21 g |

344

The scientists you are working with have measured and weighed each object. Their measurements are shown in the figure beneath each object. All of the spheres are made of the same blue material. All of the cubes are made of different, green material.

Note: **Boldface** page numbers indicate figures.

A

Absolute size vs. relative size, 61–78
  duration, 61
  exameter, 65
  femtometer, 66
  further application, 66–67
  gigameter, 65
  goals, 63–66
  interactive websites, 67
  kilometer, 65
  materials, 61
  megameter, 65
  meters, 64–65
    units in, 65–66
  micrometer, 66
  millimeter, 66
  nanometer, 66
  objectives, 61
  petameter, 65
  picometer, 66
  powers of ten, 63–66
  process skills, 61
  project overview, 62
  relative size, 62–63
  relativity, 68–69
  significance, 61
  student activity, 62–63
  student answer sheet, 70–78
  terameter, 65
  yottameter, 65
  zettameter, 65
Accuracy in measurement, 38
Adult human, size, 63
Alkanes, properties of, 306–307
Archery analogy, measurement, 38
Area-to-volume ratios, 209–222
  duration, 209
  evaluation, 213, 218
  further application, 212–213, 217
  goals, 211–212, 217
  materials, 211, 215
  objectives, 209
  procedures, 216–217
  process skills, 209
  project overview, 211, 216
  significance, 209–210, 215
  student activity, 211, 216–217
  student answer sheet, 214, 219–222
Asteroid belt, 81
Astronomical units, 83
Atom, size of, 63
Automaticity, xxi

B

Bacterium, size, 63
Behaviors, scale and, 257–344
Billion
  in measurement, 50
  parts per
    modeling, 318
    volume calculation, 321
Billionth, in measurement, 50
Blue whale, length of, 63
Body heat loss, 189–198
  duration, 189
  evaluation, 194
  further application, 194
  goals, 194
  materials, 190–191
  objectives, 189
  process skills, 189
  project overview, 191–192
  significance, 189–190
  student activity, 192–193
  student answer sheet, 195–197
Bonding, molecular, 305–316
Bumpiness, xiv

345

C

Calibration, 38
Celestial bodies, 79–94
  Asteroid belt, 81
  celestial bodies, distances, 83
  celestial body diameters, 82
  Ceres
    diameter, 82
    planetary distance, astronomical
      units, 83
  diameters, 82
  distance from Sun, 83
  duration, 79
  Earth, 81
    diameter, 82
    planetary distance, astronomical
      units, 83
  Eris, 81
    diameter, 82
    planetary distance, astronomical
      units, 83
  evaluation, 87
  further application, 86–87
  goals, 84–86
  inner planets, **84**
  Jupiter, 81
    diameter, 82
    planetary distance, astronomical
      units, 83
  Mars, 81
    diameter, 82
    planetary distance, astronomical
      units, 83
  materials, 80
  Mercury, 81
    diameter, 82
    planetary distance, astronomical
      units, 83
  Neptune, 81
    diameter, 82

    planetary distance, astronomical
      units, 83
  objectives, 79
  outer planet view, **84**
  Pluto, 81
    diameter, 82
    planetary distance, astronomical
      units, 83
  process skills, 79
  project overview, 80–81
  Saturn, 81
    diameter, 82
    planetary distance, astronomical
      units, 83
  significance, 79–80
  student activity, 81–84
  student answer sheet, 88–93
  Sun, 81
    diameter, 82
    Earth, average distance between,
      85
    planetary distance, astronomical
      units, 83
  Uranus, 81
    diameter, 82
    planetary distance, astronomical
      units, 83
  Venus, 81
    diameter, 82
    planetary distance, astronomical
      units, 83
Cell, diameter of, 49
Cell phone in Faraday cage, **298**
Centimeter ruler, 37
Ceres
  diameter, 82
  planetary distance, astronomical
    units, 83
City scales, 116
Cold virus, size, 63

346

347

348

349

NATIONAL SCIENCE TEACHERS ASSOCIATION

351

353

354

355

356

DATE DUE